Thomas Russell

Motor Boats, Hydroplanes, Hydroaeroplanes

Thomas Russell

Motor Boats, Hydroplanes, Hydroaeroplanes

ISBN/EAN: 9783954273386
Erscheinungsjahr: 2013
Erscheinungsort: Bremen, Deutschland

© maritimepress in Europäischer Hochschulverlag GmbH & Co. KG, Fahrenheitstr. 1, 28359 Bremen. Alle Rechte beim Verlag und bei den jeweiligen Lizenzgebern.

www.maritimepress.de | office@maritimepress.de

Bei diesem Titel handelt es sich um den Nachdruck eines historischen, lange vergriffenen Buches. Da elektronische Druckvorlagen für diese Titel nicht existieren, musste auf alte Vorlagen zurückgegriffen werden. Hieraus zwangsläufig resultierende Qualitätsverluste bitten wir zu entschuldigen.

MOTOR BOATS
HYDROPLANES
HYDROAEROPLANES

Construction and Operation with Practical
Notes on Propeller Calculation and Design

An Illustrated Manual of Self Instruction for
Owners and Operators of Marine
Gasoline Engines and Amateur Boat-Builders

By

THOMAS H. RUSSELL, A. M., M. E.

With

Revisions and Extensions

By

JOHN B. RATHBUN, M. E.,
Consulting Engineer and Instructor Chicago Technical College

1917
CHARLES C. THOMPSON CO.
CHICAGO, U. S. A.

PREFACE.

The purpose of this work is to provide a compendious guide to the design, construction, installation and operation of marine motors and to the design and construction of motor boats. It will be found useful and often invaluable, alike by the man who wishes to install a small motor in his rowboat or yacht, and his more ambitious or more fortunate brother who aspires to own a seagoing power craft. It is intended primarily for the man who is not a practical mechanic—and yet mechanics may study its pages with profit.

Boat-building has ever been a favorite avocation among the people of maritime nations. In the United States and Canada, blessed as they are with countless navigable lakes and rivers as well as a splendid seaboard, the building and operation of pleasure boats is a national pastime, which has been stimulated by the development of the marine gasolene engine, so that today, while thousands of small craft are turned out annually by the professional boat-builders, amateur boat-building has vastly increased. To those who are building or who wish to build their own craft, the present work offers a valuable guide.

As far as the installation and operation of marine engines are concerned, it is estimated by manufacturers of world-wide renown that fully eighty per cent of their engines are used by people who have little or no "motor knowledge." Few persons have an opportunity to operate a motor before they own one, hence the great majority of boat engines are sold to the inexperienced.

In the confident belief that most of these purchasers and users of marine engines would prefer to have at least a working knowledge of motor construction and operation, this book covers the subject thoroughly. It exploits no unproved theories, but embodies only facts and principles of construction which are recognized and accepted by the foremost builders of motor boats and marine engines. It does not profess to describe every good engine on the market, but does describe to the last detail those which are typical of the best and most advanced construction. It appeals, therefore, to all present and prospective owners of motor boats who wish to learn how to operate their craft to the best advantage.

Probably one of the most important chapters is that which treats of the elementary theory and construction of the propeller. This subject is treated as fully as possible in a book of this scope and many useful hints are given regarding the selection of a propeller. The design of a propeller is a highly technical subject, but with the data given, the amateur has at least a guide by which to work.

Hydroplanes and hydroaeroplanes, the latest development in water craft are each given a chapter. The construction of the hulls, and the principle of sustenation by reaction are fully explained in a simple manner and are clearly illustrated.

CONTENTS

Chapter.		Page.
I.	The Modern Motor Boat..................	7
	Ideal Power for Small Self-Propelled Craft—Development of the Gasoline Motor—Amateur Boat Building—Choosing an Engine, Etc.	
II.	Marine Gasoline Engines—1. The Four-cycle Type	13
III.	Marine Gasoline Engines—2. The Two-cycle Type	20
IV.	Carburation and Carbureters.............	30
	The Float-feed Principle—The Mixing Valve or Vaporizer—Spray Carbureters—The Puddle Type, Etc.	
V.	Ignition	37
	Various Methods—Dry Cells—Wet Batteries—Magneto Ignition—Make and Break and Jump Spark Systems—Installation—Wiring, Etc.	
VI.	Lubrication and Cooling Systems.........	61
	The Best Lubricants—The Splash System—Mechanical Oilers, Etc.—Air and Water Cooling Methods.	
VII.	Exhaust Devices	70
	Air and Water Mufflers—The Underwater Exhaust, Etc.	

CONTENTS—Continued.

Chapter.		Page.
VIII.	Installation of Motor Boat Engines	75
IX.	Operation and Care of Engine	91
X.	Hydroplanes	97
XI.	Choice of a Boat Model	107
XII.	Practical Boatbuilding—1. Boat Patterns and Knock-down Frames	125
XIII.	Practical Boatbuilding — 2. Form and Strength of Hull	137
XIV.	Practical Boatbuilding — 3. Structural Members and Materials	143
XV.	Practical Boatbuilding—4. Laying Down and Assembling—Finishing	151
XVI.	Practical Boatbuilding—5. How to Build a Boat from Patterns	165
XVII.	Propellers—Theory and Construction	192
XVIII.	Reversing·Gear and Propeller Wheels.	211
XIX.	Hydroaeroplanes	217
XX.	Engine Troubles and Their Remedies	225
XXI.	Don'ts for Motor Boatmen	243
XXII.	Rules of Navigation	249

CHAPTER I.

THE MODERN MOTOR BOAT.

The modern era in power boating dates from the development for marine purposes of the internal combustion engine, usually employing gasolene as fuel.

For small self-propelled craft the gasolene engine furnishes ideal power. Within the brief span of the last few years its utility, reliability and endurance have been developed to a point nearing perfection as far as pleasure craft are concerned, while its use for passenger transport and other business purposes is steadily increasing, as, for example, in the towing and fishing industries of the United States and Canada. In fact, it has already measurably lessened the burdens of many of those who go down to the sea in ships, besides adding immeasurably to the delights of the amateur boatman and the yachtsman.

Among the advantages accruing from the use of the gasolene engine are the absence of smoke, soot and heat, and the minimizing of the work required in the operation of a power boat. The boat-owner can be his own engineer—and therein lies the secret of the gasolene motor's success.

There is no delay in starting a boat with a gasolene motor—no tiresome waiting to get up steam; no waste of fuel when the engine is standing idle; no need to don overalls for protection against grime and grease; no stoking or coaling; no absolute dependence on electric charging stations. The main essential is a continuous gasolene supply—and that can be replenished almost anywhere at comparatively insignificant cost.

Just as the gasolene engine has revolutionized land transport, through its universal use in the automobile, so it is having a great effect on marine transport, especially as regards the thousands who take their pleasure afloat. Even the vetreran yachtsman, wedded to his ideas of sporting ethics, has been converted to the use of the motor for auxiliary power—and thereby has added immensely to his comfort and to his enjoyment of his white-winged craft.

While the landsman has had a hard battle to fight, against many forms of prejudice and persecution, while awaiting public recognition of the "arrival" of the motor car, the yachtsman and motor-boatman have had no such struggle at all. The sea and all navigable waters spell freedom, and those who use them are free to adopt any form of propulsion they please. It has been well said that police officers do not lurk afloat in unsuspected places, ready to time (with watches innocent of second hands) any motor-boat passing from buoy to buoy, so that they may swear to impossible records of speed being made, and thus enable heavy fines to be imposed.

The practical utility of the gasolene motor having been recognized for several years, it has gradually dawned upon the public that its reliability and endurance have been increasing apace. At the same time the motor has come within the reach of those of moderate means, so that today not only can the sailing yachtsman with a heavy purse equip his craft with an efficient auxiliary motor, but almost any man can have a self-propelled boat, always ready at a minute's notice to take him about on the water, far cheaper to buy or to build than the smallest steam launch, and far cheaper to operate because he, though not an engineer or mechanic, can operate it himself.

Amateur Boat-Building.

Amateur builders of motor-boats are abroad in the land in ever increasing numbers. The old idea was that there are many technical difficulties in the way of those who do not care, or have not the time, to make a thorough study of the subject. Such an idea is a mistake, for boat-building is well worth the amateur's attention, and is really a simple craft. Modern methods have also made it particularly easy for the amateur to construct all or part of his boat.

To be able to build a boat well and to his own ideas and plans requires that the amateur should be both a de-

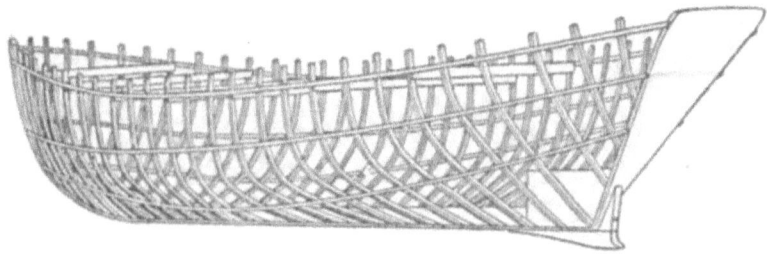

signer and a builder, which in their turn require that he should be an efficient draftsman and carpenter. No one can hope to succeed in building a boat to his own plan unless he is fully able to design and lay down the lines and body plan of the proposed craft, and added to this in many kinds of boats, such as a sailing boat or power launch, it is necessary that he should be able to calculate the displacement and the position of the center of buoyancy. With this knowledge at his command, an unlimited field is opened to the amateur boat-builder, as he will be able to build after his own ideas.

Plans and patterns can, however, now be purchased for so many different models that the amateur who does not care to attempt designing a boat has the choice of many tried and approved designs ready to his hand when he starts to build his own craft.

Choosing an Engine.

When buying an engine the novice should look for a simple machine, one easy to keep in running order, and one that requires the least possible attention. The life of an engine should be taken into consideration very carefully, that is, how long will the different parts wear before they have to be replaced? Are the bearings and the running parts of the engine designed to stand hard work without wearing out quickly? Remember, the cheapest engine in the end to buy is one that requires the least amount of repairs. Every part of a good modern gasolene engine can be readily examined and adjusted by the operator without the assistance of a machine shop.

The business reputation and financial responsibility of the manufacturers are factors which should be considered in making a selection, and where a satisfactory choice cannot be arrived at in any other manner, these points should be carefully considered in making the purchase.

There are four essential points which are the most vital on all engines: the General Construction, the Igniter, the Carbureter, and the Lubrication. By the General Construction we mean the materials used on the engine, the workmanship shown, and the mechanical principles underlying the work. The Igniter transmits the sparks and as a gasolene engine cannot be run without a spark, this point is rightly reckoned among the vital features. The Carbureter mixes the gasolene fuel and air to form the gas from which power to run the engine is developed, and is therefore an all-important factor. As regards Lubrication, every engine should be properly lubricated to run successfully, the crank-pin being the hardest to oil. The mechanical principles of all two-cycle and of all four-cycle engines are similar, but the other points mentioned are not and it is these points that should be carefully considered in choosing an engine.

Before buying an engine of any particular build, the prospective purchaser should, if possible, inspect a similar engine in operation, doing the same class of work for which he requires it. He should examine its construction thoroughly, study its principles, and learn all he can from the owner or operator as to its behavior under varying circumstances—and as to its foibles. Equipped with such information he will welcome the arrival of his new engine with a better understanding of what he may expect from it.

A 16-foot launch with a 1½ H. P. motor will have a speed of about 7 miles per hour, and the same launch with a 3½ H. P. engine will have a speed of about 9 miles per hour. A 25-foot runabout with a 5½ H. P. engine will have a speed of 8 miles per hour, but the same boat may be fitted with anything up to a 25 H. P. engine, with which a speed of about 21 miles per hour can be reached. When a completed hull is purchased from a reputable builder of motor-boats there need be little fear of installing an engine which the hull will not stand, for the boats are usually guaranteed to stand any power, if properly installed, that the hull will accommodate for space. Upon being informed as to the speed desired from any stock model boat the builders will advise the purchaser as to the engine which, in their opinion, will be best adapted for it. Some builders make no extra charge for installing an engine. but list the latter separately as a convenient method of permitting a choice of power.

Cabin Cruisers.

The past few years have seen a wonderful advancement in the construction of cruiser craft. In the past decade the gasolene engine and the motor-boat have revolutionized the field of sport and recreation. but only of very recent years have people come to realize the real utility and practicability of the cabin cruiser, and that such boats are capable of cruising safely in any waters of the globe. The four boats which in 1909 entered the New York to Bermuda contest ranged only from 42 to 85 feet in length and raced across the open Atlantic 800 miles.

To anyone living upon the coast, the Great Lakes, the Mississippi system, or any of the rivers tributary thereto, the cabin cruiser affords the greatest opportunities for healthful and delightful recreation. It is as cool, convenient, and comfortable as a summer cottage, never grows monotonous, because of continual change of scene, and can be operated at very small expense. Realizing the advantages of this type of boat, and that its popularity must increase with each succeeding season, the leading boatbuilders have, during the past few years, exerted every possible effort to perfect the design of their models and to improve the interior plans in order to secure the greatest serviceability and comfort, and the most pleasing general appearance at the least possible cost.

"The greatest need in the motor and boat business," says an acknowledged authority, "is more information on marine engines." We shall, therefore, first describe and illustrate the principles, construction and operation of the various marine gasolene engines in present day use—and then proceed to the subject of practical boat-building.

CHAPTER II.

MARINE GASOLENE ENGINES.

1. The Four-Cycle Type.

Two distinct types of gasolene engine are in successful use on motor-boats, these being known respectively as the two-cycle and the four-cycle type.

The principle of operation of both types is based on the now well known facts that gasolene vapor or a fine spray of gasolene when mixed with air forms a highly inflammable mixture, and that if this mixture be confined in a closed chamber and ignited by a flame or spark it will explode and expand. This is just what is done in a gasolene engine, the expansion being used as the motive power.

In modern practice the engines used for propelling motor-boats and launches are, in the great majority of cases, of the internal combustion type, using gasolene (sometimes kerosene) as fuel; the exceptions are in the case of steam launches and electric power boats, using respectively steam engines and electric motors.

In all engines, of whatever type, providing a source of power, something must be consumed. In a steam engine coal or liquid fuel is consumed to furnish heat and the steam generated by the heat given off is used to produce power. The internal combustion engine is so named because the fuel used is burned or consumed inside the engine itself. It is for this reason that it forms a very simple and satisfactory way of producing power for driving a boat, launch or yacht and is in increasing use for heavier marine duty.

Power for power, the internal combustion engine is much lighter than any form of steam engine and boiler, besides having other very important advantages. For instance, the steam engine is at a disadvantage in comparison with the gasolene motor in that an additional process is passed through in converting the fuel into motion. Thus the steps are:

Gasolene motor—Fuel, combustion, motion.

Steam engine—Fuel, combustion, generation of steam, motion.

And, unfortunately for steam, the extra step always involves the expenditure of a large quantity of fuel. Further, the steam generator or boiler occupies a lot of space and much time is required in getting up steam for the start.

An internal combustion engine can use various kinds of fuel, but all of them are hydrocarbons. Heavy oils are used in some marine engines, especially for what is known as heavy duty, such as towing, but the engine almost universally used in motor-boats burns the very light and volatile hydrocarbon known as gasolene, petrol or petroleum spirit. It is from this that the gas is produced which is burned inside the engine.

The production of the gas from the hydrocarbon is usually obtained by means of a carbureter. In a few engines the carbureter is dispensed with, small doses of gasolene being injected into the cylinder at frequent intervals and the gasolene mixture formed therein as required, but this is an exceptional practice, and the use of a carbureter is the rule.

The gas, being expansive or explosive when ignited, is used to force a piston of a cylinder outward, this piston being connected by means of a connecting rod to the crank in such a manner that when it is forced out by the expansion of the gas in the cylinder it turns the crank and the power is developed, to be communicated through the shaft to the propeller wheel at the stern.

CONSTRUCTION AND OPERATION

But the mechanism which is required to produce this apparently simple operation has other functions to perform, especially in the case of the earlier form of internal combustion engine known as the "four-cycle" engine, to which we will first refer.

Before the gas can be exploded in the cylinder it is necessary to admit it or draw it in, which means that there must be some opening in the cylinder through

Buffalo 4-cylinder, 10-40 H. P. Engine—Front View.

which it may pass. Before it can be exploded so that it will drive the piston down in the cylinder, there must be some means of closing up the entrance through which it has passed into the cylinder; while, again, before the operation of exploding the gas can be repeated, it is essential to get rid of the exhaust gases generated by the explosion. Also, some method of igniting the gas so as to cause it to expand must be provided. This latter requirement is usually attained by means of an electric spark.

Another fact to be noted is that the explosive gas drawn into the cylinder will give out greater power when ignited if it is first compressed, and, therefore, the engine has also to perform the function of compressing the charge.

Thus, the engine has four different duties to perform:

First, it has to open an inlet valve and to draw in the charge.

Second, it has to close the inlet and compress the charge.

Third, it has to fire the charge so as to force the piston out to do work.

Fourth, it has to expel the exhaust gases.

It is owing to these four operations having to be performed in sequence that the internal combustion engine of this type, as used in motor-boats, is known as a "four-cycle" engine. The term is somewhat erroneous, as there is but one true cycle of operations, embracing four steps or parts.

On the completion of the four steps or operations all the parts of the engine are in the same position as at the beginning and the four-step cycle of operations is repeated rapidly, time after time, as long as the engine is kept at work. The cycle includes two outward and two inward strokes of the piston, or four in all, so that the flywheel is revolved twice during each complete cycle.

Working of the Four-Cycle Engine.

In the illustrations, Fig. Nos. 1, 2, 3 and 4, we show in diagrammatic form the working of the four-cycle type of internal combustion engine used in many motor-boats. In arrangement of details engines vary considerably, but in the main features they are all practically alike. A is the cylinder and B is the movable piston, hollow and like an inverted tin pail. This piston B is capable of sliding freely up and down inside the cylinder A, but it is provided with spring rings, which make it fit tightly and prevent any gas passing by it. D is the connecting rod which connects the piston to the crank E, which crank

CONSTRUCTION AND OPERATION

forms part of the engine shaft, and it is by the rotation of this that the boat is driven. The piston B, when it is forced down in the cylinder, pushes round the crank E and so turns the shaft. F and F1 are respectively the inlet and exhaust valves.

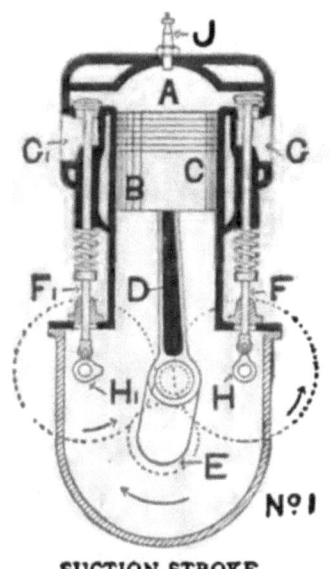
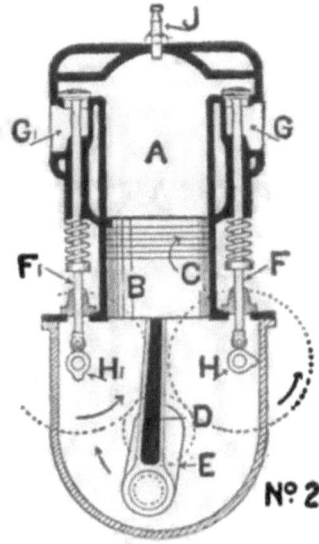

SUCTION STROKE. **COMPRESSION STROKE.**

The gas from the carbureter enters at G and after having been ignited is expelled through the port G1. The valves F and F1 are operated by the engine itself by means of cams H and H1. These cams are carried on shafts which are driven by the engine crankshaft, but at half its speed. The dotted lines indicate the gear wheels on the two shafts and on the engine, by means of which the shafts are rotated. It will be seen that the cam on either of these shafts will lift its valve once in every two revolutions of the crankshaft.

In Fig. No. 1 we see that the cam has lifted the inlet valve F. At the same time the crank is in such a position that the piston is just descending in the cylinder. As the piston descends it acts as a suction pump and draws in the gas from the carbureter through the valve port G. As soon as the piston has reached the bottom of its stroke the cam H allows the valve F to fall on its seat. The flywheel on the crankshaft of the engine, however, through its stored momentum, continues to rotate the crank, and, therefore, the piston B is pushed back again into the cylinder (Fig. No. 2), but as now there is no exit from the cylinder, the gas inside it is compressed into the combustion space. This compression proceeds

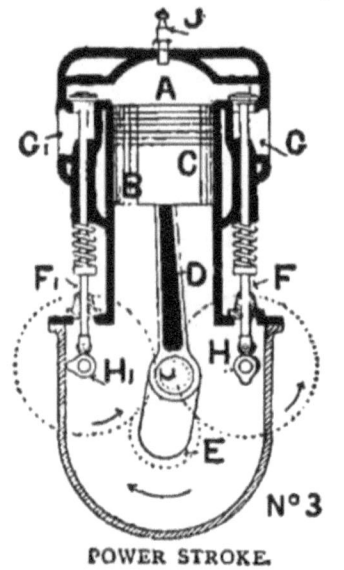 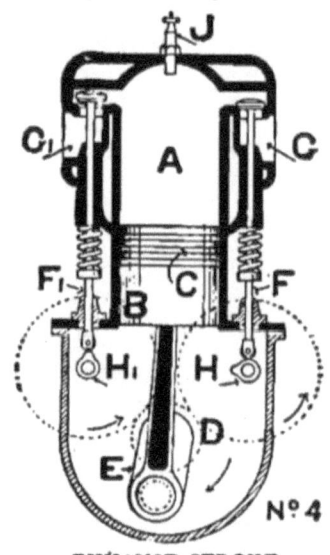

POWER STROKE.   EXHAUST STROKE.

until the piston has reached the top of its stroke, and at this point a spark is caused to pass across the points of the spark plug J. As soon as this occurs, the gas charge is ignited and expands very rapidly, this expansion forcing the piston B down in the cylinder and, through the medium of the connecting rod, turning the crank E. This is the power stroke (Fig. No. 3).

Immediately before the piston reaches the bottom of its stroke, the cam H1 lifts the exhaust valve F1, the inlet valve F of course remaining closed. The momentum of the flywheel carries the crank round and forces the piston

CONSTRUCTION AND OPERATION

back up the cylinder, it in turn forcing the exhaust gases out through the exhaust port G1. This is the exhaust stroke (Fig. No. 4).

The engine is now in a position to perform the same cycle of operations as before, the next stroke drawing the piston down and bringing in a fresh charge through the inlet G, which in turn is compressed, ignited and expelled as before. It will thus be seen that the engine during two revolutions of the crankshaft has performed the four operations which are necessary to its proper working. The operations in sequence are as follows:

1. Down stroke of the piston—Gas charge is drawn in.
2. Up stroke of the piston—Gas charge is compressed.
3. Down stroke of the piston—Gas charge, being ignited, is rapidly expanding.
4. Up stroke of the piston—The exhaust gases are being expelled.

These four strokes of the piston, respectively, are known as the Suction, Compression, Power and Exhaust strokes, as indicated under the diagrams.

As the initial operation is to draw in a charge of gas, it will be seen that before the engine can be started it is necessary to rotate the crankshaft, by turning the flywheel or some starting device, a starting crank or starting ratchet and lever, so that a charge is drawn in and compressed. This is then fired and the engine will continue to operate automatically.

CHAPTER III.

MARINE GASOLENE ENGINES.

2. The Two-Cycle Type.

In modern motor-boat practice, especially for the smaller boats, the two-cycle type of gasolene engine is now in large and growing demand. Various advantages are claimed for it, among these being (a) the small number of moving parts—namely, the piston, connecting rod and crankshaft with flywheel; (b) adaptability for reversing, the engine running equally well in either direction; (c) absence of complicated valves, cams, etc.; (d) simplicity and reliability.

The word "cycle" can be defined as "a succession of events necessary to complete an operation." For instance, every internal combustion engine when running does the four following things every time it produces a power impulse:

First, draws in a charge of explosive mixture.
Second, compresses this charge.
Third, fires or expands the charge.
Fourth, exhausts the burned or expanded charge.

The four-stroke engine (commonly called four-cycle engine) requires four strokes of the piston, two up and two down (or two revolutions) to complete the above cycle and, therefore, operates in a four-stroke cycle.

The two-stroke (commonly called two-cycle engine) performs all of the above functions with two strokes of the piston, one up and one down (or one revolution) and, therefore, operates in a two-stroke cycle.

In the two-stroke or two-cycle engine of the internal combustion type there is an explosion of the fuel mixture at every revolution of the crankshaft. In this type of engine the cylinder is not utilized for the purpose of compressing the charge, although the piston is. The airtight crankcase acts as a supplementary air-chamber into which the gas to be exploded can be drawn and then forced into the cylinder under pressure. The incoming gas charge forces the exhaust gases out.

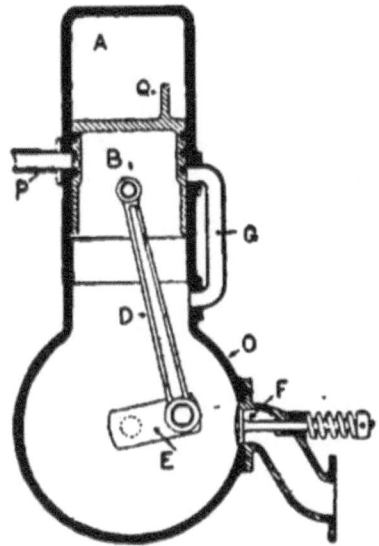

FIG. 1.—A TWO-CYCLE ENGINE.

A diagrammatic view of a simple arrangement of the two-cycle engine (which is made in a great many different designs) is shown herewith. A is the cylinder and B the piston, D the connecting rod and E the crank. The crank-case O is made as airtight as possible and an automatic inlet valve F is arranged so as to admit the gas to the crank chamber. There is a pipe leading from the crank chamber to the inside of the cylinder A, this pipe being shown at G. When the piston is at the bottom of its stroke it uncovers the top of the pipe G, so that the cylinder A comes into communication with the crank-case O.

P is the exhaust port, which is uncovered by the piston when it reaches the bottom of its stroke. Q is a baffle plate, which, when the piston has opened the top of the pipe G, comes opposite to that opening and directs the incoming gas charge in an upward direction. The cycle of operations is as follows:

The first upstroke of the piston draws the charge of gas into the crank-case through the valve F. The piston then descends, compressing the gas charge in the crank-case. When it reaches that point at which the top of the pipe G is uncovered, the compressed gases in the crank-case rush through the pipe G into the cylinder A. The piston then ascends and when it reaches the top of its stroke the charge is fired and the piston descends until it reaches that point at which the exhaust port P is uncovered. This is the power stroke, following the impulse of the explosion and expansion of the gaseous charge. During this power stroke another charge of gas, which came into the crank chamber owing to the upward suction of the piston, is being compressed, and just after the exhaust P is opened this compressed charge rushes up through pipe G into cylinder A; the returning piston further compresses it there, and when it is at the top of its stroke the charge is fired. The incoming charge, during the time that the piston B has uncovered both the exhaust port P and the top of G, violently pushes the exhaust gases out through P. By this arrangement an impulse is given to the piston on each revolution, so that there is no need for any mechanically operated valve, the only valve being the automatic one at F. Such engines, though not largely used for motor vehicle purposes, are very popular for motor-boats and, in fact, for this purpose have proved themselves to be among the most efficient of internal combustion engines.

The "Three-Port" Type.

In some two-cycle engines the necessity for a check valve leading to the crank-case is avoided by what is known as the "three-port" design. In this type of engine the piston creates a partial vacuum in the crank-case by its upward movement, and no fresh charge is taken in until near the end of the up-stroke, when the lower edge of the piston uncovers a port through which the fresh charge enters with a rush.

Knox Single-Cylinder, 2-cycle, 3-port Engine.

The successful performance of a two-cycle engine depends on the correct design of the exhaust and transfer ports and the baffle plate or deflector, all of which are matters for experiment. It also depends on the piston being a reasonably good fit in the cylinder, since a loose piston allows the compressed charge in the crank-case to leak past it out of the exhaust port. It is further necessary to have the crank-case substantially airtight and to adopt suitable means to prevent blowing by the crankshaft bearings. For this reason, grease is largely used for bearing lubrication in these engines.

Two-cycle engines are frequenty oiled on the splash system, but this is considered by other engine-builders to be wasteful of oil, since an unnecessary amount of oil spray is carried into the cylinder through the transfer port. Some engines have mechanical oilers and use special means of conveying oil to the crank pin and piston.

A two-cycle engine will run in one direction as well as the other. A four-cycle engine runs in only one direction, unless a special arrangement is used to open the valves at the proper time for reversing.

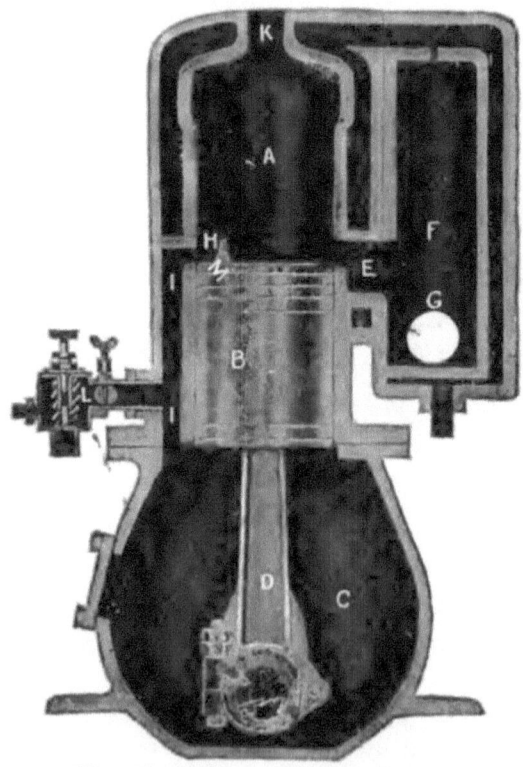

The Two-Cycle Detroit Engine.

A—Cylinder.
B—Piston.
C—Crank-case.
D—Connecting rod.
E—Exhaust port.
F—Expansion chamber.
G—Exhaust pipe.
H—Inlet port.
I—Transfer passage from cylinder to crank-case.
K—Spark plug.
L—Carbureter.
M—Deflector or baffle plate.

A Typical Two-Cycle Engine.

The actual working of a typical two-cycle engine is explained by means of the illustration as follows:

We will start with cylinder A full of fresh mixture. Piston B travels upward drawing a mixture of air and gasolene from carbureter L through inlet into crank-case C. At the same time it compresses the fresh mixture in cylinder A, at the top center an electric spark is thrown across the points of spark plug K which lights the charge and makes it expand and drive the piston downward, while the gas in the crank-case C, being held in same by non-return valve in carbureter, is slightly compressed. The piston first uncovers the exhaust port E and the highly expanded gases pass out of same into expansion chamber F, where they are instantly condensed by a fine spray of water. The inlet port H opens and admits the gas compressed in the crank-case—which rushes up through passage I to fill the cylinder. This gas strikes the deflector plate M and shoots straight toward the top of the cylinder. As the port opens to full width the stream of gas traces a fan-shaped path and blows before it all the remainder of the burned gas from the previous explosion.

The Offset Cylinder.

The efficiency of the modern gasolene engine is increased by the adoption of what is known as the "offset" cylinder, which slightly increases the length of the stroke and secures a more direct effect upon the crank at the time the explosion occurs.

A good idea of the construction of the offset cylinder can be drawn from the illustrations, figures 1 and 3. It will be observed that with the piston at the top of stroke, its center, as compared with the center of crankshaft, has a slight deviation. Fig. 2 shows the usual method of construction with the center of both crankshaft and cylinder in perfect alignment.

It is the common practice of motor-boat men to operate their engines, while at cruising speed, on either a late spark or with the firing point at the top of the piston stroke. In the latter case by reference to Fig. 3 it will be observed that the impulse of the explosion is not directed

Fig. 1

upon the dead center as in Fig. 2, but the transmission of the energy is exerted upon the crankshaft in a turning position as in Fig. 3. The connecting rod in descending on the impulse stroke has practically a vertical position, thus more directly transmitting the energy from the piston to the crankshaft.

The offset cylinder procures from the motor its maximum power and efficiency, reduces and equalizes the side thrust upon the cylinder wall on the impulse stroke and furthermore eliminates the knock which always tends towards loosening of parts, and premature decay of the motor.

The line drawing, Fig. 2, represents the ordinary construction with straight center line. The position of the piston as shown is at explosion center. The explosion exerts no turning effort to the crankshaft, for the thrust is exerted on the dead center and falls on the bearings.

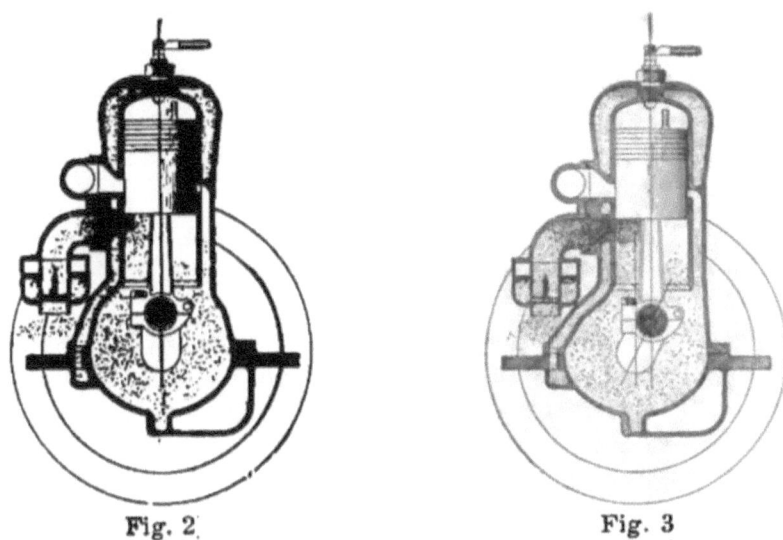

Fig. 2.   Fig. 3

In Fig. 3, the offset construction is represented with the piston in same position as Fig. 2, at firing center. It will be observed that the crank, however, is not at dead center, and that the impulse or thrust will be imparted to it in a turning position. No energy is wasted, and no undue shock is given the bearings.

Kerosene Fuel Devices.

There is a growing demand for engines that will use kerosene as fuel, and manufacturers have recently been giving some attention to this matter, with the result that there are now in the market a number of engines that, it is claimed, will burn kerosene, distillate, naphtha, benzine, alcohol, etc., as well as gasolene. The usual plan is to start the engine on gasolene, then shut off the gasolene supply and turn on kerosene, etc. Special instructions for the use of other fuels are issued by the engine-builders and these must be carefully followed to secure good results.

The Detroit two-cycle engine, built by the Detroit Engine Works, is fitted with a device known as the Detroit fuel injector when kerosene or other fuels than gasolene are to be used, and it is understood good results are thus obtained. This device is not applicable to four-cycle engines.

The Buffalo Gas Motor Company has evolved a kerosene device for its four-cycle Buffalo engines, starting on gasolene, but an engine so arranged will not show full power on gasolene only, as kerosene being a heavier fuel compression in a kerosene engine must necessarily be lower than in a regular gasolene engine.

Ferro motors and others can also be run on kerosene, and the use of this fuel may be developed to give more generally satisfactory results. The increasing price of gasolene is an important factor in the operation of internal combustion engines and a cheaper fuel will be welcomed.

One present difficulty with kerosene is its tendency to deposit carbon in the cylinder and on the piston and rings—for which the only remedy is to take out the piston and remove the deposits.

Naphtha Engines.

The naphtha launch was the immediate precursor of the modern gasolene craft, and was popular for over twenty years. Its extreme simplicity in operation, its reliability and safety, commended it everywhere, and only the largely increased cost of the fuel militated against its use where economy was a primary consideration. The consumption of fuel, however, in the smaller sizes, 1 to 10 horsepower, is not so material as to be of much weight. For use in launches of 16 to 30 feet, and especially for tenders on large yachts, the naphtha engine is still much in evidence. The illustrations show the form of naphtha engines of recent construction.

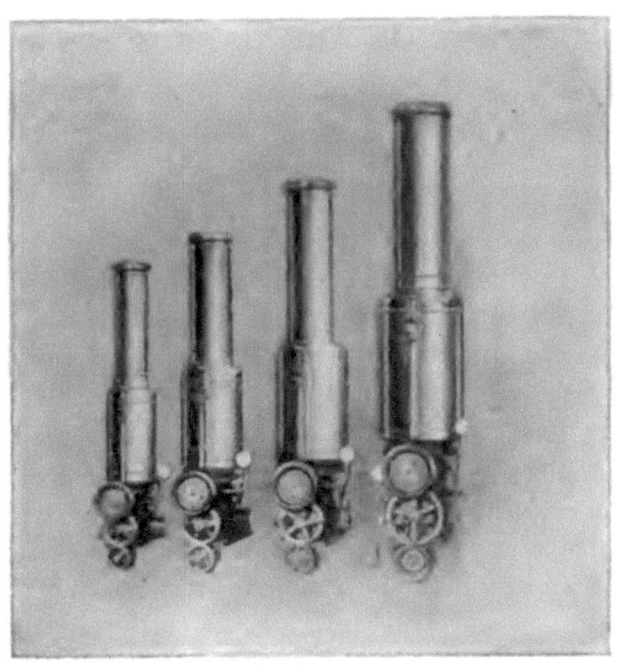

Naphtha Engines.

CHAPTER IV.

CARBURATION AND CARBURETERS.

Gasolene vapor being explosive only when mixed with air in approximately such proportions that each molecule of vapor finds a certain quota of oxygen, a mechanical device to secure the proper mixture is an essential part of a gasolene engine. Mixtures, which are either too "rich" or too "lean"—that is, those in which there is too great or too small a proportion of gasolene vapor—are not explosive, and are ignited with difficulty, thereby interfering with the proper running of the engine.

The carbureter is the device usually employed to feed the gasolene to an air stream in suitable proportions to form an explosive mixture. In the commonest form of this device, a stream of air is drawn at high velocity past a nozzle, from which the gasolene is sucked and broken into spray, the gasolene entering the carbureter by gravity from the supply tank, a means of control being duly provided.

Numerous forms of carbureters are employed with gasolene engines, but the type almost universal on motorboats is the spray carbureter. In this, the gasolene is drawn through a nozzle or jet by the engine, and as it leaves the jet in the form of spray, it mixes with air which is sucked into the engine at the same time.

The Float-Feed Principle.

Now, as the air must be charged with a certain proportion of gasolene vapor in order to obtain the best results, it will be apparent that the form and dimensions of the carbureter must be carefully designed, and that the flow of gasolene must be properly regulated. To accomplish the second object, a float valve is employed. Instead of being led directly to the nozzle the gasolene is fed through a pipe into a chamber in which is a float, nearly filling the same.

In some carbureters the floats are principally made of cork, but they are generally constructed of thin metal.

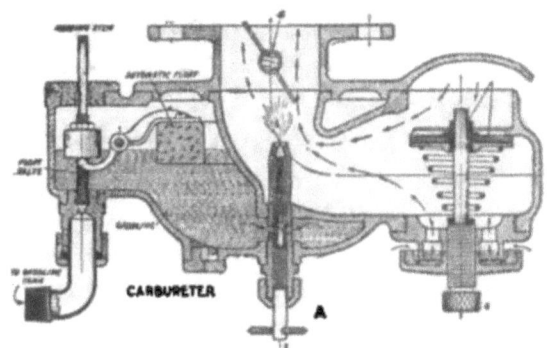

The Ferro Carbureter.

Pivoted to the top and bottom of the chamber of a typical carbureter are two weighted levers. The outer ends of these levers bear against the float; the inner ends engage in a grooved collar fixed to a wire or needle. This needle has a conical point adapted to fit into a corresponding conical seating at the point where the gasolene enters the chamber. As the gasolene gets deeper in the chamber it raises the float, the outer ends of the lever rise, the inner ends are forced down, and the pointed end of the needle is thrust farther and farther into the seating, so that when the gasolene has reached the desired height in the chamber the supply is cut off.

There is a small passage communicating between the float chamber and the nozzle, consequently the gasolene will stand at the same height in the nozzle as in the chamber. Usually the float valve device is arranged to keep the gasolene at about one-sixteenth inch below the level of the top of the jet.

More gasolene vapor being sucked into the engine when it is running at high speed, a proper air supply is important to maintain a mixture of the same proportions at high and low speeds. To meet this requirement numerous forms of automatic carbureters have been devised, most of which admit additional air at high speeds by a light valve opening against a spring. This is usually called an auxiliary air valve and the air thus automatically admitted at high speeds, reduces the richness of the mixture to the proper point.

Regulation of Spray Carbureters.

The flow of gasolene through the spray orifice is controlled either by an adjustable needle valve or by regulating the opening of the air intake. Reducing the size of this intake increases the suction and therefore the richness of the mixture, unless the auxiliary intake is separate, in which case reducing the primary intake weakens the mixture after the auxiliary valve is open. Changing either the needle valve or the primary air intake will increase or diminish the gasolene supply at all speeds, It is customary in adjusting a carbureter to begin by setting the needle valve or the primary air intake to give a good mixture when the engine is running on a low throttle with little or no opening of the auxiliary air valve. This insures easy starting and good control at low speeds. For medium and high speeds the auxiliary air valve is adjusted by regulating its spring tension and its maximum opening at high speed.

The Mixing Valve or Vaporizer.

If a marine engine is to be run at approximately one speed all the time, a simple mixing valve is often found to give good results. With this device, however, the mixture must be regulated by hand. This was the original method of mixing gasolene vapor and air in due proportions for combustion and the device is variously called a mixing valve, generator or vaporizer. It consists chiefly of an air chamber or passage in which a needle valve is situated. This valve is practically the same as the needle valve on the common gasolene stove in that it sprays the gasolene into the burner. The burner in the stove would represent the mixing chamber. In connection with this passage or mixing chamber with its gasolene valve is a check or disk valve which operates in holding the vaporous gases in the motor as they pass from the mixer. At every up stroke of the engine piston, with the two-cycle motor, the partial vacuum or suction in the crank-case causes an influx of air through the mixing valve. The force of the incoming air lifts the check valve. This valve when it lifts, uncovers a small gasolene port, allowing it to spray the liquid into the air chamber, and become mixed with the inrushing air. When the engine piston starts downward, compressing the charge in the base, the check valve closes, holding the charge and also closing the gasolene port until the next similar operation.

This type of generator works very successfully but lacks the feature of a steady constant feed of gasolene where the gravity flow varies, as it does with a full or nearly empty gasolene tank. Again the varying speeds of the motor will affect the feed of gasolene into the mixing chamber. In both these cases it requires an adjustment of the needle valve, by the operator. This feature of constant care with the generator valve is often a worry to the operator under the conditions mentioned.

The improved float-feed type of carbureter is designed to obviate the difficulty of maintaining a constant flow of gasolene under all circumstances.

The "Puddle" Type.

In a new form of carbureter known as the puddle type,

a float maintains the gasolene nozzle at such a level that it forms a small puddle in the bottom of a U-shaped mixing tube. The inflow of gasolene to this puddle is controlled by a needle valve and this adjustment, in connection with the depth of the puddle itself, determines the quality of the mixture. This carbureter does not act by spraying except at high speeds. At all lower speeds the gasolene is simply swept along the walls of the intake pipe and evaporated. The essential difference between the puddle and the spraying types is that in the former the gasolene feeds itself to the air at low speeds, instead of requiring a certain minimum degree of suction for that purpose. It will therefore make a mixture at lower speeds than the ordinary spraying carbureter. It has, however, certain peculiarities in operation, and very accurate adjustment of the float is necessary to prevent over-richness of the mixture.

Schebler Carbureter, Model D—Front View.

The Schebler float-feed carbureter in use on many motor-boats is known as Model D, and is illustrated herewith. It is manufactured by Wheeler & Schebler, of

Indianapolis, and is made in four pipe sizes, from one to two inches. It has been improved recently by the addition of a butterfly shutter placed in the air intake. This should be attached to a wire, running to some convenient place near the starting crank. When cranking, pull the shutter closed. This draws a rich mixture into the cylinders, causing the motor to start on the first or second turn of the crank.

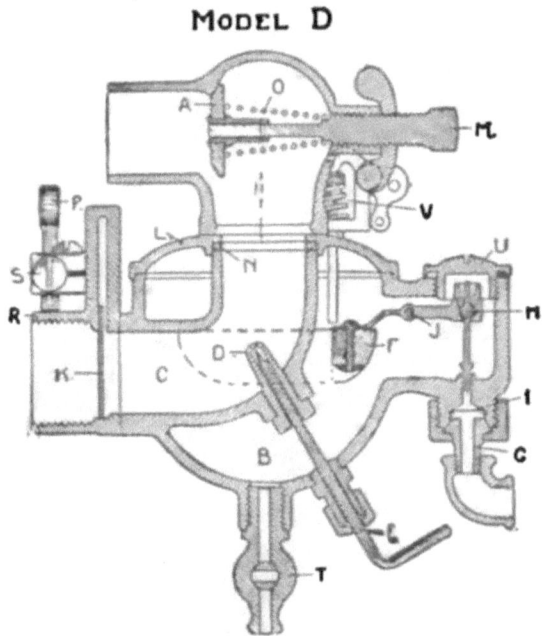

Schebler Carbureter, Model D—Section.

Another improvement has been made on the air valve adjusting screw. A strong friction spring is placed around the adjusting screw between the lock nut and air valve casting, preventing the lock nut from jarring loose and thus allowing the air adjustment to change.

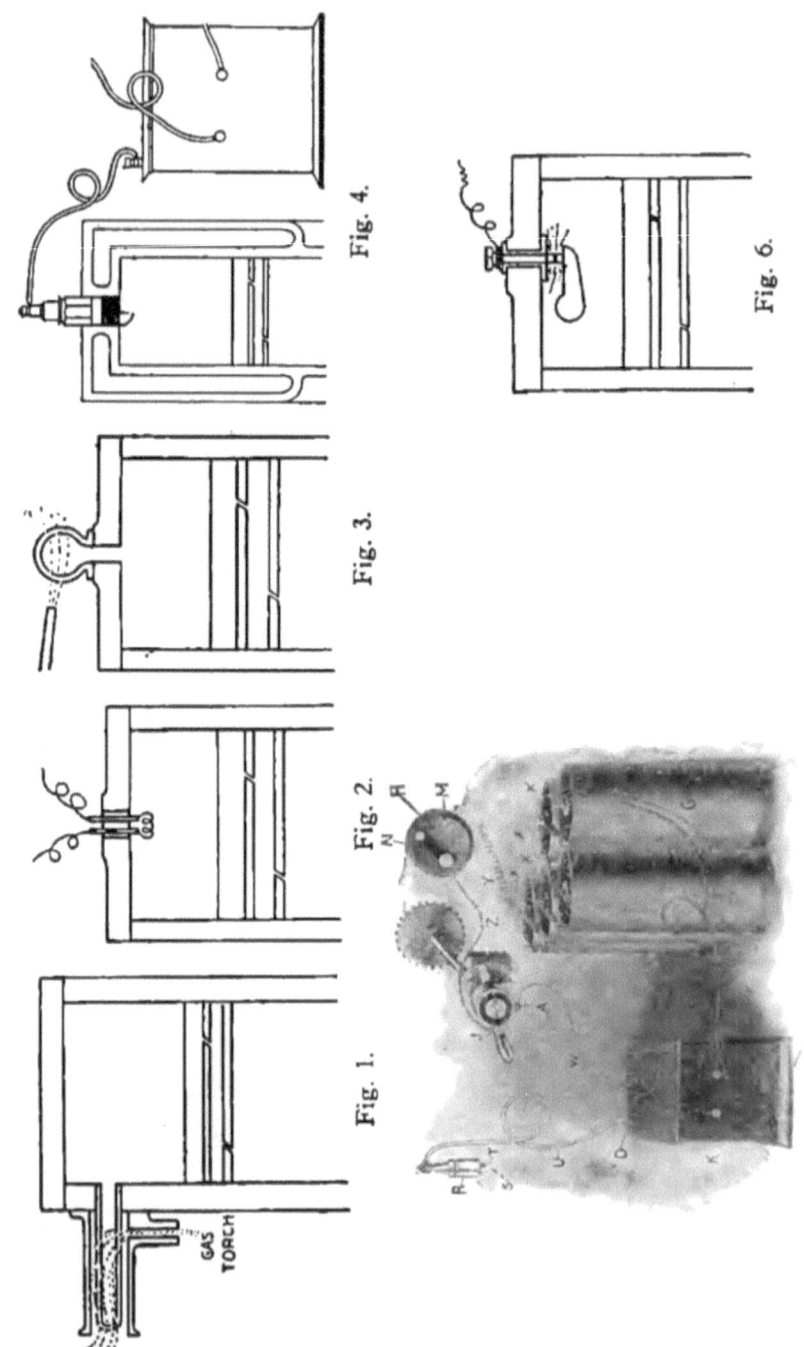

CHAPTER V

IGNITION.

In order to explode the charge of vaporous gases that are drawn into the cylinder of an internal combustion engine, some means must be provided for supplying heat in the proper amount and at the proper time. This heat may be furnished by various methods, namely, the hot tube, the incandescent filament, a heated surface or an electric spark. The first three methods, illustrated in Figs. 1, 2 and 3, belong to the period of development of the gasolene engine and are practically obsolete. (See full page illustration.)

With the electric spark, Fig. 4, the method consists of sending an electric current to a spark coil, where it is transformed and sent on to the spark plug in the top of the cylinder, terminating in two points of the plug which are separated about one thirty-second of an inch from each other. At the proper time the current is sent through these wires, causing a spark in the cylinder at the spark plug. This method is in universal use today. Its advantages over the old time system of the hot tube, the heated surface and the filament, lie in the fact that it is simple, more reliable and easily controlled.

There are two distinct kinds of electric current in use, namely, the high tension or jump spark and the low tension or make and break spark. Briefly, the high tension system consists of leading an electric current from dry or wet batteries, magneto or dynamo to a transformer or spark coil, thence to the spark plug, Fig. 5, which is usually located on the top of the cylinder. In order to control this spark, that is, to make the spark occur at just the proper moment, the current is thrown on and off by the use of a sparking device or timer, located outside the cylinder. When the current is thrown on, a spark jumps across the gap at the spark plug S-T inside the cylinder, thus igniting the charge.

A low tension system consists chiefly of leading an electric current to a coil, whose functions are not the same as the coil used in the jump spark system. From this coil the current is led to two movable contact pieces inside the cylinder. (See Fig. 6.) These contact pieces are operated from without in such a manner that they come together and separate at just the proper moment to make a spark and ignite the charge.

The electric current used in producing the spark is usually drawn from one of three sources: 1, a dry cell; 2, the storage battery; 3, the magneto or dynamo.

Dry Cells.

The dry cell (group Fig. 5) consists usually of a carbon and zinc element immersed in moistened salts. By chemical action this combination has the power of delivering an electric current. Since the gasolene engine has come into prominence and the demand for an efficient, reliable and inexpensive source of current supply has been developed, the dry cell has been brought to commercial perfection. It is clean, not very heavy and occupies a small amount of space. A set of dry cells is regularly supplied with the best marine engine outfits. If properly installed, the dry cell will last a long time and any one cell may be removed from the set if defective and replaced by a new one.

Wet Batteries.

Wet batteries have become very popular for some classes of marine ignition work. There are a great many different companies supplying batteries of the wet type that are very efficient. In purchasing a set of wet batteries the following points ought to be remembered: They should be slop-proof and all renewals required should be easily obtainable.

The jars ought to be as substantial as possible and constructed so that chemicals will not "creep" over the edge of the jar or evaporate.

When space allows and first cost is not of utmost importance, these batteries give excellent service when used for either system of ignition.

The advantage of this type of batteries is that the current is practically constant and the elements usually zinc and copper oxid; and liquid solution may be renewed, so that it is not necessary to buy a new set of batteries when these wet cells have become exhausted.

Magneto Ignition.

A magneto is a machine for generating an electric current by employing the use of permanent electric magnets. Most people are familiar with the ordinary horseshoe magnet, used in picking up needles, etc. This

Magneto.

same sort of magnet is used in the construction of the modern magneto. (See illustration.) The shaft is wound with copper wire. When this shaft, called an armature, is revolved, the wire rotating between the ends of the magneto is influenced by them and an electric current is set up in the wire. This current can then be led to the spark coil and become transformed in the same manner as that of battery current. Every year finds the use of the magneto increasing.

There is now such a variety of these machines on the market that if care is taken in the selection of the apparatus and proper installation, such an equipment will give perfect satisfaction.

The electrical requirements of the jump spark and make-and-break systems are not the same, so that it is necessary to construct and install magnetos adapted to these different ignition systems somewhat differently. The best magnetos for either make-and-break or jump spark systems, however, have been developed to a point of perfect service.

The Dynamo and Storage Battery for Ignition and Lighting.

The storage battery system consists of a dynamo and storage battery used in connection with any standard electric ignition. It can also be used to supply electricity

Lackawanna Electric Light Plant.
(For 60 Lights.)

for a number of low voltage incandescent lamps for lighting the launch.

The storage battery may be used singly or in series of several numbers depending upon the capacity or duration of current required to operate a system without re-charging. The dynamo furnishes the electricity to the batteries and from them it is fed to the ignition and lighting systems. The dynamo is usually belted to the flywheel of the motor but can be driven with friction wheel or spur gears. An automatic speed governor is generally furnished with the dynamo and serves to maintain a steady volume of current to the battery. An automatic switch also serves to break the dynamo circuit when the batteries have been charged to their full capacity.

This system furnishes a constant and steady current and obviates the necessity of replacement or renewals, as with dry and wet batteries.

It is hardly possible to depend upon the dynamo alone without any batteries to start a motor, unless the speed of the dynamo can be made high enough by cranking the motor to furnish sufficient strength of electricity for ignition. Therefore it is advisable to use some source of current other than the dynamo to start the motor.

The Timer (or Commutator) for Jump Spark Ignition.

The timer is a mechanical device for controlling the time for ignition of the gas in the cylinder. At eight hundred revolutions, the timer in a three-cylinder two-stroke engine is called upon to make 2400 perfect electrical contacts per minute, or one perfect contact every $1/40$ of a second, consequently it is necessary to provide a segment long enough (at least thirty-five degrees) to care for the rapid movement. Taking the timer of the well-known Ferro engine as an example, it is tested up to 1800 revolutions, 5400 contacts per minute, without missing. It has an adjustment of ninety degrees, and gives economy of battery power. It is driven by bronze gear meshing with a similar gear on the flywheel. A circuit relief button is in a convenient position for stopping the engine instantly, by simply pressing with the thumb while the hand grasps the timer lever. A tight bronze cover closes the contact box. The timer spool and contact box are occasionally cleaned with gasolene and a daub of vaseline oil spread on the spool for lubricating it. It is only necessary to unscrew a taper screw less than one half a turn to instantly remove all wearing parts.

Make-and-Break vs. Jump Spark.

The make-and-break or mechanical ignition is the original device that was used with the marine gasolene motor. Although the jump spark device has very largely replaced the mechanical ignition, still the old method has several features of advantage over the jump spark, which make it most commendable for the commonly used open launch, such as the utility boat or fishermen's craft. The make-and-break igniter by virtue of its low tension electric current, which is supplied direct from batteries or a dynamo to the sparking device, is not subject to short circuit or leakage of electricity, as is the possibility with the jump spark, due to its transformed high voltage current, where the latter is poorly installed. The damaging elements of water, moisture and even salt air, that affect the unprotected jump spark system, have no detrimental action on the unprotected make-and-break system, where, with the motor, it is exposed to weather, spray and moisture.

It is a universally recognized fact that the jump spark igniter is a more efficient one than the make-and-break, under the conditions already mentioned, but where the jump spark is not adapted and the right care and precaution are not given to the installation and operation of it, then its features of efficiency must give way to something better and more reliable, namely the mechanical spark.

CONSTRUCTION AND OPERATION

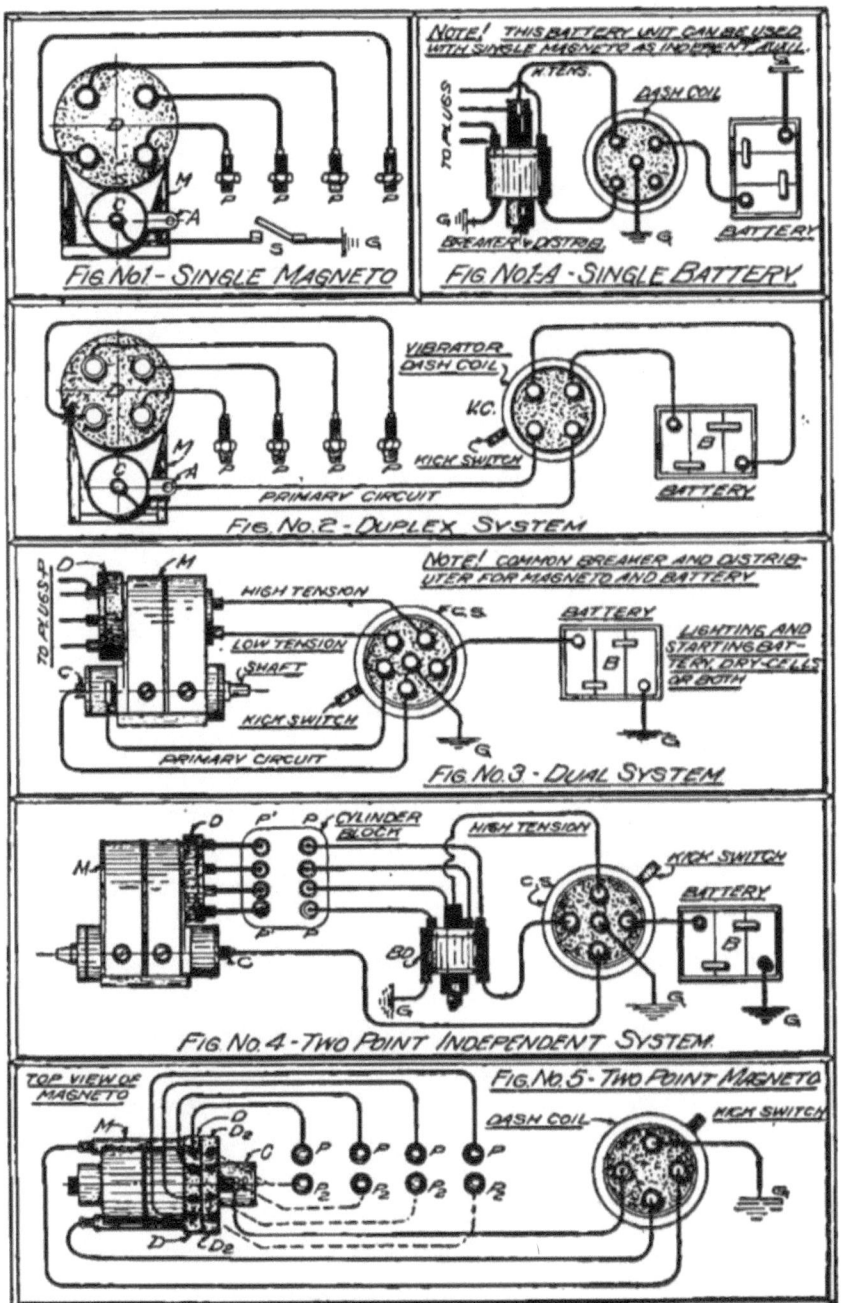

Magneto Connections.
(See Page 49.)

One of the advantages presented with the jump spark ignition is its flexibility in timing the spark. The seeming difficulties in developing this feature with the Ferro timing device, mentioned above, have been overcome in that an early or late spark is controlled by a lever in operating the motor either left or right hand direction.

Thus it is that many engineers advocate the make-and-break ignition where it is to be placed in an open boat, unprotected, and also where it is more desirable to the operator to be confronted with simple mechanical adjustments rather than a more complex electrical adjustment of the jump spark equipment.

In the improved Ferro make-and-break system the spark is generated in the cylinder at the same location as with the jump spark, and is the result of breaking an electric circuit at two points or electrodes. The mechanism consists of the sparking device set in a brass bushing. The sparking points are operated by a trip rod. The timing device with its lever is so constructed as to advance or retard the action of the trip rod and hence gives a late or early spark.

The merit of this mechanical spark lies in the fact that it is extremely simple, consisting of the least number of working parts. Its mechanical action is short and consequently capable of high speed with the motor and accompanying accuracy in the time of required ignition. All the movable parts are constructed of case-hardened steel, offering the greatest strength and durability. The electrode points are of nickel steel, free from any tendency to rust and always maintaining a clean electrical contact.

The Jump Spark System.

The high tension or jump spark system is so called because the spark which it produces has a voltage sufficiently high to jump a fixed air gap. This system has no moving parts in the cylinder, and the mechanism is consequently very simple and not liable to get out of order by wear. On the other hand, the spark current must be very carefully insulated, since metallic contact is not necessary for a leak, and dirt, an air gap of ¼ inch or less, or simple moisture about the igniters, or spark plugs, will permit sufficient leakage to destroy the spark.

The spark plug has a central insulated stem surrounded by a porcelain or mica tube which is a gastight fit in a steel shell screwed into the cylinder wall. At the inner end a spark jumps from the central stem to an extension of the steel shell. After jumping the spark gap the current grounds itself in the engine and completes its return to the coil through the primary circuit. The effect of the action of the trembler or vibrator used in this system is to induce a high tension current in the secondary winding of the coil every time the trembler breaks contact with its screw, thereby producing a stream of sparks at the spark plug.

Installation of Ignition.

Wiring diagrams are usually furnished with marine gasolene engines in order that the ignition system may be properly installed and the purchaser should preserve the diagram so that he may understand the system in case of emergency. There are several points that should always be borne in mind. For instance, in a high-tension system the heavily insulated secondary wires, that lead from the coil to the spark plug are high tension wires conducting a high voltage of electricity and the utmost precaution must be taken to avoid short-circuiting by the wire coming in contact with any object that also serves as a conductor for the electric current.

All portions of the jump spark wiring system as well as the batteries, coil and plugs must be well protected from water, spray and even moist air, for they all have a detrimental effect upon it. Nothing but the very best grade of wire should be used, particularly for the secondary current, to insure satisfactory results at all times. It is essential to have every wire connection made with a clean contact and rigidly fastened so that it cannot work loose with vibration and cause failure of ignition perhaps when least expected.

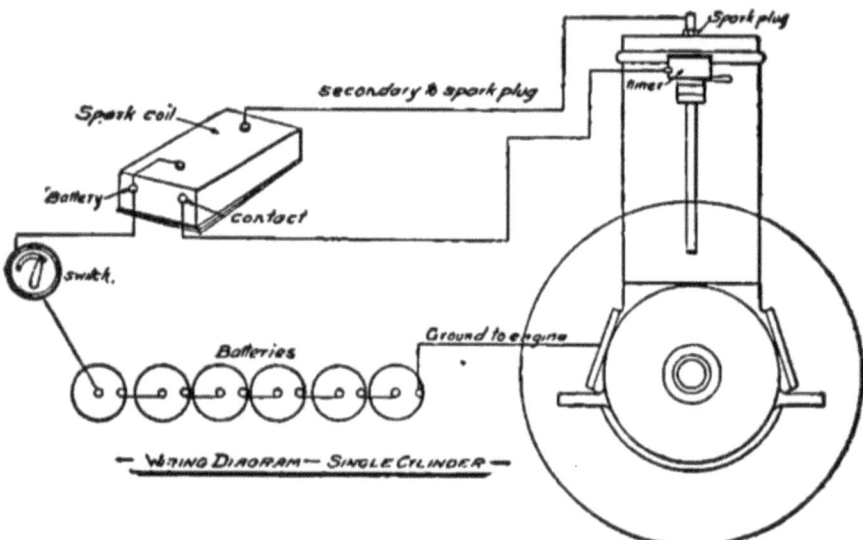

Wiring Diagram For Single Cylinder Engine.
(Fairbanks, Morse & Co., Chicago.)

When using batteries only, it is well to have two sets of five or six each, switching from one to the other alternately. This allows one set to recuperate while the other is in operation. It will be found to add greatly to the life of the batteries. Where a motor is receiving steady use, it is advisable to install a magneto, depending upon the batteries to start with only, or for emergency in case of possible mishap to the magneto.

The make-and-break ignition system, although somewhat similar to the jump spark, is much simpler to understand and install. The wiring diagrams will show the most satisfactory method used with batteries or the combination of a dynamo. The same arguments in favor of this combination are true with the make-and-break system as they are with the jump spark.

There are no high tension currents of electricity with make-and-break ignition, but nevertheless care should be exercised that wires do not cross or come in contact with one another so as to destroy the proper course of the electricity. The coil used with this system differs from that of the jump spark in that there is no vibrator to it. The construction of this coil, in a word, is a spool of

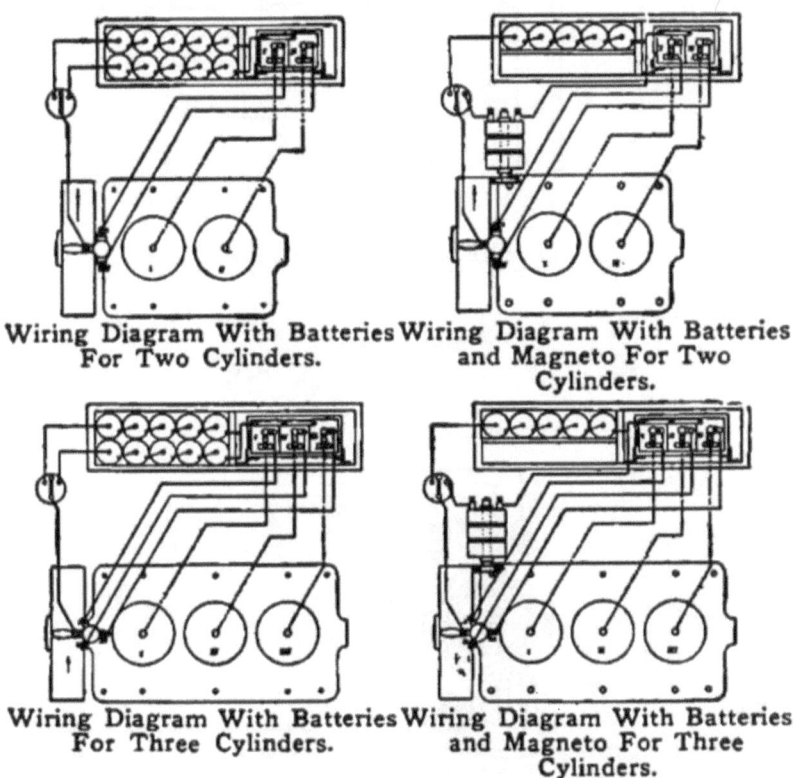

Wiring Diagram With Batteries For Two Cylinders.

Wiring Diagram With Batteries and Magneto For Two Cylinders.

Wiring Diagram With Batteries For Three Cylinders.

Wiring Diagram With Batteries and Magneto For Three Cylinders.

wire wound around an iron core. It serves to store the electricity for each successive operation of the igniting points, thereby imparting greater force to the current, resulting in a bright hot spark in the cylinder. The sparking points must be kept free from accumulation of burnt carbon or it will interfere with a good spark, if not result in total failure. It is of course essential to keep the mechanism of the make-and-break system amply lubricated with the frequent application of a first-class machine oil.

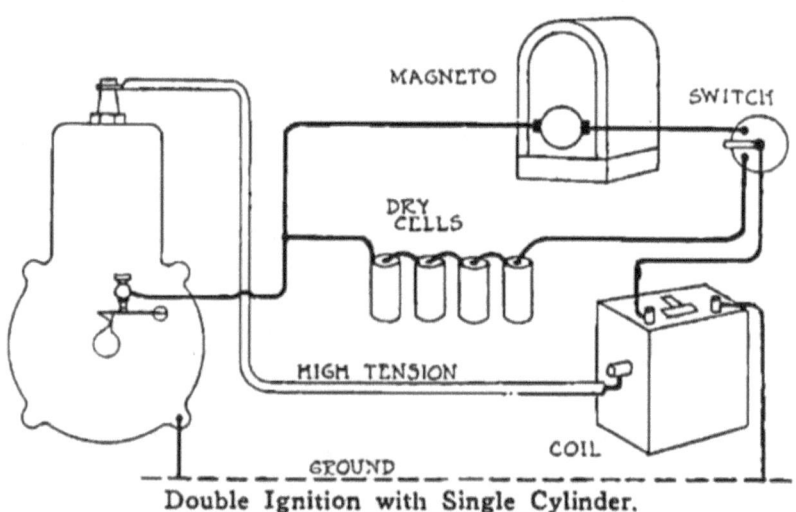
Double Ignition with Single Cylinder.

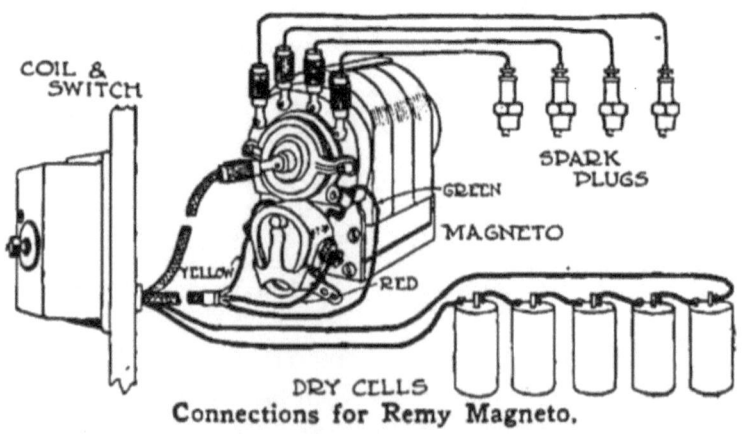
Connections for Remy Magneto.

High-Tension Magnetos.

Types of High-Tension Magnetos—To overcome the mechanical complications of the low-tension make-and-break system and the electrical troubles of the battery system, the high-tension magneto system has been almost universally adopted. Depending on the method by which the low-tension primary current is stepped up into the high-tension current, these magnetos may be classified into three general groups.

(1) **Dynamo Type**—The dynamo type of magneto is generally driven from the engine by a belt or friction pulley.

(2) **Transformer Type**—The transformer type is geared to the motor so that the armature position has a definite relation to the piston. A primary circuit breaker is incorporated in the magneto that breaks the primary at the end of the compression stroke. The low-tension primary current generated by the magneto is led to a non-vibrating spark coil. Only a single spark is produced at the time that the circuit breaker opens.

(3) **True High-Tension Type**—In this type of magneto the armature generates high-tension current directly without the use of a spark coil.

Direct Current Magnetos—The direct current magneto is commonly used on stationary engines. As the speed of the device is comparatively high, it is driven with a belt or friction pulley a governor being used to keep the voltage constant. It can be used for charging storage cells. A separate circuit breaker or timer must be used. In substituting this generator for a battery it is only necessary to disconnect the batteries and reconnect the same two wires with the dynamo.

Alternating Current Dynamos—Alternating current dynamos may be either belt, friction, or gear driven from the motor. This type is not installed with reference to the crankshaft and must be provided with a separate timer. No governor is necessary with the alternating current type, as the generator is to some extent self-regulating. This class cannot be used for charging storage batteries. It is placed in the circuit in the same way as the direct current dynamo.

True High-Tension Type—This is by far the most common type of high-tension magneto for the reason that it is compact and self-contained. It requires no coil except that used for a battery auxiliary. In the true high-tension type there are two windings on the armature, a primary and secondary, the secondary like the secondary of a spark coil, being composed of thousands of turns of very fine wire. The primary is of coarse wire and is interrupted by a circuit breaker. A spark is produced at every break in the primary circuit.

The outer end of the secondary wire is connected to the high-tension distributer through a slip ring mounted on the armature shaft. The distributer is driven from the armature shaft by a gear so that it revolves at camshaft speed. This type is geared to the motor in a definite relation, the armature shaft running at exactly crankshaft speed in the two and four cylinder types, and one and one-half crankshaft speed in the case of the six-cylinder motor. The primary circuit breaker is then so placed that it opens when the piston is very near to the end of the compression stroke, thus igniting the charge on the upper dead center.

A lead from each spark plug is brought to the distributer so that as the distributer arm revolves it comes into contact with the terminal of each plug in the correct firing order. A low-tension lead runs from the breaker box to the cutout switch, so that when the switch is closed the primary winding of the armature is short-circuited, thus stopping the motor.

Advance and retard in this type of magneto is had by shifting the casing of the circuit breaker back and forth so that the primary current is interrupted earlier or later in the revolution.

Typical True High-Tension Type.

In the accompanying figure is shown a perspective view of a true high-tension type magneto, the magnets and pole pieces being omitted for the sake of simplifying the drawing. The armature lies between the pole pieces and magnets. At the right of the perspective is a section through the armature showing the actual arrangements of the two windings on the armature. The shuttle armature of "H" form is indicated by H in both views.

The body of the armature in general is built of laminated sheet steel to prevent the generation of useless currents and to increase the magnetic flux through the winding. The primary winding is grounded to the core at Y, and is then given several turns around the core K, the outer end of the winding being connected to the bolt 2B at M.

From the point M, the secondary consisting of thousands of turns of very fine wire is started. The inner end of the secondary being connected to M makes the secondary a continuation of the primary. This is not shown in the perspective as it would complicate the drawing, but the true arrangement can be seen from the section at the right in which J is the primary and L is the secondary. The entire series of winding is insulated from the core by the insulation indicated by the heavy lines. Primary current is carried to the circuit breaker jaw 2A and the switch 2D, through the insulated connection bolt 2B. The outer end of the high-tension winding is carried to the high-tension collector ring E by means of the insulated pin 2E. A brush at 2B carries primary current to the grounding switch 2D, which when closed stops the generation of high-tension current.

A primary circuit breaker jaw 2A, connected to the primary winding, and insulated from the shaft, revolves with the shaft and makes intermittent contact with the jaw X at the point Z. The jaw X is grounded to the

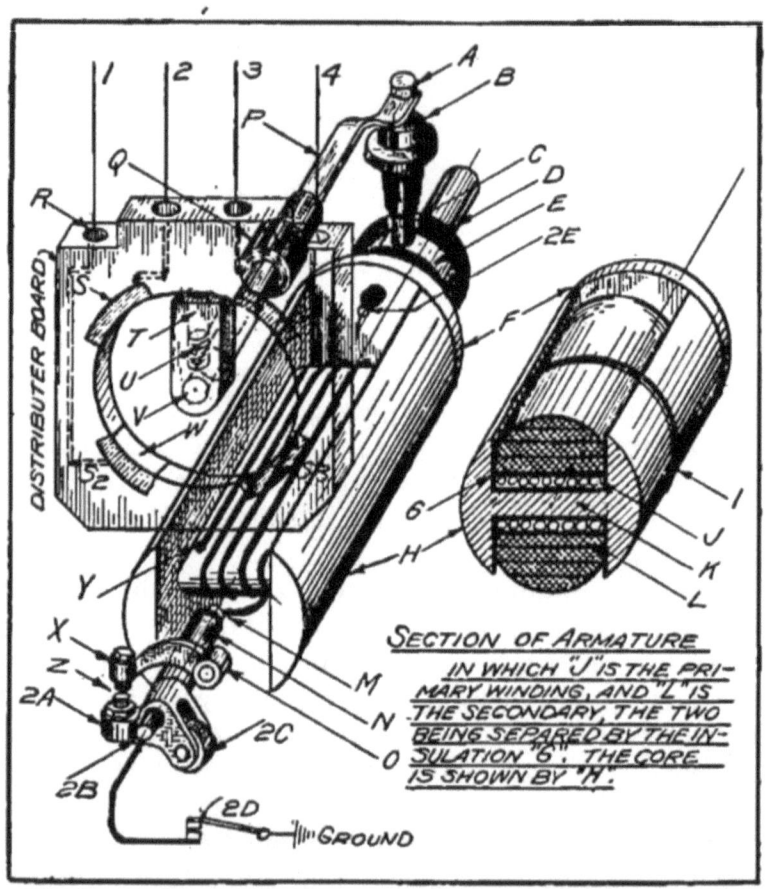

Typical True High Tension Type Magneto Showing Construction and Circuit in Diagrammatic Form.

shaft and revolves with it so that the two contact points are always opposite to one another. The opening and closing of the jaws is accomplished by means of a stationary cam which acts on the cam roller 2C. When the contact is broken, the primary circuit is opened which gives a heavy current impulse to the secondary winding. This impulse results in a spark at the plugs. The spark therefore occurs at the instant when the breaker opens the circuit.

By shifting the breaker housing to the right or left by means of lever, the breaker jaws open sooner or later in the revolution of the armature, causing the advance or retard of the spark. This is similar to the effect produced by rocking the housing of the battery timer.

A distributer board is shown in the perspective which contains the metal sectors S-S2-S3-S4, each of these sectors being connected to the wires 1-2-3-4, which lead to the spark plugs in the cylinders. These sectors receive high-tension current from the brush T contained in the revolving distributer arm V, each sector being charged in turn as the arm revolves. The distributer board is built of some high insulating material such as hard rubber or Bakelite, and is shown as if it were transparent so that the armature parts may be seen.

High-tension current from the secondary winding passes from the connection 2E to the collector ring E, this ring being thoroughly insulated from the frame by the hard rubber bushing D, shown in solid black. The high-tension current is taken from the collector ring by the brush C, through the insulating support B, and to the terminal A. From A the current passes through the bridge P to the distributer arm U through the brush holder Q and the connector V. The current passes to the plugs through 1-2-3-4, and the plugs being grounded, the current returns through the grounded frame to the armature coil. The distributer arm V is driven through a gear (not shown) from a pinion on the armature shaft N.

The following table will give the armature speeds for different numbers of cylinders. It should be remembered that in all cases the distributer runs at camshaft speed, and that there are as many distributer sectors as there are cylinders. The magneto must run twice as fast for a two cycle engine.

(Four-Cycle Type Motors Only.)

No. Cylinders	Distributer Gear Ratio	Armature Speed	Note
One	No Dist.	Crankshaft Speed	
Two	No Dist.	Crankshaft Speed	
Three	½ to 1	¾ Crankshaft Speed	
Four	2 to 1	Crankshaft Speed	
*Five	No Dist.	5/4 times Crankshaft Speed	Rotary Motor Dist. on Motor
Six	3 to 1	1½ times Crankshaft Speed	
*Seven	No Dist.	1¾ times Crankshaft Speed	Rotary Motor Dist. on Motor
Eight	4 to 1	2 times Crankshaft Speed	Single Magneto
Eight	2 to 1	Crankshaft Speed	Two Magnetos (each 4 cyls.)
*Nine	No Dist.	9/4 times Crankshaft Speed	Rotary Motor Dist. on Motor
†Ten	5 to 1	2½ times Crankshaft Speed	Radial Aero Type
Twelve	6 to 1	3 times Crankshaft Speed	One Magneto for Twelve Cyls.
Twelve	3 to 1	1½ times Crankshaft Speed	Two Magnetos (each for 6 cyls.)

* Denotes the arrangement used with rotary engines in which no magneto distributer is used, the plugs of the rotating cylinders coming into contact with a stationary brush held by the magneto. The magneto is of the single-cylinder type.
† Denotes a radial arrangement of cylinders, all cylinders being stationary. Seldom used.

Bosch High Tension Magneto.

The Bosch DU4 type is a true high tension magneto, the armature containing a primary and secondary winding. The circuit diagram will serve as a guide to the actual construction. For clearness, the armature is shown in side elevation, while the distributer and circuit breaker are front elevations. The primary wiring is shown by solid

CONSTRUCTION AND OPERATION

heavy lines, the secondary by fine solid lines, and the grounded circuit by dots and dashes.

Since the secondary winding is simply a continuation of the coarse wire primary winding it is shown as a single coil. The high tension is collected at the left of the armature by means of a collector ring and brush, the lead from the upper terminal of the brush being connected to the safety spark gap on its way to the distributer. The distributer brush as it revolves makes successive contact with distributer segments 1-2-3-4, leads from these segments, running to the respective spark plugs 1-2-3-4 shown in the upper lefthand corner of the diagram.

A condenser is housed with the armature at the right whose purpose is to absorb the spark at the breaker

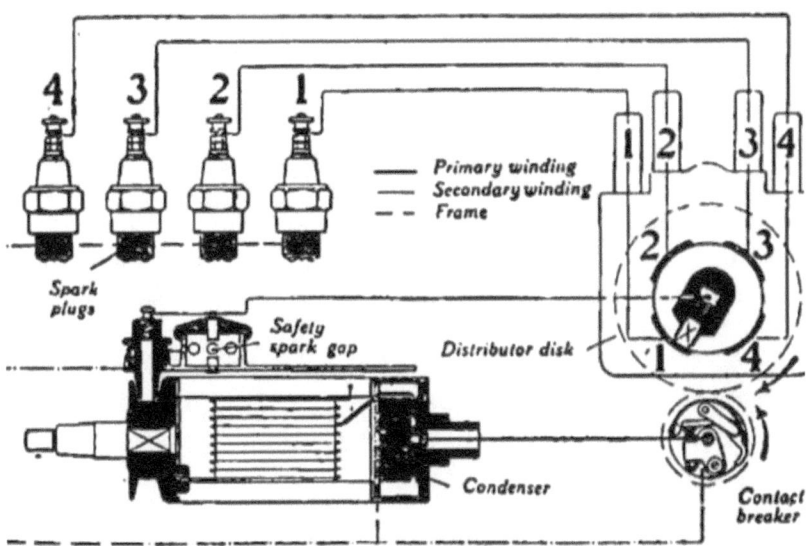

Bosch High Tension Magneto Circuit.

points. One end of both the primary winding and the condenser is grounded. The outer shells of the spark plugs, the frame, and the armature are all grounded as will be seen from the dot and dash lines. In the longitudinal section the high tension current from the secondary winding is led to the high tension collector ring 9. A brush 10 pressing on this ring collects the current, and through the spring 11, the bridge 12, and the brush 13, it passes to the rotating distributer brush or arm 15. In rotating, the brush makes successive contact with the distributer segments. A terminal shown projecting from the bridge 12 into the safety spark gap housing is placed opposite to another terminal fastened to the top plate of the armature tunnel. This gap prevents an excessive voltage that might be caused by a loose or broken high-tension connection.

Primary current is led from the armature to the circuit breaker through the insulated connection bolt 2, an intermediate connection being made to this bolt from the condenser 8. The outer end of the bolt 2 is connected to the interrupter or circuit breaker jaw 3, an insulating strip 4 separates the block from the metal of the frame. At the end of 2 a spring controlled brush carries current to the terminal 24 through the spring 26 and the clip 25. A connection from 24 is led to the grounding switch whose purpose is to stop the engine. The supporting block 27 is insulated from the clamp 23 which holds the distributer cover 22 on the distributer disk 16. A hard rubber hub 14 carries the brush 15. The prolonged shank of the hub 14 rotates in the bearing at the left of the hub, the bearing being thoroughly insulated from the current conducting rod that runs from the brush 13 to the brush 15.

The end of the primary winding is connected to the plate 1 into which the connecting bolt 2 is screwed. This plate is insulated from the frame by the strip of hard rubber shown between the end piece and the condenser 8.

Current from 2 enters the breaker block or jaw 3, which on referring to the front elevation, will be seen to carry the platinum breaker point retained by screw 5.

These parts are both insulated from the breaker disk 4 which carries the rotating parts. A contact breaker lever 7 (grounded to the frame) carries a platinum screw 29 which makes contact intermittently with the first platinum point 5. These points are normally forced into contact by the flat spring 6. It should be remembered

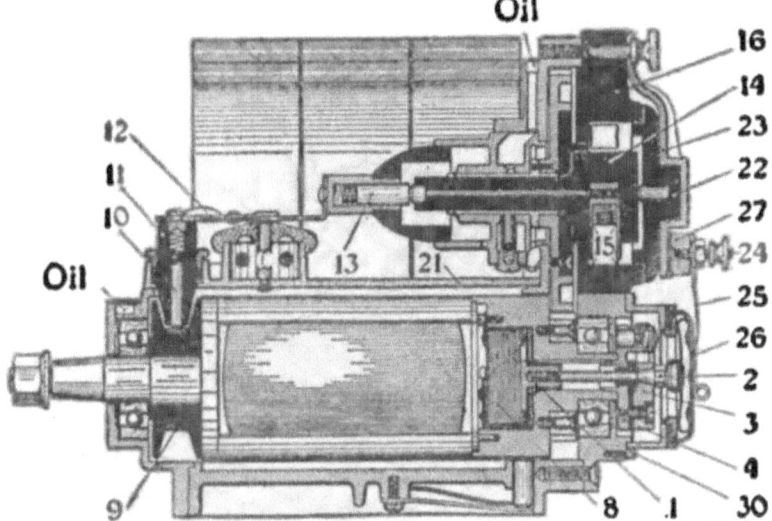

FIG. 4.—Longitudinal Section Through Bosch Four Cylinder High Tension Magneto.

that the contact block 3, points 5 and 29, the lever 7 and the spring 6 are mounted on the armature front plate 4 and revolve with it.

Two fiber cam disks 19-19 mounted in the breaker housing make contact with the toe end of the lever 7, causing the platinum points to open every time that the end of the lever passes the cams. As this is a shuttle armature giving two current impulses per revolution, there are two cams to open the breaker at the highest voltage peak of each impulse. A rocker arm 20 is connected with the breaker housing so that the housing and the cams can be rocked for advance and retard.

The brush 15 carried in the distributer arm 14 receives

the high tension current. The distributer segments connect with plug sockets 16 into which are pushed the plugs or spring jacks 18 that carry the high tension cables to the spark plugs in the cylinders.

There are as many segments and plugs as there are cylinders. With single and double cylinder engines there is no distributer, the high tension current being carried

Inductors of K. W. Magneto.

directly to the spark plugs from the high tension collector rings. In every other respect the construction is the same. The distributer brush is driven from the armature shaft by a gear and pinion.

Needless to say, the Bosch magneto must be geared or chain driven by the engine, since there is a positive relation between the piston position of the engine and the time at which the circuit breaker opens the primary circuit.

"K. W." Inductor Type Magneto.

The primary winding of the K. W. inductor magneto occupies the space between the two revolving inductor masses, and gives four current impulses per revolution. The construction of the K. W. system is shown below in which I and I^1 are the inductors and C is the primary winding. As the inductors are double ended and at right angles each inductor cuts the magnetic field four times per revolution, two times for each end.

This magneto may be used either as a low tension, low tension transformer type, or as a true high tension magneto. When used as a true high tension type the usual circuit breaker and high tension distributer are mounted directly on the instrument.

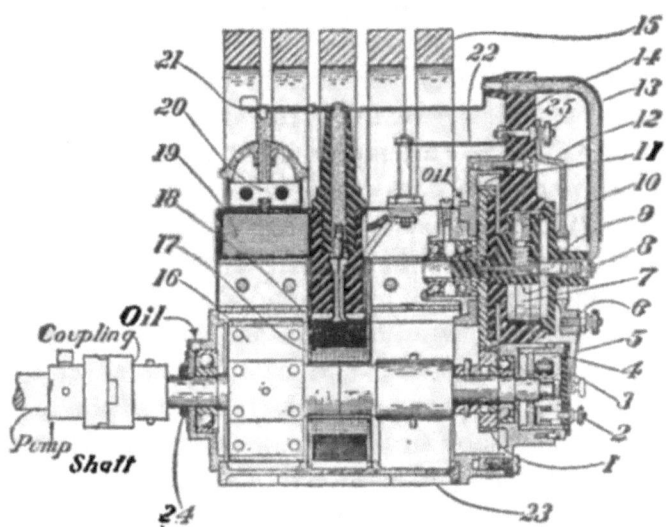

Longitudinal Section Through K. W. High Tension Magneto.

Like all magnetos, the true high tension K. W. is positively driven from the engines through gears or chain, and as there are four impulses per revolution instead of two, the speed relative to the engine is half that given for the shuttle type armature.

"K. W." High Tension Magneto.

The "K. W." high tension magneto generates high tension current directly without the use of a spark coil. The arrangement of the coil and inductors is practically the same as in the case of the low tension K. W. magneto except for the fact that the generating coil carries both a primary and secondary winding.

A longitudinal section is shown above in which 16-16 are the inductors and 17-18 are the primary and secondary coils respectively. A hard rubber insulator carries the high tension lead from the secondary coil to the point where it connects with the bridge 21. The current from the primary winding is led to the circuit breaker through the connectors 22, 25, and 12, the final connections coming from 12 to the terminal 6, and then through strip 5 to the breaker jaws.

High tension current from the bridge 21 splits two ways, one way being to the distributer through 13, and the other being to the safety sparks gap 20. Current enters the porcelain cap through a point, and if a sufficiently high voltage exists it jumps across the gap 20 to the point mounted on the condenser case 19, and thence to the frame and ground. A condenser 19 is connected across the primary winding. As one end of the primary winding is grounded, one side of the condenser is also grounded to the condenser. The free end of the primary winding is closed and broken by the interrupter contacts.

High tension current from the lead 13 enters the distributer by the way of the brush 9,

CHAPTER VI.

LUBRICATION AND COOLING SYSTEMS.

The friction between moving parts of a machine produces heat and consequent loss of energy. Hence to minimize the loss and prevent wear of the surfaces in contact, lubrication is necessary. This is especially true of the moving parts of an internal combustion engine, and every owner of a gasolene motor finds it essential to see that the system of lubrication performs its function thoroughly under all conditions.

The best lubricants for the motor boat engine and reversing gear are usually specified by the manufacturer, and it is well to follow the advice thus given. Owing to the fact that the cylinder walls are exposed to direct flame on the explosion stroke, only pure mineral oil of high fire test can be used. Such oil is known as "gas engine oil," and can be bought in different viscosities and qualities to suit different conditions. The oil may be fed to the cylinder walls and piston in various ways, but the best systems are those known as the splash system and the mechanical oiler system. In the former, the crank-case is filled with oil until the crank ends dip slightly and splash the oil throughout the interior of the crank-case. The oil is supplied to the crank-case either by sight feed oil cups or by a mechanical lubricator run by the engine. In the second system the mechanical lubricator feeds oil through small pipes directly to the cylinder, usually on the side against which the piston presses during the explosion stroke. The crank-pin bearings are usually oiled by splash, and the main crankshaft bearings receive oil either by splash from pockets over the bearings inside the crank case, or by direct feed from a mechanical oiler. The main shaft bearings may be lubricated by oil or grease according to design. The reversing gear is generally packed with grease, mineral grease being preferable.

As stated, oil may be fed to the pistons either drop by drop as required, or by internal splash in the crank-case. If oil cups are used their rate of feed requires constant watching, as it is greatly affected by changes in temperature, etc. A good mechanical oiler is very reliable.

A lighter oil than usual may be used in cold weather.

The Splash System.

Where positive pressure oiling systems are supplied, some manufacturers also furnish the regular "splash-feed" system, as an auxiliary safeguard against careless-

Crankshaft Oil Hole.

ness or ignorance. It often consists of two wicks in the end of the connecting cap, operating on the crank-pin, which constantly feed oil to this bearing. The oil which settles down into the bottom of the crank-case forms a pool which is splashed all over the interior by the rapid revolutions of the crank, and thus gives the system its name. This system, while not always a reliable one for general oiling, is valuable as an emergency feature, and should only be depended on as such.

There are, broadly speaking, four vital points in a gasolene engine which must positively be oiled—the cylinder, piston, crank-pin and crankshaft main bearings.

When the "splash system" of lubrication is used it is essential to keep the oil level such that the cranks dip into it very slightly. Too much oil will make a smoky exhaust and foul the igniters with soot and grease. Usually a sight-feed or mechanical oiler supplies the crank-case, but it may be necessary to add extra oil from time to time. When the oil in the crank-case gets black it should be thrown away, the crank-case interior flushed with kerosene, and the engine run a few moments to wash the bearings; after which the kerosene is drained off, fresh oil introduced, and the engine run again for a minute or two without load to splash the oil into the bearings.

The crank-pins may receive oil by simple splash, or it may be fed to them through oil ducts in the cranks from the main bearings or from individual supply pipes. The main bearings themselves may receive oil from a mechanical oiler, from individual oil cups, or from pockets over the inner ends of the bearings, into which oil is splashed by the cranks. Whatever arrangement is used should be well understood by the owner, so that he will make sure that sufficient oil is supplied.

The main bearings of two-cycle engines are frequently fed with grease, the object being to prevent air leakage from the crank-case. Grease may also be used in the main bearings of a four-cycle engine if they tend to run hot. Spring compression cups are best for this purpose.

A Typical Oiling System.

The plan of lubrication adopted in single and multiple cylinder Ferro engines of the most recent construction is a positive pressure sight-feed oiling system. This system, it is claimed, takes nothing for granted and provides a system which works just as surely as the engine works, forcing a uniform constant supply of oil to every bearing surface in the exact amount for each. It starts automatically and works with the engine. The simplicity of the entire device is notable. The oil reservoir, a separate airtight compartment, is cast integral with the crankcase. A short tube with a check valve, connects the

Ferro 3-cylinder Engine.

crank chamber to the reservoir. At each revolution pressure is stored in the reservoir, and thus serves to force oil up to the sight-feed distributer through a feed tube. From the bottom of each sight-feed valve, an oil tube leads directly to the vital part of each bearing. In a single-cylinder engine there are four sight-feed valves and tubes; in a two-cylinder engine, six, etc.

The system of distribution is as follows: The tube leading to the cylinder conducts the oil direct to its inside wall at a point in line with the hollow piston pin and oil grooves of piston. The oil passes through the piston pin to opposite walls of cylinder and is collected in the oil grooves, picked up by the piston rings and distributed by the up-and-down motion of the piston to every portion of the rubbing surface. The tube leading to each main bearing cap conducts the oil through the caps to the rotating crankshaft, and thence through holes drilled from main bearing portions of crankshaft to crank-pin. Each ball thrust bearing also receives its quota of oil from the adjoining main bearing cap. Thus it will be seen that every vital bearing is supplied directly with a positive feed supply of lubricating oil. Each sight-feed valve can be instantly adjusted to deliver a "drop by drop" supply to its respective bearing. As an additional precaution a tube is led to the carbureter, where the oil is vaporized and fed to all interior parts of the engine.

The regular splash-feed system, as above described, is also supplied with Ferro engines.

COOLING SYSTEMS.

A high degree of heat being developed in the cylinder of a gasolene engine by the combustion of the fuel mixture lubrication is not sufficient to prevent the walls of the cylinder from becoming overheated. Unless this tendency is counteracted, the result will be the cutting and scoring of the piston and cylinder walls where they come into contact. Hence, it is absolutely necessary to remove excessive heat in the metal. There are two methods commonly used for this purpose, both being in successful operation at the present time. In the first and most common, water is used for cooling the cylinder, while in the second a current of air exerts the cooling influence.

The Water Cooling Method.

The water method consists essentially of a pump and a jacket around the cylinder, usually cast integral with it. This jacket forms a hollow pocket around the cylinder, through which the water is forced and kept in constant circulation, thus carrying off the excess heat in the metal.

In the best modern practice the engine design is such as to allow for independent expansion between the cylinder and its jacket, so that the cylinder may expand and contract without reference to the jacket or barrel.

The pump to supply the cooling water, by means of a cold water intake and seacock, may be either a reciprocating plunger operated by an eccentric on the crankshaft, or, in the case of a four-cycle engine, the valve camshaft. Rotary pumps are also sometimes used.

A certain amount of heat is required for the successful operation of an internal combustion engine and care must be taken by the engine designer that the cooling system does not remove too much heat from the cylinder. If the cylinder becomes overheated, there is danger of injury to both piston and cylinder, but on the other hand, if too much heat is removed, the efficiency of the engine will be lessened. The gasolene engine is essentially a heat engine and in the cooling system a happy medium is the object to be desired.

The Air Cooling Method.

The air method of cooling an internal combustion engine consists of a series of ribs or fins arranged around the cylinder, thus presenting a large radiating surface over which is usually blown a constant stream of air by employing a rotary fan similar in design to the ordinary electric fan. For marine work, where water is at hand, it is far more practical and convenient to employ it as a means of cooling the cylinder than air. The air-cooled cylinder is more liable to become overheated, unless some further means is employed to increase the circulation of air.

Air Cooled Cylinder.

It was realized long ago by the foremost engine builders that the cooling problem of the gasolene engine must receive careful study or power and efficiency would be sacrificed, to say nothing of money for needless repairs. Hence the former idea that any sort of water cooling arrangement would suffice so long as it provided water in contact with the exterior walls of the cylinder, is fast passing away. In the best modern engines the proper degree of efficiency is secured in the water system in the simplest and most direct way, the cooling water pursuing in its course clean-cut straight lines, free from air pockets.

The coolest water in the cylinder jackets is near the bottom. The hottest part of the cool part of the jacket is where the exhaust comes from the engine. At that point the cold water supplied by the pump enters, in a typical modern system, and passing up and around between the walls of the cylinder and jacket, discharges at the extreme top of the cylinder. A generous sized concealed trunk main delivers the water to the cylinder, and a similar concealed duct receives the discharge from the cylinder jacket and carries it to the exhaust condenser, which leads the exhaust noiselessly to the side of the boat or through the bottom.

In frosty or freezing weather particular attention must be given to the draining of all water jackets and channels. This can be done, in the representative system referred to above, by simply removing the water drain plug at the end of the water channel under the crank-case and loosening the vent plug in top of the cylinder. If desirable for greater convenience, a pet cock may be inserted by the owner in place of the channel plug.

Pumps.

The pump is a very important part of the motor and should be specially designed to supply water to the cylinder jacket, in as steady proportion as the speed of the motor may require. It is sometimes a slighted feature of marine motors, its importance not being always properly recognized, but the tendency of modern construction is towards perfection of this feature of the engine, and very satisfactory pumps are furnished by some of the leading engine-builders.

The illustration shows the course of water circulation in the Ferro engine, which is equipped with a patent circulating pump. The latter consists of a small barrel with stuffing-box, in which a hollow piston works, driven by an eccentric, whose strap is pivoted to the piston by a pin. The eccentric is bolted to the crankshaft by a screw. The suction nipple is connected by a hose with seacock and intake passing through the bottom of boat, by which means the water is admitted to the valve chamber.

The stem of the suction valve slides in the discharge valve. Both valves drop into the valve chamber and make tight, easy fits on their respective seats. The bonnet which closes the valve chamber permits of instant inspection. The pump discharges into a concealed feed

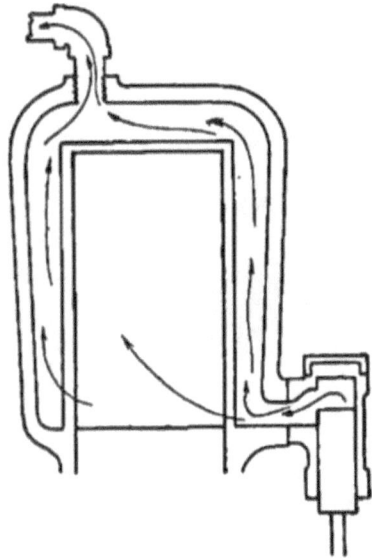

Water Circulation—The Ferro Engine.

main, where it bolts by a flange to the engine frame. A trycock drains the entire pump. If grit should cut the valve seats, it is a simple operation to grind them in by applying a little emery and oil on the valve seats and turning both valves in place by the wings on top of the discharge valve.

The action of the pump may be facilitated in drawing the water from the seacock or intake, by placing a scoop over the opening of the intake pipe. This scoop is a crown-shaped disk with two long openings on the side that catch the water when the boat is moving forward.

CHAPTER VII

EXHAUST DEVICES.

The noise and odor of the exhaust gases escaping from a gasolene motor being continuous and objectionable, some device is necessary to deaden them. The device in universal use on land for this purpose is an air muffler and for marine gasolene engines the air muffler is also often used. It is usually made in the form of a cylindrical chamber attachable to the exhaust pipe. It is fitted in-

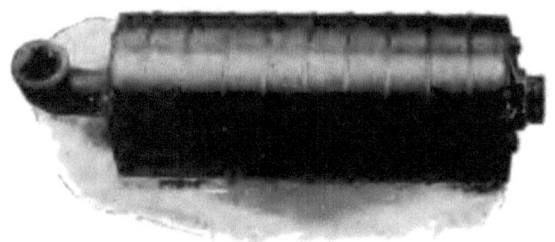

A Common Form of Marine Air Muffler.

side with baffle plates, against which the exhaust gases expand and then escape into the air at the open end by the way of an attached pipe leading through the side of the boat at a point above the water line.

Water Mufflers.

The air muffler serves best, however, on land, for automobiles, etc. In boats, different conditions exist. On account of the well known condensing action of water and consequent reduction in pressure where cool water is mingled with the exhaust gases, it is possible to both silence the noise and increase the power developed by the engine. Besides, as the water is being pumped through the cylinder jacket constantly, an automatic feed to the exhaust pipes may be had, keeping them almost cool to the touch.

The first form of muffler consisted of a water jacket around an air muffler through which the waste cooling water was led and then piped overboard. Then another method was tried, namely, running some of the water directly into the exhaust pipe, between the engine and the muffler. In this case it was necessary to make the

A Common Form of Marine Water Muffler.

muffler water-tight, while the air muffler is not water-tight. The immediate result was a great reduction of noise and pressure in the exhaust. It required careful regulation of the water, also a drain for deposited water in the muffler.

The Under-Water Exhaust.

The under-water or submerged exhaust is an effective way of muffling the exhaust noises, but it must be installed properly to be a success.

A submerged exhaust should never be put in a boat without a relief valve leading to a free opening, so that when starting, or at any time that it may be necessary, the exhaust may be turned out into the open air.

The depth below the water and the location of the outlet on the bottom of the hull are dependent greatly upon the general lines of the boat.

Choice of Exhaust Devices.

All boat owners are interested in the question, What method of discharging the exhaust in motor-boats is most efficient in reducing the noise and odor without impairing the power of the engine or interfering with the interior arrangement of the boat?

This question was asked of its readers recently by the popular magazine, Motor Boating, and the prize-winning answer by Mr. L. Kromholz, of New York City, was as follows:

"The choice of a muffler must be made from a study of the circumstances governing each case. That an arrangement of apparatus gives complete satisfaction on one boat does not necessarily mean that it will be equally successful on another.

"For open launches an expansion chamber and a large pipe leading aft to the stern and out under water is a good and simple method. The difficulty of water getting back into the pipe and filling the cylinders, can be overcome by running the exhaust pipe in a straight line (under the side seats) from the motor to the outboard fitting. This will be well above the waterline and have enough pitch so as to drain easily. A relief cock should be fitted to assist in starting the motor. The loss of power, if any, will be slight, in fact in some cases .it is claimed more power can be obtained with the submerged exhaust than without it.

"On high speed runabouts all of the cooling water from the motor can be let through the muffler, but the piping must be in a straight line without any quick bends where the water is likely to collect and choke the exhaust. A completely water-jacketed exhaust from the motor to the outlet at the stern is an efficient device. The straight lead aft to the stern will cause but litttle back pressure if the pipe is of good size.

"A water-jacketed muffler or one with the cooling water running through it with the exhaust outlet under water and near the engine, is a good arrangement for cabin cruisers. Another way would be to wrap asbestos around the exhaust pipe and lead it under the seats or berths in the cabin, under the flooring in the cockpit to the muffler in the stern and out. In this way the piping would have a fairly straight lead with no sharp turns and would not interfere with the accommodations to any extent. Letting the exhaust out at the stern is good practice, as there is hardly a chance of the odor being blown over the occupants of the cockpit.

"On the larger motor boats or yachts the best and most popular way is through water-jacketed mufflers in a false funnel or stack. But while a stack will improve the appearance of many yachts it cannot always be made a thing of beauty.

"Sharp turns, bends or ells in the exhaust pipe should strictly be avoided as they decrease the speed of the boat a great deal."

Another experienced boatman, Mr. J. B. Sadler, of the Navy Yard, Norfolk, Va., also writing in Motor Boating, advocated the under-water method of muffling as follows:

"For reducing the noise and odor of the exhaust in motor-boats and at the same time increasing the efficiency of the motor, the submerged exhaust system is without an equal.

"By this system the exhaust is conducted from the motor to the expansion chamber, which must be located above the load waterline of the boat and from thence to a special fitting or nozzle, located in the bottom or side of the boat below the waterline.

"As it is desirable that the flow of the exhaust through the exhaust nozzle be continuous, the expansion chamber must be placed between the motor and the nozzle, and should have at least six times the cubic capacity of the motor cylinder.

"Before the exhaust passes overboard it must be cooled and contracted to its original volume, otherwise the contraction will take place beneath the boat and result in an annoying jar to the hull. To accomplish this, the general practice is to lead a part of the circulating water into the top of the expansion chamber or the exhaust pipe leading to it, but as the circulating water is somewhat heated, it is better to pump cold water direct.

"The pipe leading from the expansion chamber to the exhaust nozzle should be larger than the exhaust pipe, and the exhaust nozzle should have the same area as the enlarged pipe.

"The exhaust nozzle should point aft and be located away from the propeller, for if located in front, it tends to slacken the speed of the boat.

"To facilitate starting the motor and prevent water being drawn into the engine cylinder in case of backfire, a three way cock should be placed in the exhaust line. This cock should be so arranged as to have the exhaust opened to the atmosphere and closed to the sea when starting the motor. The pull exerted on the exhaust of a boat equipped with the submerged exhaust system, has the effect of increasing the speed of the engine. In some cases this increase has been as much as 50 revolutions per minute."

Ferro Intake and Exhaust Header For a 3-cylinder Engine.

CHAPTER VIII

INSTALLATION OF ENGINES.

As a rule, it may be said, the installation of a marine gasolene engine is a comparatively easy matter. By reference to the diagrams and instructions presented in the following pages, which apply to well known engines' of typical make, the amateur will be able to install an engine properly in a canoe, rowboat, launch, flat-bottom boat, sailboat or yacht without special tools or expert experience. These instructions—or those furnished by the engine builders in the case of engines not referred to here—should be read with care, and each part of the work should be done in the order named. After each part has been done the work should be examined to see that it has been done properly before taking up the next part.

In selecting practical instructions for installing a few well-known engines, the object has been, not to show any discrimination in favor of the engines mentioned, but to cover by actual illustration all the points likely to arise in installing an engine of any make. There are many good, reliable engines in the market besides those named in these pages and the power boatman has a wide range of choice. No matter what engine he may select, however, he will find among the instructions given below many general points applicable to all engines alike—and these are the points most essential to observe. The installation features peculiar to any particular engine are always clearly indicated by the manufacturer or sales agent.

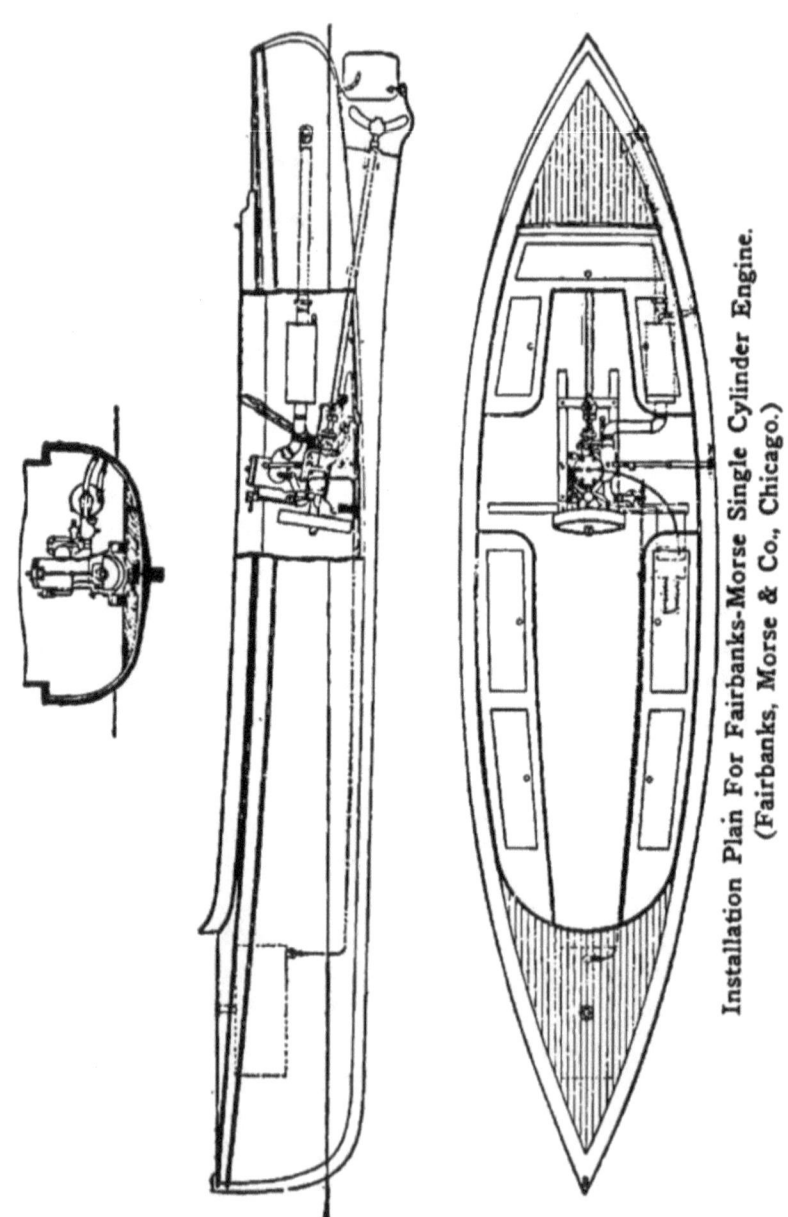

Installation Plan For Fairbanks-Morse Single Cylinder Engine. (Fairbanks, Morse & Co., Chicago.)

It is impossible to get satisfactory results from your engine unless the foundation is right and the engine is properly installed. The foundation should be so constructed as to take up the thrust and distribute the engine vibration over a large part of the bottom of the boat. The following is a foundation recommended for the Ferro engine. It is simple and easily installed and yet fulfills all the essentials of a good foundation:

It is assumed at the outset that the skeg or shaft-log is in place ready to receive the propeller shaft. Stretch a string so that it passes exactly through the center of the shaft hole and fasten it in this position, having the forward end a little in front of where you plan to place your

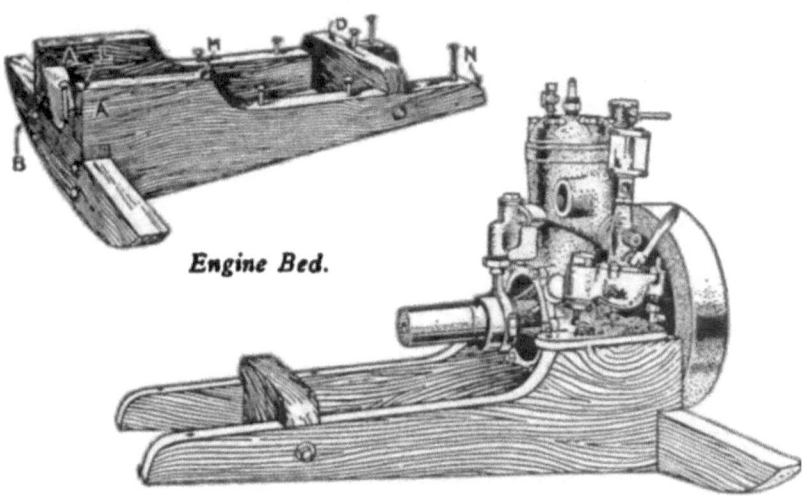

Engine Bed.

Ferro Special on Engine Bed.

engine. This string will be about ⅝ inch higher than the level of the top of the engine bed (the thickness of the crank-case flange). Another method is to place a piece of gaspipe in the shaft hole, making it long enough to reach forward of the engine bed. When this pipe is leveled up it will give you almost exactly the level of the engine bed.

Get out two fore-and-aft pieces (AA) first. All the foundation timbers should be of oak if possible, or other hard wood if oak is not obtainable. For engines below about 15 H. P. two-inch stock can be used, but pieces three inches thick should be used for engines over 15 H. P. Lay off on the bottom of the boat the position of the fore and aft logs, having the inside width between them about an inch less than the width between the crank-case holes as shown on the engine dimension sheet.

The bottom of these timbers should of course be shaped to conform to the bottom of the boat in the position laid off. They should be laid on top of the ribs and not notched out to receive them. The height of these fore-and-aft timbers can of course be determined by leveling

Parts of Engine Bed.

up a straight-edge on top of the string or pipe and measuring the height from this to the boat ribs, allowing about ½ inch in using the wire and the thickness of the pipe in using that.

The distance L-M, the engine bed proper, is of course determined by the length of the crank-case, and must be increased when using the reverse gear, as shown in an illustration, but how long the after-end of the log (M-N) should be must be determined by circumstances. It is a good plan to make it nearly or quite as long as the forward distance (L-M) and in case of a single-cylinder engine it will do no harm to have it even longer, provided you place your engine in such a position as to make this possible.

Remember a single-cylinder engine requires a heavier bed proportionately than a multiple cylinder engine.

Notch out underneath the forward ends of the fore-and-aft timbers about two-thirds of their height to receive the forward crosspiece (B) as shown in the diagram. This crosspiece should be cut to extend the extreme width of the boat and should be carefully shaped to fit the bottom of the boat at this point.

Reverse Gear on Engine Bed.

Another crosspiece (D) ties together the after ends of the fore-and-aft timbers, being notched out at both ends to receive them. This piece can run the whole width of the boat and should be full height and shaped to conform to the bottom of the boat. In installing engines of 15 H. P. or over, it is also well to add a crossbrace between the fore-and-aft timbers just forward of the pump and of as great height as possible and yet give plenty of clearance. Crosspieces should be about 1½ inches thick for the smaller engines and 2 inches for the larger ones.

After all the timbers are got out they should be nailed down temporarily and the engine and shaft put in place to test the foundation and see if it is of the proper height and slant so the shaft will be in line when the engine is in place. If ribs do not come under the engine bolt holes, put in extra ones that will, so you can bolt through them. If this test shows the foundation to be right or nearly so, the logs may be bolted down as shown in the diagram. Note that all crosspieces are bolted through the keel and the fore and aft pieces bolted through rib and planking at intervals of every other rib. In no case should bolts be fastened through the planking only, as this will work the planking loose. Put good-sized washers coated with white lead under the boltheads on the bottom of the boat so as to prevent possibility of leakage. Note that the crosspiece is lagged to the fore and aft pieces in front and the middle crossbrace lagged through them from each side.

With the foundation thus fastened in place, the engine is now ready to be installed. The final lining up should be done when the boat is in the water, for then it changes its alignment somewhat. If your boat has no skeg, but an outboard bearing, place your inboard stuffing-box on the shaft, but don't fasten it in place until you have lined up your engine and shaft. But if your boat has a skeg, put your stuffing-box outside in place first and see whether the shaft turns freely before it is fastened to the engine. If not loosen the box and pack around it until the shaft turns freely, then screw the box in place. The hole in the shaft log should be ¼ inch larger than the diameter of the shaft. Fill with white lead between the stuffing-box and its seat.

After putting the engine in place fasten half of the flange coupling to the propeller shaft and hold this up against the flange coupling on the end of the engine crankshaft. Note whether the two halves come together evenly all the way around. If not, move the engine sideways or pack up, or cut away under one end as the case may be until four strips of paper placed between the two

CONSTRUCTION AND OPERATION

parts of the coupling on opposite sides are held with even tension as the coupling is pressed together. Now bolt down the engine in the four corners and try the strips of paper again. If all are held evenly, bolt the engine down permanently; if not change the position of the engine as before until the right position is found.

This done, take the spark plugs out of the cylinders and note how much force is required to turn the engine over. Then bolt the coupling together and again try turning the engine over. It should turn as freely as before. This is important. **The engine must turn as freely when coupled to the propeller shaft as when uncoupled.**

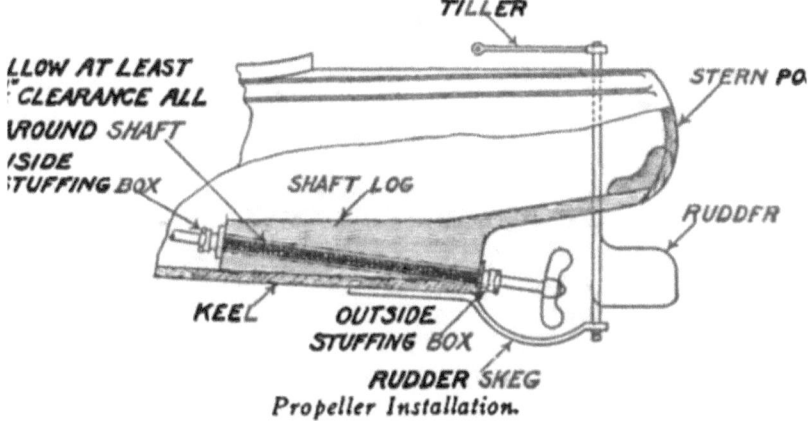

Propeller Installation.

If it does not, something is out of line and must be changed or serious loss of power and perhaps worse trouble will result. Unbolt your coupling and go carefully over your alignment again as described above. Pack the stuffing-box between the nut and body with hemp or candle wicking soaked in grease and screw up just tight enough to stop water leak but not enough to bind the shaft.

To Install a Reversible Propeller—Before connecting shaft to engine coupling locate the lever, quadrant, thrust and clamp collars and inside stuffing-box. Place quadrant with pin towards the engine. Allow space between fork and stern bearings for moving the lever forward to unlock the header when pin is removed from the forward end of quadrant. On long shafts place bearings every five feet along the tubing. Be sure the shaft does not bind in any way. Use grease between shaft and sleeve and in blade joints. Place the reverse lever in a vertical

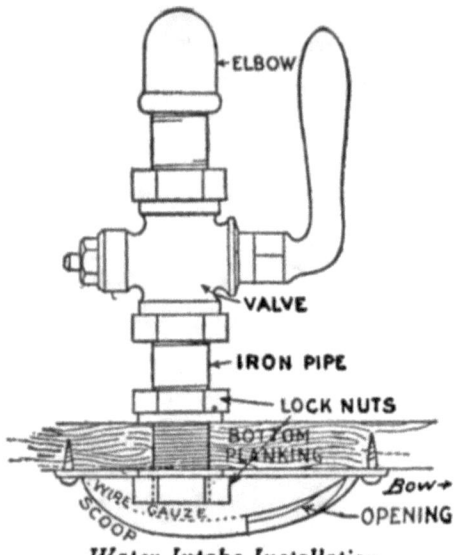

Water Intake Installation.

position with tips of blades square with shaft. Then securely bolt clamp collars against center thrust collar. The blades will then have the same pitch whether full lead ahead or reverse. To remove the blades, take out the pin in the forward end of the quadrant, moving lever forward until the blades are unlocked from fork, then unscrew the blades from the hub.

Bore the hole for your water intake in such a place that the piping between the pump connection and intake will have no sharp turn in it, and never reduce size of this pipe. A short piece of hose can be used as a joint for flexibility, but we would caution you against making this hose connection too long, as you will have leaks and pump trouble. As good an intake connection as any is to take a short piece of gas pipe threaded to take a lock nut on the inside and one on outside of planking. Pack the lock nuts inside and out with two or three turns of candle wick soaked in white lead. It is well to connect a cut-out valve to the intake connection. Outside this intake connection fasten the scoop, putting the fine wire screen inside and turning the scoop opening forward in fastening it to the bottom of the boat.

Installing Lamb Engines.

The following instructions for installing the well known Lamb engines, built by the Lamb Boat & Engine Company, of Clinton, Iowa, are remarkable for clearness and conciseness and contain many excellent hints applicable to the installation of engines in general:

Lamb 4-cylinder 24 H. P. Engine.

Keelson and Bilge Keelsons—In constructing a power boat, a keelson is usually notched over the ribs and bolted to the keel. In addition to this, bilge keelsons or stringers are recommended, one on either side, and running nearly parallel to the keelson.

These keelsons also should be notched to fit over and securely fastened to the ribs and planking. The keelsons, coming under the motor foundation timbers and over a number of ribs, distribute the strain over a large area and contribute largely to the stiffness of the structure.

Shaft Hole—The shaft hole should be bored the size given in table of motor dimensions in the catalogue, taking care that it is of such a pitch or angle that the propeller will be entirely submerged, and that no part of motor bed or flywheel will come in contact or touch the inside of boat aside from the foundation timbers.

With properly constructed deadwood, there is no shaft hole lining needed except where the stuffing-box is placed on the inside of the boat. With the last named arrangement a brass or iron tube may be used, the stuffing-box fastened to the inboard end and the stern bearing to the outboard end.

The shaft hole being bored, stretch a fine line through the **center** of it; fasten the outboard end to a stick nailed to the stern of the boat; make the other end fast inside of boat; go over the line carefully and see that it is in the exact center of hole throughout its length, and if the shaft hole has been properly bored, a plumb-bob held beside the line should point to the center of the keelson, provided the boat sits level.

The face of the stern-post must be absolutely smooth and at exactly right-angles with the line which has been stretched where the center of the shaft should be.

Foundation—In the table of motor dimensions in the catalogue see distance from the center of the shaft to the bottom of floor flanges. This distance being known, the foundation timbers, which should be of good sound oak, should be securely fastened to keelsons at the given distance from the line, and at the same pitch or angle as the line.

These foundation timbers may run either athwart ship or fore and aft; in either case they must be securely fastened to every timber and plank over which they pass. The table of motor dimensions gives all necessary measurements, but it is well to check your measurements over when you receive the motor.

Placing Motor—Place the motor on the foundation at the proper position fore and aft, and in line with the center of the shaft. The shaft now being in place, compare the faces of flange couplings and see that their faces come together fairly. The least variation at this point, if allowed to remain, will cause undue friction and heating.

With motor securely bolted down and faces of flanges on the couplings coming up perfectly fair, you may feel reasonably sure your motor and shaft are in line. **This is important.**

Stern Bearing and Stuffing Box—Bolt the stern-bearing to stern-post with a film of white lead between. See that the shaft turns perfectly free after the stern-bearing is fastened to place. If it binds the shaft, it would indicate that the face of the stern-post is not exactly at right-angles on the shaft and must be dressed off until the shaft works free.

If a log is used, the inside stuffing-box is bolted to the inboard end, after having squared the end the same as described for the stern-post. If no log is used, insert a sleeve, one end of which screws into the stern-bearing, the sleeve being long enough to extend into the boat far enough to admit of the stuffing-box being screwed on the inboard end.

Piping—Use care in cutting threads on all pipe so that they will make up tight, using white lead on all joints of water pipe and soap on all gasolene connections.

Make all pipe runs as direct as possible, avoiding elbows and bends. Water pipes should be all brass where the boat is used in salt water, but for fresh water, common iron pipe will answer.

For the sea-cock or intake to the pump, the pipe should have long running thread cut on the end intended to go through the planking. The hole should be bored through the bottom of the boat small enough so that the pipe will screw tight into planking. Have a lock-nut both inside and out after the pipe is screwed through the planking far enough to admit of a full tread on the lock-nut outside. Put a few turns of white-leaded candle wicking under the lock-nuts and screw down firmly, tacking a dish screen over the end of pipe to keep all foreign matter out of the check valves.

A stop-cock should be placed just inside of the boat that the flow of water may be regulated to suit conditions. It is also advisable to place a tee just above the stop-cock, taking the water from the side of the same with a plug in the end. In case of pipe getting clogged, the plug may be removed and a small rod of wire used to clean same.

The discharge from the water-jacket overboard should be above the water line if possible and should be fastened as described above for the sea-cock pipe; all water pipe to be no smaller than the openings in or out of the motor for same, and larger will do no harm.

Gasolene Pipe—Gasolene pipe should be of copper, tin, brass or lead, never iron, and should be run from the tank to the carbureter as directly as possible along the keelson.

See that the gasolene pipe is thoroughly cleaned before making up, as a very small amount of dirt or scale will clog the carbureter.

Gasolene Tank—The gasolene tank should be placed as high up in the bow of the boat as possible so that the gasolene will have sufficient head to flow to the carbureter good and strong.

The gasolene tank should have a strainer over the outlet opening, inside of the tank. A hole should be cut through the deck to correspond to the filling plug in the tank and the gasolene should be **thoroughly strained** when filling the tank. Chamois skin makes the best strainer as no water will pass through it. The tank must be securely fastened in the boat to avoid straining of joints in the gasolene pipe, should the tank shift.

Exhaust Pipe—Either of two styles of mufflers is furnished with Lamb engines. The one most to be desired is of the automobile type, and can only be used on boats with a fixed roof. The mufflers are light and are securely fastened to the roof, the exhaust pipe from the motor running up through the roof to the muffler, with sheet-iron hood running from the motor to and through the roof, covered by a cone to shed water. This hood should be two inches larger than the exhaust pipe, thereby furnishing a one-inch air space around the exhaust pipe, which is sufficient to carry off the heat from the exhaust pipe.

The other style is the stern muffler, to go under the stern deck, with outlet from muffler running out from either side of the stern. This style of muffler necessitates the running of the exhaust pipe under the floor of the boat to the stern, connecting to the muffler and then out as previously described.

Where this type of muffler is used it is advisable to admit a small amount of the discharge water from the water-jacket into the exhaust pipe to keep it cool. There should be a valve placed in the water pipe to the exhaust pipe that the amount may be regulated, as too great an amount of water in the exhaust pipe tends to choke same and to check the speed of the motor.

Batteries—Lamb motors are regularly furnished with two sets of dry-cell batteries. These should be placed in a dry place in the boat and connected as shown by the wiring chart accompanying each motor. Where dynamos or magnetos are used, one set of batteries are cut out and the generator wired in their place. A dynamo or generator will give much better satisfaction if used in connection with a storage battery.

Wiring—If there is one thing more important than another in motor installation, it is the wiring, which should be done carefully and well. All wires should be visible and above floor if possible; for instance: We will explain the method of wiring the Lamb 4-cylinder 4-cycle motor. The wiring chart fully describes or shows the manner of connecting batteries to the spark coil and from the spark coil to the motor; the circuit-breaker or timer has four binding posts marked 1, 2, 3, 4. These indicate the post to run the primary wires to for each cylinder, for instance: Taking one end of the coil as No. 1, run the primary wire from this end coil to the binding post marked (1), also secondary wire from same coil to the spark plug on the top of No. 1 cylinder on the motor.

Run wires on numbers 2, 3, and 4 cylinders in the same manner. Having completed the wiring as described, remove spark plugs from the cylinder heads and lay them on top of the cylinder, so that they make contact the same as if they were in place. Now beginning with No. 1 cylinder, place piston on the upper center after having completed the compression stroke. **Be sure it is the compression stroke.**

Now set your timer to spark at this point and you should have spark on No. 1 spark plug. Then try the next cylinder, which should be No. 3; be governed by the numbers stamped on the timer for the sequence in firing.

After timing each cylinder perfectly your motor should start readily.

Installing a Mianus Motor.

(Mianus Motor Works, Mianus, Conn.)

If the motor is to set in a boat, allow at least three inches under the rim of flywheel so as to give the hand plenty of clearance in starting. If possible set the motor so that there will not be over one and one-half inches pitch to foot of propeller shaft. After the motor is set turn the carbureter connections so that it will stand

Mianus Single Cylinder Engine.

plumb, otherwise the valves may not work freely. All circulating pipes for salt water should be of brass. The gasolene feed pipe should be of brass or copper. Great care should be exercised in making up the connections for the gasolene supply, so that there will be no possibility of a leak. Make up all threaded joints with shellac or common bar soap and solder. Exhaust pipe is usually of galvanized iron. Avoid placing the exhaust pipe nearer than one inch to any woodwork—two inches would be better. Cover if possible with asbestos.

Set the gasolene tank above the level of the carbureter; three or four inches is enough. In a boat the tank is nearly always in the bow, as that is the highest point. For auxiliary installation we would recommend placing the tanks aft on deck under the lockers or seats if possible; this will avoid the necessity of running the gasolene pipes through the cabin or other inclosed parts of the boat. In connecting the gasolene supply use two stop-cocks, one at the tank and one at the engine, also use two unions in the same way; then either tank or motor may be removed without removing the other. All air must be forced out of the gasolene pipe before motor can be started. All water connections should have stop-cocks or seacock with aircock to drain all piping. Be sure that the inlet has a suitable screen to cover the opening to keep out dirt and other foreign matter. Water-jacket and pipes must be kept drained in cold weather when not in use.

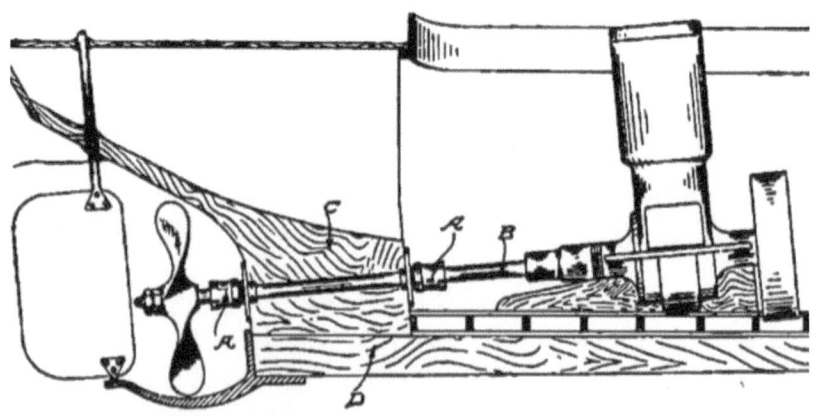

Mianus Motor Installed With Two Stuffing-Boxes A A.

CHAPTER IX

OPERATION AND CARE OF ENGINE.

There are three important points that must be carefully looked after before any gasolene engine will operate successfully:

First: You must be sure that your engine receives a good spark.

Second: You must know that your engine receives a proper amount of gas.

Third: You must see that all the bearings are properly oiled.

Some marine engines are so simple that they are claimed to be as easy to run as an ordinary sewing machine. The amateur will have no trouble in learning how to operate one of them perfectly if he follows instructions carefully.

But don't make your first attempt thinking that you know all about it and can make the engine run at the first turn; for if you do, you are likely to be disappointed and might get discouraged.

Remember, that the makers have assured you that you can learn to operate their engine without much trouble; and you can. But you must be patient, careful, sensible, self-reliant, and follow the makers' instructions closely. If you don't get results at first, don't condemn the engine or blame the builders until you know that either the engine or the builders are to blame. Every engine has probably been run for hours on its own power before leaving the factory and if it does not run for you, look for the trouble in the way you operate it, for there you will most likely find it.

Don't listen to advice or suggestions from self-styled experts, and don't experiment or "monkey" with the engine.

If, after fair trial, you are unable to make the engine run, write the builders and tell them all about your trouble, and they will then offer such suggestions as are needed. They won't let you fail, and you won't fail if you do your part. Just use sense, study the instructions and keep trying. You will soon get the knack of running the engine and then all will be pleasant.

The Lamb Four-Cycle Engine.

The following instructions for the operation and care of Lamb engines will be found interesting by many owners:

Starting and Running Motor—Fill the gasolene tank. Fill the oil tank and oil all moving parts of the motor. Oil the clutch through the plug-hole in the top of the case. Turn the motor over several times and see that everything works free. Throw the clutch lever in neutral or center position. Open the valves in the gasolene pipe at the tank and at the carbureter to be sure gasolene flows freely.

It is advisable on first starting the motor or in cold weather to prime the motor by putting a small amount of gasolene in each of the priming cups and letting it into the inlet valves by means of the cock below the cup.

Set your lead-changer so that the motor fires just **after passing** the center to avoid kicking back. Open the throttle valve on mixer about half way. Throw the switch on the batteries. Stand on the carbureter side of the motor and throw the top of the flywheel towards you.

After the engine gets to running regulate the speed of the motor by the throttle lever on the carbureter and by the lead-changer. See that the sea-cock is open and that water is coming out of the over-flow pipe. See if pump is working by means of pet-cock.

Gasolene Regulation—Just enough gasolene should be used to give the motor its maximum speed, the carbureter being automatic. The gasolene flow, if adjusted at slow speed, should be right at all speeds.

The varying heights of gasolene in tank will make no difference in the flow of gasolene, as this is controlled by a float in the chamber of the carbureter.

Advancing Spark—After throwing in the clutch, the speed of motor may be increased 25 per cent by advancing spark to fire ten to fifteen degrees before center. This is

Connecting Rods—The Lamb Engine.

Piston and Rings—The Lamb Engine.

variable according to speed of motor. The higher the speed of the motor the more lead the motor will stand without pounding.

Loss of Compression—May be caused by leaky valves or by the piston packing rings becoming gummed or inactive by the use of poor cylinder oil. An occasional dose of kerosene will be found helpful in the latter case.

When everything is perfectly tight, it will be found hard to turn motor over with relief valves closed.

Inlet and Exhaust Valves—The inlet and exhaust valves are both mechanically operated, and may be easily removed for regulating or inspection as follows: Loosen the nuts above the saddle, turn the saddle slightly from under the nuts and the valve caps may be lifted off; then compress the valve spring and slip up the spring collar and remove spring; the spring and collar will then drop off and the valve can be lifted out of the chamber. If necessary to regrind valves, use a fine grade of emery and oil, using a screw driver in the slot in top of valve to revolve same.

Igniters—These are of the jump spark type in the Lamb engine. In running, the motor should ignite ten to fifteen degrees before the crank reaches the upper dead center, in order that the charge may be properly fired by the time the power stroke starts.

In starting the motor, the ignition should not occur until the motor has passed dead center, otherwise the motor will kick back, and starting will be difficult.

To fulfill the foregoing conditions, it becomes necessary to provide a means of regulating the time of ignition. This in the Lamb engine is provided for in a movable circuit-breaker, controlled at the front of the motor by a handle with a notched segment.

Ignition Troubles—If after reasonable trial the motor refuses to start, set the motor on a dead center and place circuit breaker or timer in position to spark, then throw on the switch to see if the vibrator works or buzzes. Try all cylinders in same manner.

Testing Spark—Remove the spark plugs from the cylinders. Lay them on top of the cylinder so that the body of the plug is ground the same as if they were in place in the cylinder head. Now test each one for a spark by turning the motor from point to point of contact or by using screw-driver or other instrument across the points on the circuit-breaker.

Vibrator—Adjust the vibrator until you obtain a good hot spark and the vibrator has a good strong buzz. If the vibrator works and no spark shows across the points of the spark plug, it would indicate that the spark plug

CONSTRUCTION AND OPERATION

was short-circuited, caused by either water, soot, oil or broken insulation, cracked porcelain, etc.

Spark Plug—Use a small brush to keep the points of spark plugs clean and free from scale, soot, oil, etc. Broken or cracked insulation must be replaced by new parts.

Timer—The interior or moving parts should be kept well oiled.

Wiring—Go over the wires carefully and see that all connections are tight and no bare wires come in contact

Reverse Clutch—The Lamb Engine.

with other wires or parts of the motor. Wires should not pass through bilge water; all bare wire and joints must be wound with tape.

Batteries—Must be kept in a dry place and allow no tools of any kind to lie on top of batteries, as they will become short-circuited and useless in a short time.

Motor Knocking—May be caused by the flywheel being loose, too early ignition, one or more cylinders missing, mixture too light, (not enough gasolene). Motor cylinders heating caused by stoppage of water circulation.

Reverse Clutch—Where the motor is furnished with a reverse clutch, the mechanism consists of six spur gears, two friction clutch rings, and a retaining casing. The internal clutch ring is securely keyed to the propeller shaft and forms the forward motion to the shaft.

Going Ahead—A spur gear is rigidly secured to the crankshaft and engages the four long spur pinions that extend to and engage the spur gear that is secured to the wheel shaft. The after clutch ring or external one is secured to the motor bed by lugs, and by friction engages the casing. When the forward or internal ring is frictionally connected by means of a sliding cone to the casing, the casing with its contained gears (the gears remaining inoperative), carries the propeller shaft with it in rotation with the crankshaft.

At Rest—If neither clutch ring is connected to the casing, the resistance of the propeller in the water holds it idle while the motor revolves and the gears in the casing run idle.

Going Astern—Should the after or external clutch be frictionally connected to the casing the casing is held still and the crankshaft gear engaging the four long spur pinions and these in turn with spur gear on the propeller shaft, cause the propeller shaft to revolve in an opposite direction.

Adjusting Clutches—It is necessary that both clutch rings be so adjusted as to hold the full power of the motor.

Slipping—Slipping of forward or internal clutch is indicated by motor racing and the casing heating over the clutch ring.

Adjusting—In adjusting the forward clutch, loosen the lock nuts on the adjusting screws on the clutch dogs, and adjust the screws that engage on the cone; care must be taken that each screw be adjusted the same. Neglect of this will cause the clutch to slip even though it may be very hard to get the cone under the points of the screws.

CHAPTER X

HYDROPLANES.

Buoyancy.

When a solid object, such as a block of wood, is thrown into water it will continue to sink until the weight of the water displaced is equal to the weight of the block. When this occurs a position of equilibrium is reached which is called "floatation," and the body will rest with more or less of its mass above the surface. Should the weight of a solid block be more per cubic foot than the weight of a cubic foot of water it is evident that no such point of equilibrium will be found and that such a body will sink until the bottom is reached. As an example we will work out the following problem to show the relations between weight and floatation:

A box 10 feet long, 4 feet wide, and 3 feet high, weighs 200 pounds. How far will it sink in water weighing 62.5 pounds per cubic foot?

The water displaced will be equal to the weight of the box, and will have a volume of $200 \div 62.5 = 3.2$ cubic feet. To immerse the box 1 foot will displace $10 \times 4 \times 1 = 40$ cubic feet of water, so that the weight of the box will sink it $3.2 \div 40 = 0.08$ foot, or very nearly 1 inch. Consider that a boy weighing 100 pounds is placed in the box causing the total weight to be 300 pounds. The volume of water displaced will be $300 \div 62.5 = 4.8$ cubic feet, and the depth of immersion will be $4.8 \div 40 = 0.12$ foot or 1.44 inches.

From the above it will be seen that the supporting force must be equal and opposite to the weight of the floating body. This is known as the "buoyant force" or buoyancy of the water. Since the weight of a cubic foot of water varies with the temperature and with the amount of salt in solution it is evident that a boat will float higher in cold sea water than in warm fresh river water. If the depth of immersion is an important factor in the design, such as would be the case with craft intended for use in shallow streams, the items listed above must be taken into account. By knowing the volume of the hull and its weight it is possible to locate the water line accurately by the above method.

While iron and steel are much heavier per volume than water it is possible to construct metal boats by having the volume of displacement increased to such a point that the weight per cubic foot of hull is less than the weight of a cubic foot of water. By the judicious distribution of material it is possible to have a metal boat that is lighter per cubic foot of displacement than an equivalent wood hull, and therefore one that will ride less deeply in the water.

Displacement Boats.

All ordinary boats are supported in the water by the weight of the displaced water on the principles outlined above. To distinguish them from a class of racing craft known as "Hydroplanes," such boats are commonly called "displacement" boats from the method of floatation.

Hydroplanes.

When a flat plane surface is held at an angle near the surface of the water and is pushed rapidly forward, the water is forced downwards by the inclined surface and an upward pressure is brought against the plane by the impact of the deflected stream. By suitably arranging the angle of the plane and the forward speed it is possible to derive enough upward force to suspend the entire weight of a hull and its passengers without the aid of the displacement buoyancy. Such support of course is only possible when the boat is moving at a considerable speed, and therefore the boat must have sufficient buoyancy to float the load when at rest. A boat which is supported by the reaction of a moving stream of water against an inclined surface is known as a "Hydroplane."

Hydroplanes are almost invariably built as speed boats or for racing and at present hold all speed records in the gas driven field. They are quite different in construction from the usual motor boat, are exceedingly light and heavily powered. The bottoms are broad and flat with the greater part of the weight arranged in the stern so as to maintain a particular angle with the surface of the water. At full speed, the reaction of the water on the inclined bottom causes them to skip over the surface much on the principle of a skipping stone. The bow and fore part of the hull stand well out of the water with the greater part of the weight carried by the after portion of the bottom.

As the hydroplane at speed is only barely immersed, the area of skin friction is reduced to a minimum as is also the energy required to split the water. By reducing these losses it has been possible to considerably exceed a speed of 60 miles per hour. When at full speed it has been possible to see "daylight" between the water and the hull for a distance of fully two-thirds of the length of the boat. As the speed drops the boat gradually sinks deeper and deeper into the water until it reaches its full displacement depth when at rest.

Owing to the small amount of surface resting on the water and to the absence of keels it is not stable when at speed and is very likely to "skid" sideways after the manner of an automobile on a wet pavement. It is not adapted for use on rough choppy water since the impact of waves of different heights not only disturb the fore and aft equilibrium but also are likely to strike the bow and cause the plane to "stub its toe" and probably to cause it to dive to the bottom. Because of this instability in the fore and aft balance many hydroplanes have taken a sudden dive to the bottom carrying passengers and all with them. For this reason the average hydroplane is not a safe proposition for the inexperienced motor-boat operator.

Being of an unusually fragile construction, any degree of rough water is likely to break the back of the plane. In many cases a 500 or 600 H. P. engine is carried in a hull with only a $\frac{3}{16}$ or $\frac{1}{4}$-inch mahogany shell so that when the weight of the motors, the operators and the fuel are considered it will be seen that there is not a large factor of safety even with the most careful operation and under the most favorable conditions of water.

Probably the most important single factor in the construction of a hydroplane is the balance or the manner in which the weights of the motors, fuel, etc., are distributed. With a proper weight distribution, proper propeller and plenty of power almost any displacement boat can be made to act as a hydroplane with more or less success, but with improper balancing even the most efficiently designed hydroplane hull will perform indifferently or not at all. Again, the angle which the bottom makes with the surface is a factor and this varies not only with the loading but with the speed. The proper assembling of a hydroplane plant is therefore not a rule of the thumb proposition but a matter of experience and judgment—and still further, a matter of individual experiment with each hull. Even the most experienced designers and constructors of planes are occasionally compelled to discard a hull and consign it to the scrap heap through their inability to exactly forecast these conditions.

In gradually starting from rest, the planing bottom makes only a slight angle with the surface of the water, the weight of the engine and fuel being placed at the rear so as to point the nose slightly upwards. As the speed increases, the increased pressure due to the impact of the water raises the nose still further and increases the angle. As the angle increases the center of pressure, or the effective point of application of the stream, moves steadily toward the rear, thus reducing the leverage of the engine and fuel, and finally causes the forward weight to overcome that in the rear. This of course now tends to reduce the angle after a certain speed is reached which is fairly correct balance since an excessive angle causes loss in the water and elevates the bow so that the wind resistance is high.

These losses due to excessive angles and wind resistance are especially noticeable at the higher speed now reached since the power required to overcome them varies as the cube of the speed. As the sustaining effect is now great, the angle can be reduced to a certain extent and still maintain sufficient support. By properly adjusting the weights, etc., the angle can be made to adjust itself to the proper degree at any speed, so that the losses are at a minimum and the power most effective. The movement of the center of pressure is the uncertain factor in arranging the balance, and can be compared in effect with the movement of the support under a "teeter board." If we know the point of support at any one instant we can easily arrange the weights to balance, but as the center moves irregularly and not at all according to any known law, the matter is not an easy one to solve. This is further complicated by the effect of differently shaped planes on the pressure movement, a slight curve giving widely different results from those produced by a flat plane.

In general, a hydroplane may be defined as a boat in which the power is used to lift the boat out of the water, to reduce the resistance, as well as to drive her forward.

In the faster hydroplanes, the power plant is divided into two groups with twin screws, the "Oregon Kid" and the "Disturbers" being equipped in this manner. In this case, the engines must be driven at very nearly the same speed to prevent a tendency to skidding or "yawing."

Planes in Water.

To illustrate the principle of the Hydroplane clearly the accompanying sketches 1, 2, 3, 4, 5, 6, 7, have been prepared, which show the application of the plane in progressive steps.

In Fig. 1 is shown the plane surface AC completely immersed in water below the surface or water line WL. The force or thrust T is pushing the plane from right to left as indicated by the arrow T. As the plane is pushed forward, the water in front of the surface is compressed with a pressure F, causing the water to rise at D and E and to pass over the top and bottom of the plane at A and C. Since the water streams cannot close up instantly after passing the plane there is a partially open and vacuous space left at G which is more or less occupied by turbulent spray and air motions indicated by the whirling lines. As the vacuum acts to the left as shown by arrow G it opposes the propelling force T, causing the latter to compensate for the compression F plus vacuum G. The top and bottom streams are shown reunited at R.

The plane in this case is normal, or at right angles, to the direction of motion, and in this condition will balance when T is applied at the plane center B. This point at which the forces of all the minute stream lines are supposed to be concentrated is known as the "center of pressure" or, in other words, is the point at which the sum of the forces acting on the face produce no tendency to turn the plane either to the left or to the right. (Position of equilibrium.)

A second condition is shown by Fig. 2 in which a part of the plane AC is above the water level WL, an arrangement that considerably changes the stream lines. The thrust T is as before and acts in the same direction, but is now nearer the edge C as the pressure on the plane is now only between D and C. With the old center of pressure at the center of the plane at B, the new center has now moved down by the distance I to H. It is evident that the less there is of immersion, the lower will be the center of pressure. The water still rises in front of the plane as at ED but passes at the ends instead of the top as in the former case. The vacuous turbulent space G still exists but is no longer closed by the stream ED at the top. This open space allows the air to enter at N which destroys the vacuous drag to some extent, though not all together. In all cases, it will be noted, the force T has been principally engaged in overcoming the impact of the water in front and the effect of the inertia of the water at the rear. The inertia, or movement of the water is responsible for the vacuum established at G since this property prevents instant closure of the stream.

In Fig. 3 the plane AC is shown inclined to the direction of progress by the angle X. Inclining the plane now divides the water forces into two components, one being a vertical force L, and the other, the old thrust T employed in overcoming the resistance. As we now have a vertical force L, acting upwardly and against gravitation, we can use this force to support the hull instead of a buoyant force. This is the elementary principle of the hydroplane. It is evident from examination that the smaller we make the angle X the smaller will be the propulsive force T in relation to the lift L, although with the other conditions constant we will have a smaller total lift. To maintain a constant lift, say equal to the weight of the hull, with a decreased angle we must increase the speed to correspond with the reduction of X. For the smallest amount of thrust T to support a given load we must have a very small angle X and a high speed. At low speeds the efficiency of the drive is decreased on account of the large angle necessary for

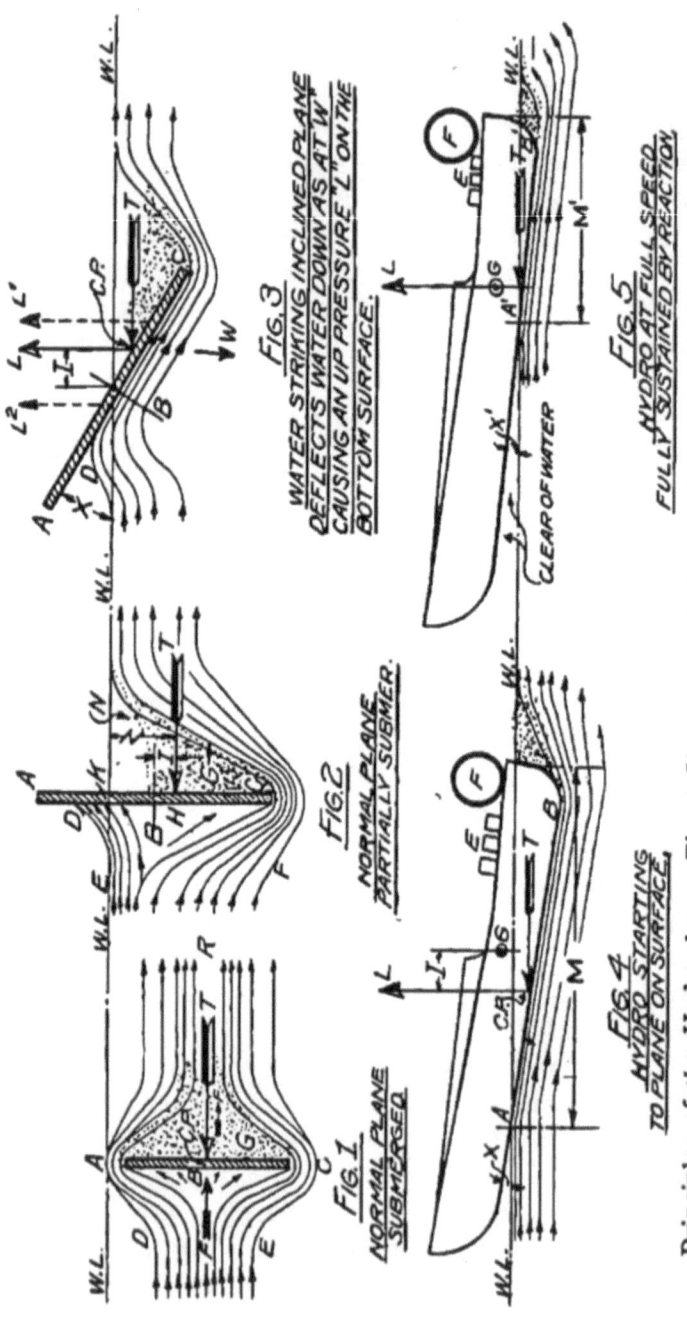

Principles of the Hydroplane. Fig. 1 Shows Board Forced Through Water at Right Angles to Line of Motion. In Fig. 2 Board Is only Partially Submerged. Fig. 3 Shows Lifting Effect of Inclined Plane, and Fig. 4 Is the Application of the Incline Plane to a Boat. Fig. 5 Shows Hydroplaning.

L and the ensuing low ratio between L and T. The point B, center of plane, marks the old center of pressure in Fig. 1 with the normal plane. It will be noted that the new center has moved back by the distance I.

Unfortunately the center of pressure varies widely and irregularly with a change in the angle X so that the center of pressure at different angles may cause the center of gravity to be moved to L^1 or L^2 according to conditions. For stability the center of pressure and the center of gravity should be coincident to prevent the plane from assuming a new angle. Since in a boat, practical conditions make the shifting of the load impossible, the location of the gravity center is usually a compromise between extreme conditions.

Fig. 4 shows the application of the principle to a "monoplane" hull (Single plane) in which AB is the bottom planing surface, L is the lift numerically equal to the weight less the buoyancy, and M is the wetted surface. The force T is the thrust applied at CP, the center of pressure, and at the intersection of L and T. The arrows show the stream direction. The weight of the engine E plus the fuel F, plus the passengers causes the center of gravity G to be slightly to the rear of the lift line L, by an amount I. This at low speed, the condition shown, causes the hull to make the angle X with the water line WL.

In Fig. 5 the hydroplane is shown at full speed, the increased lift due to the high speed lifting the greater part of the hull out of water. The length of wetted surface M^1 has been greatly reduced from the wetted length M in Fig. 4 and hence the resistance and frictional power requirements have been greatly reduced. The angle X^1 has been reduced owing to the high speed, and the center of gravity now lies on the lift line L, or in stable position for the most efficient angle. It will be seen that L has moved back to G.

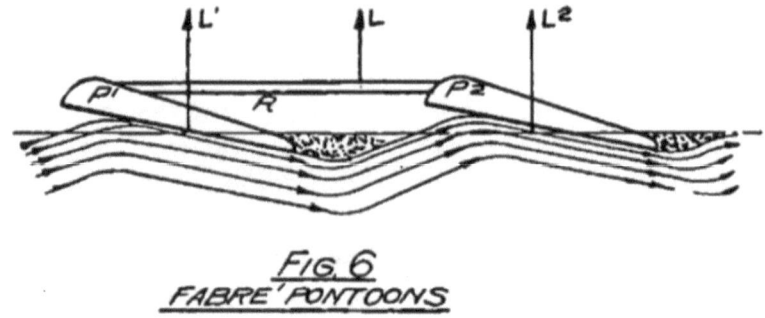

FIG. 6
FABRE' PONTOONS

Fig. 6 shows one of the early pontoon arrangements built by Henri Fabré which is composed of the two floats P^1 and P^2, connected by the bar R.

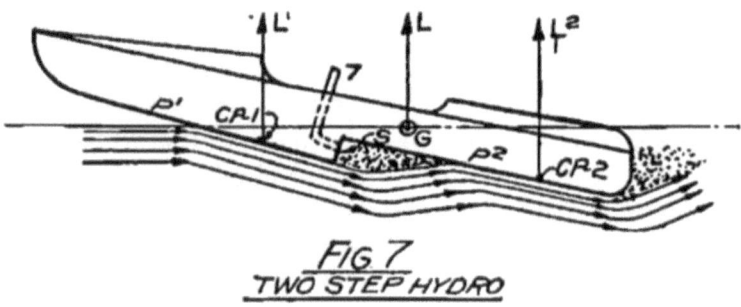

FIG. 7
TWO STEP HYDRO

In Fig. 7 is shown a "biplane" or "two-stepper" which in principle is similar to Fig. 6, the structural difference being that the two planing surfaces are combined in one hull. This type is very extensively used. As shown, the hull is divided into two separately inclined surfaces, P^1 and P^2, separated by the step S. The action of the water is clearly shown by the curved lines as in the previous examples, the lifts due to the two planes being shown by L^1 and L^2, and the total lift by L. As shown by the dotted area at the rear of the step, there is a considerable suction which produces drag. In many types an air tube 7 is inserted in the step so that air will be admitted to break the suction.

CHAPTER XI

CHOICE OF A BOAT MODEL.

In making a choice of a boat model, whether for the purpose of amateur boat-building or in buying a completed hull, there are several main considerations to be taken into account. First of these is the question of seaworthiness. If the boat is to be used on the seacoast or the Great Lakes, the possible range of travel and the depth of the waters to be navigated demand a greater beam and greater stability in other respects than are required in craft intended for the navigation of narrow and shallower waters.

The problem of the form and structure of the boat involves the selection of a craft having the proper carrying capacity, stability and comfort, designed along lines that will present the least resistance at a required speed.

If the inquirer intends to build his own boat or to install his own engine in the hull he selects, the weight of the engine to be installed is an important factor. He will do well to obtain the views of an experienced boatbuilder or of a marine engineer, capable of making the necessary calculations of the displacement of a boat.

If his object is to secure a boat to run at high speed, he will need a model in which the lightest possible construction is combined with the strength required to support the engine and resist the stresses set up by its vibration.

If he desires only a moderate speed boat, he may select a model of safer and stronger construction, of greater beam and higher freeboard, having the advantages of more room and carrying capacity; in other words, a craft of a more seaworthy and general safer character.

The infinite variety of boat models now offered to the public in all stages of construction, including patterns, knock-down frames and completed hulls, offers a wide range of choice. Many of these models of approved construction, popular among boatmen East and West, are illustrated in these pages. On every body of water other models can usually be seen and as a rule the person who starts out to purchase a boat or to construct a hull for himself has a fair general idea of the kind of craft he requires.

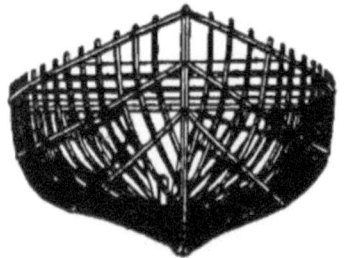 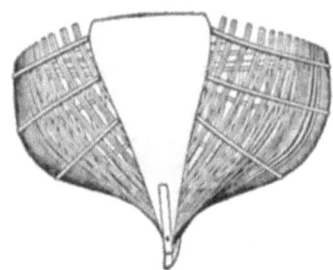

18' and 23' Dories.
(Pioneer Boat & Pattern Co., Bay City, Mich.)

A number of the boats illustrated in this work have come, by reason of long and successful operation, to be regarded almost as standard models and the novice in motor boating will not go far wrong if he selects one of these boats of generally approved design.

As stated elsewhere, the novice should be careful to avoid "freaks," that is models in which some peculiar individual idea or ideas have been embodied at the expense of recognized lines of construction. Freaks are apt to prove expensive, even as experiments, and the wise boatman usually sticks to approved designs, leaving it to skilled naval architects to originate new ideas in design and have them thoroughly tested before recommending them for general adoption.

The matter of the proportion of the length of the boat to its beam is one upon which no definite rule can be laid down. The higher the speed required, the narrower the proportional beam as a rule. The limit in present practice is the ration of 9 or 10 to 1 for high speed boats and the ratio ranges down to 4, 4½, or 5 to 1, which is the proportion of the length to beam in small and low speed boats. Moderate sized craft designed for fair speed, seaworthiness and comfort may show a ratio of 5½, 6, or 7 to 1 between length and beam.

The following table shows the length and beam, engine horse power, etc., in a typical series of boat models built on the New England coast:

Length	Beam	H. P.	Number of Cylinders
16 ft.	4 ft. 6 in.	1½ to 2	1
18 ft.	4 ft. 8 in.	2½ to 3	1
20 ft.	5 ft. 6 in.	3½	1
22 ft.	5 ft. 8 in.	4	1
25 ft.	6 ft. 3 in.	5	1
25 ft.	6 ft. 6 in.	6	2
28 ft.	6 ft. 6 in.	6	2
28 ft.	6 ft. 8 in.	7	2
30 ft.	6 ft. 10 in.	8	2
32 ft.	7 ft.	8	2
32 ft.	7 ft. 3 in.	10	2
35 ft.	7 ft. 10 in.	10 to 13	2

Careful sailors agree that, speaking generally, a launch should have a beam about one-fifth of her length on the water line, when it is intended for seagoing or to withstand heavy weather. In small boats the beam should be about one-fourth of the length on the water line. This applies only to boats of moderate to fair speed.

The draft of a boat is determined by the form of the hull and weight of the loaded structure. Increase of the beam results in lessening the draft, and vice versa. As a rule, except for very shallow waters, the question of draft need not deeply concern the purchaser of a boat. It will take care of itself, provided the length and beam are suitably proportioned and the lines of the boat are of approved design.

General Form of the Hull.

As regards the general form of the hull, there are certain principles that may be mentioned here; as, for instance, the flare at the bow and sides from the water line

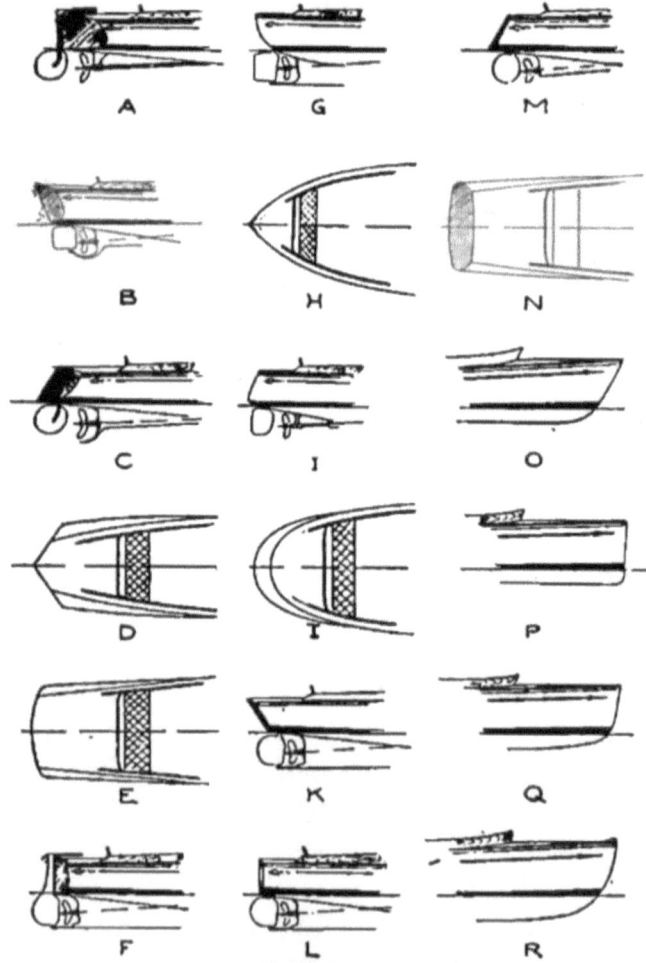

Types of Stems and Sterns.
(Bath Marine Construction Co., Bath, Me.)

to the sheer. The greater the flare outward, as a rule, the less water the boat will ship in a seaway, but flare retards speed, while adding to comfort and safety. This is seen in the seagoing dory with its splendid stability in all weathers.

For seagoing craft a wedge-shaped bottom is preferable and in heavy weather adds greatly to the comfort of the occupants.

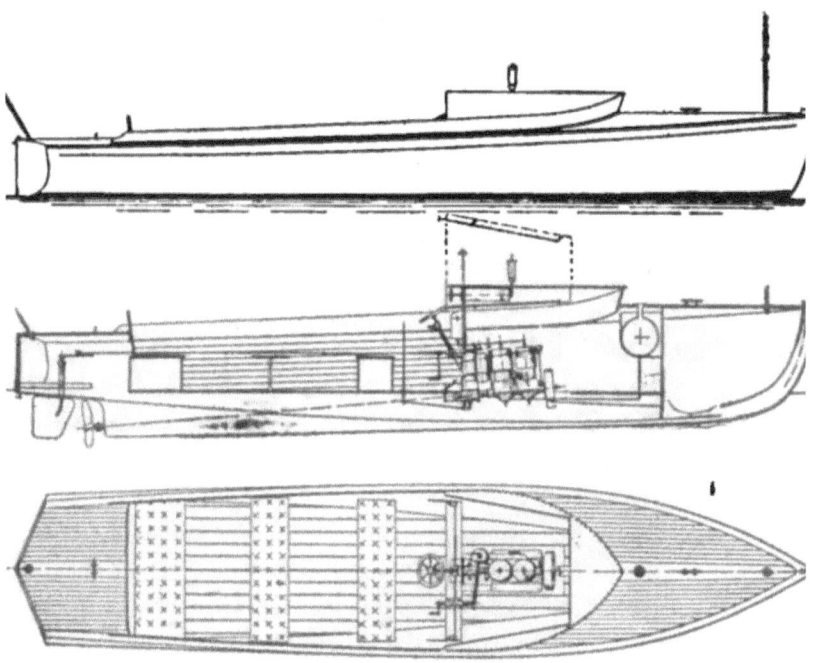

21′x4′ 6″ Runabout.
(Bath Marine Construction Co., Bath, Me.)

A certain amount of sheer or rise at bow and stern is another desideratum in seagoing craft and this applies to boats intended for use on the Great Lakes, where heavy weather is apt to be encountered and conditions often strongly resemble those encountered on the seacoast.

The sheer is always greater at the bow than at the stern and adds to the lifting power of the hull in a seaway.

A certain amount of decking should be fitted in all open launches at the bow and stern. The forward deck helps to keep the boat dry and the decking aft protects the occupants in heavy weather from "following" waves climbing over the stern. Such decks do not decrease the capacity of the boat since the space beneath can be used for stowage, and they add greatly to comfort and safety, by keeping the machinery, accessories, clothing, etc., dry. A certain width of deck should be fitted the whole length of the boat on either side and these side decks should not be made too narrow.

The height of the coaming or washboard around the cockpit is a matter of choice and is governed by considerations of appearance and convenience. A high coaming helps to keep out spray.

Cruising Craft.

Cruisers are distinguished mostly by the character of the cabin fittings. Some have a short cabin with a large cockpit, while in others most of the interior space is occupied by the cabin, with a small cockpit aft.

Cabins are often of what is called the trunk type, a gangway to the bow being left on either side of the trunk. Another type of cruiser has a flush deck forming the cabin top, in which case the sides of the boat are brought up flush and the deck may be slightly rounded to form a "turtle back." This style of cabin affords more room inside and by many is regarded as less liable to leakage in a heavy sea.

Naval architects have rung the changes on these two leading types of cruisers, so that a wide range of choice is offered to the amateur builder or purchaser, and cabin cruisers nowadays may be a delight to the eye by their handsome appearance while at the same time affording a maximum of accommodation for comfortable cruising.

Finished Boats.

The large boatbuilders endeavor to maintain a stock of completed boats ready for immediate shipment, but as the majority of purchasers prefer an interior arrangement and finish to meet their own tastes, their principal stock is often of bare hulls, which can be completed on short notice, thus giving to each purchaser a boat built to his special order but at regular prices and without delay. Each purchaser is often given the option of various interior arrangements, or such special arrangement as he may specify. Or, if special size, design, or construction is desired, they will build to your special order upon receipt of plans and specifications, or will submit plans for approval if you give them an idea of what you wish, and quote you special prices for such construction.

Boatbuilders' Terms.

The following are typical boatbuilders' terms:

"Twenty-five per cent with order and balance when notified that goods are ready to ship, or by sight draft attached to bill of lading, as directed. Full amount with order will generally facilitate shipment.

"On patterns: Cash with order, or builders will ship by express C. O. D. subject to examination and approval. All patterns guaranteed to be perfectly accurate in every phase and particular. If you find that they are not; in fact, if you are not thoroughly elated with them after you have tried them, notify the makers and they will return your money cheerfully."

Specifications For Wooden Launch Hulls.

The following are up-to-date specifications for wooden launch hulls, covering the regular form of construction of a leading New York engine and boatbuilding concern, the Gas Engine & Power Co. and Charles L. Seabury & Co., Consolidated, of Morris Heights on the Harlem.

These specifications may be regarded as typical of the best—which is often the cheapest—construction.

Timber—All timber thoroughly seasoned and free from large, loose and rotten knots, sap and shakes, or other imperfections of growth detrimental to satisfactory service.

Keel—Best oak, in one piece where practicable, and where splicing is necessary on account of length, the scarfs long and locked, and through fastened with copper bolts, riveted.

Sternpost—Of oak let into keel, secured by brass dovetail plates on each side, fastened with copper rivets, and the counter dovetailed into the sternpost. Stop-waters put in all joints below the water line.

Frames—Of oak or elm, spaced 10 inches center to center, straight grain, steam bent, in one length from the keel to gunwale, fastened to deadwoods with composition nails and brass screws.

Floor Timbers—Of elm or oak, running well up the side of each frame and fastened with copper rivets and galvanized iron boat nails. Limbers cut in frames between the water-tight bulkheads.

Keel Battens—Of quartered oak, fastened with brass screws and with copper rivets through planking.

Risings—Of oak, spruce or elm, fastened with galvanized wrought-iron boat nails.

Clamps and Stringers—Of yellow pine in long lengths, through fastened where practicable with copper rivets.

Planking—Selected white cedar, or cypress, in long, narrow strakes, fastened on each edge at each frame with copper nails; all fastenings bored for (not driven), riveted on copper burrs; all nail and screw holes countersunk for wood plugs set in white lead. Butts of planking coming together between frames, fastened to quartered oak butt blocks, fitted from frame to frame and through fastened, with at least ten rivets in each butt block, same style as the plank fastenings. The forward and after ends fastened with brass screws. All planks to be planed on the inside and made to fit snugly on the frames. The outside planking planed perfectly fair, smooth and even, thoroughly sandpapered before painting. The seams of planking caulked with cotton, payed with white lead paint

28' 8-10 H. P. Hunting Cabin Launch—Gas Engine & Power Co. and Charles L. Seabury & Co. (Consolidated.)

and filled with marine putty; all through fastenings of copper clinched over copper burrs. All joints well painted before being put together.

Water-Tight Bulkheads—Of clear white pine, cedar or cypress, with flush lap seams, the laps and ends fastened with copper rivets and brass screws. Seams caulked with cotton and payed with white lead paint. Stop waters put in seams of planking at the bulkheads to insure water tightness. All bulkheads finished with tongued and grooved chamfered edge hardwood ceiling.

Upperstrake—Of quartered oak, fastened the same as the planking.

Planksheer, Coaming and Guard Moldings—Of quartered oak, fastened closely with brass screws. The coaming fitted with two bronze oarlocks and sockets, and the planksheer with bronze fender cleats.

Decks—Of quartered oak in narrow strakes, caulked with cotton, payed with paint, and filled with marine putty. Hatch with brass lifts fitted over the tiller, and over the trap screw on gasolene tank. A six-inch diameter bronze deck ring fitted over a wrought-iron galvanized hawser ring, which is fastened to the inside of the stem with two galvanized iron screw bolts.

When a sternpost projects above the planking, a wrought-iron galvanized ring bolt will be fastened through same, for lifting the boat and making fast the hawsers.

Deck Beams and Framing—Of oak; the deck over gasolene tank constructed in such a manner that it can be removed in one piece, so that the tank may be readily inspected if so desired.

Seat Ledges and Framing—Of quartered oak, fastened with brass screws.

Seat and Interior Trim—Of white ash, fastened with brass screws. Lockers where specified will have lids on top of seats fitted with brass butts and lifts. Inside of the lockers sheathed with soft wood, tongued and grooved ceiling, and the fronts with white ash tongued and grooved ceiling, secured at the floor with quarter-round moldings, and with facia on top.

Floor Beams—Of oak on each frame, with stanchions where required.

Flooring—Of white pine tongued and grooved, in narrow strakes, with hatches in the center well battened and secured with bronze flush floor buttons.

The frames and clamps above seats finished with white ash or oak.

All fastenings in the joiner work countersunk, and the heads covered with wood plugs set in with marine glue.

Painting and Varnishing—Inside of the hull to have two coats heavy lead paint. Outside of planking to be given, first, a priming coat of lead, and afterward two more coats of white lead paint above water line, and two coats of the best anti-fouling composition paint in red or green color on under body. Floor and inside of lockers is given two coats best lead color paints. Decks, coaming, guard moldings and interior trim are finished with three coats of best spar varnish.

Miscellaneous—Cotton-covered wire core steering line. Brass rudder and post. Brass skeg fastened with brass wood screws. Brass quadrant keyed on post and fastened with brass set screws. Brass rudder post guide with stuffing-box inside, fastened with brass or Tobin screw bolts set up with nuts on washers, or a heavy brass pipe screwed into the wood with a large stuffing-box on the upper end.

One pair ash oars fastened in cockpit with leather straps, with buckles.

Square sterns rabbeted to receive the end of planking, reinforced on the inside with a heavy hackmatack knee fastened with copper rivets clinched over copper burrs.

Rudders for square sterns of oak, with bronze braces, gudgeons, cap and tiller; the tiller fastened to cap with brass screw bolts, arranged so that the rudder may be readily unshipped.

Transom knees of oak, hackmatack, or chestnut, fastened to transom and through clamps and upper strake with copper rivets, clinched over copper burrs.

Steering gear pulleys of heavy bronze fastened with bronze or brass screw bolts where practicable, otherwise with brass wood screws.

Stem band of half-round brass, drilled and countersunk, well fastened with brass wood screws, all finished smooth and fair. The upper end to extend and fasten to the planksheer, and to run well under the keel.

Motor compartment of yacht tenders lined with sheet brass from keel to about 12 inches above floor.

Gasolene tank made of heavy copper, with both riveted and soldered seams, reinforced inside with galvanized sheet-iron stiffening plates, riveted and soldered, arranged with safety valve and trap screw on top, and tank placed in copper pan with drip pipe leading overboard, and a vent pipe to the outside of hull, all rigidly secured in compartment separated from body of hull by water-tight bulkhead. Wherever practicable, the feed pipe from tank to motor is carried on outside of the hull, to insure additional safety by water insulation.

The above specifications are for boats and launches for use in salt water, hence galvanized and copper hardware is specified throughout.

Typical Western Construction.

Typical construction on the Great Lakes is exemplified in the motor-boats built by the DeFoe Boat and Motor Works, of Bay City, Michigan. As there are special features found in the DeFoe boats not found in any other, we give the following detailed description of their construction:

"The entire frame is of perfect, straight-grained white oak. Ribs are steam bent and closely spaced, from 4 to 8 inches apart, depending on the size of boat and thickness of planking. The sheerstrake is of either oak or mahoganized birch to correspond with the decks and coaming, and balance of planking of clear Louisiana red cypress, with all fastenings either screwed, bolted or clinch nailed, making the strongest possible construction.

"All joints are reinforced between frames with oak butt blocks. The plank seams are caulked with cotton, payed with white lead and puttied flush, nail heads countersunk and puttied and screw and bolt heads plugged, leaving a perfectly smooth surface.

"Inside, beneath the covering boards, heavy oak clamps are bolted to the sheerstrake and ribs, adding strength and firmness to the whole frame. Deck beams and breast hooks are sawed to shape and firmly fastened in position. Covering boards cut to shape. Decking laid in narrow stuff, caulked, payed and puttied flush—the only way to make a perfect deck.

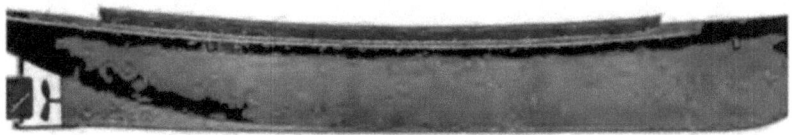

DeFoe Fantail Stern Launch.

"Bulkheads at each end of the cockpit are paneled with doors, giving easy access under the decks. The gasolene tank is so arranged that it can be easily removed at any time, and is of extra heavy galvanized iron with swash plates fore and aft and athwartship to prevent undue strain by the shifting of the gasolene in a seaway. The floor is covered with linoleum and entire cockpit is artistically paneled throughout.

"Rudder is of steel plate. Steering boards clear, but with all parts of the steering gear easily accessible at any time for repairs. Steering wheel of polished brass with mahogany grips and drum. Cleats, chocks and all other deck and interior hardware of polished brass."

A Special Michigan Steel Boat.

A fine example of a steel motor-boat in popular demand is the 1910 Special 18-foot model built by the Michigan Steel Boat Company, of which two photographic illustrations are shown. This boat has a beam of 4 feet 6 inches and the cockpit is 11 feet 4 inches long. The depth is 2 feet amidships, 2 feet 7 inches forward, and 1 foot 10 inches aft. Equipped with a 3½ H. P. Detroit

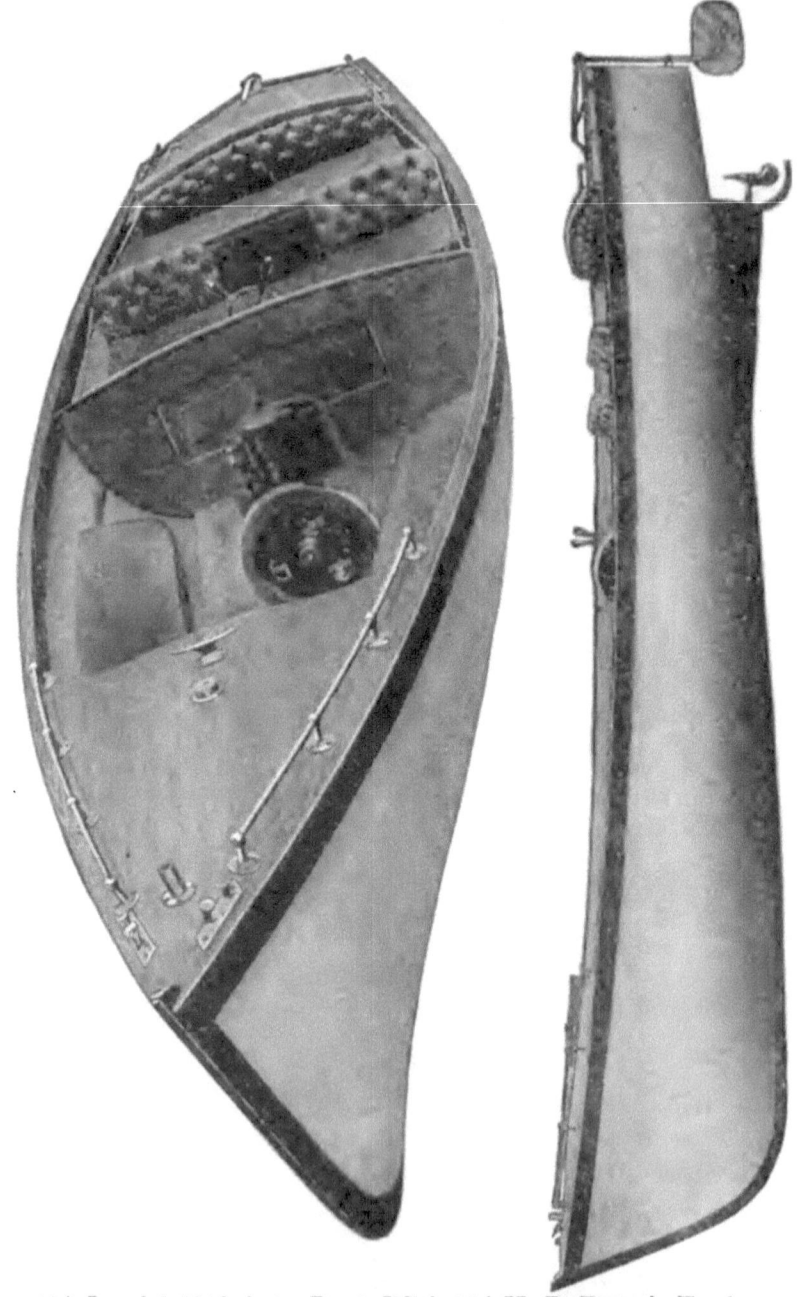

18' Special 1910 Auto Boat, With 3½ H. P. Detroit Engine.
(Michigan Steel Boat Co., Detroit, Mich.)

engine, the boat makes a speed of 10 miles an hour. It seats ten persons in all, the forward cockpit seating six, having seats 4 feet 6 inches long and 10 inches wide. The net weight of the boat is 650 pounds; crated for domestic shipment, 850 pounds. The measurements boxed are 18 feet 3 inches by 4 feet 8 inches by 3 feet 4 inches, or 284 cubic feet. The price of this model complete with engine installed ($147, crated, f. o. b. cars at Detroit) brings it within the reach of the most moderate incomes. In materials, workmanship and power, this 1910 boat is fully up to the well-known standard of the Michigan Steel Boat Company in every respect.

The launch can be equipped with an engine as large as 12-14 H. P. if desired. With such an engine installed it has made actual speed over a measured course of 19 miles an hour. Of course the price with the larger engine is comparatively higher.

"Matthews" Craft.

Among the boat-builders who have aided greatly in the recent development of motor-boating by the produc-

tion of excellent and popular models is The Matthews Boat Company, of Port Clinton, Ohio. The methods of

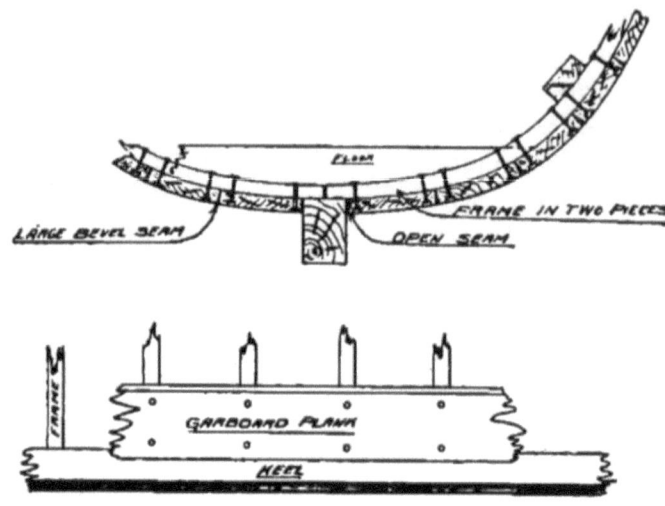

Usual Method.

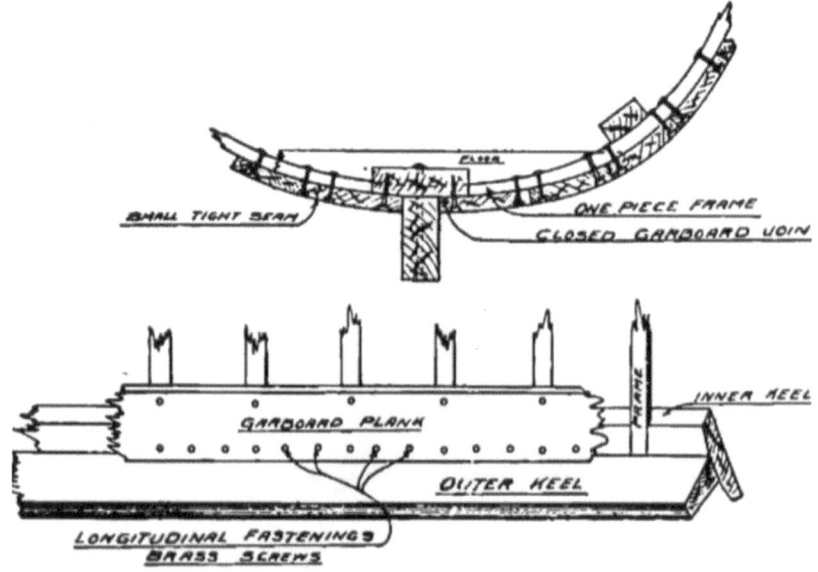

Matthews' Method of Construction.

construction adopted by this concern possess many features of general interest.

For example, as shown in the illustration, the method of construction followed by some builders includes a small single keel; two-piece frames on top of keel, cut at the weakest point; large bevel seams in planking, stuffed with calking; open seam at garboard, to cause "garboard leakage," and garboard plank fastened to frames only. The Matthews method includes stronger "backbone" construction; garboard plank lapped under keel, to obviate open seam and give longitudinal fastenings; single-piece frames, rabbeted or slotted under inner keel to increase strength where most needed, and small, tight seams of planking, with small strand of calking.

The Matthews open launches have been built in large numbers and have attained popularity as moderate-priced outfits. Their cabin cruisers are also well-known craft.

These boats are mentioned only as illustrations of the wide range of choice offered nowadays to the man who would a-boating go. No matter whether his main desideratum is speed, safety or luxury—or a combination of all these points—the boat builders stand ready to supply his needs at short notice.

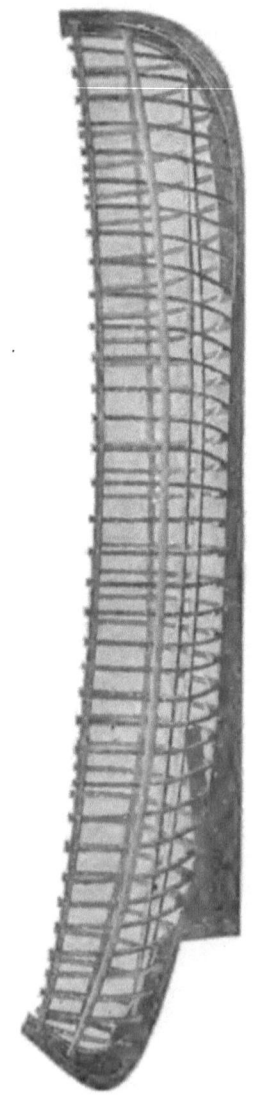

"Pioneer" Frames Set Up.

CHAPTER XII

PRACTICAL BOATBUILDING.

1. Boat Patterns and Knock-Down Frames.

The amateur boatbuilder of the present day enjoys immense advantages over his predecessor of the past. He need no longer work by rule of thumb or rely on his own ingenuity in the important matters of design and working plans. For a few dollars he can buy all the necessary boat patterns, selecting his design from among hundreds offered for his choice by the boatbuilders who make a specialty of this feature of the business. In obtaining such patterns, care should be taken of course to order them of recognized experts in boatbuilding whose patterns may be depended upon to be those of tried and approved models. This is particularly important when the amateur contemplates building a seagoing craft or one for the navigation of the Great Lakes and deep waters generally. In the construction of water craft it is always best to err on the side of safety. In ninety-nine cases out of a hundred, there is more pleasure for your friends in a roomy and thoroughly seaworthy craft than in a boat built according to plans that sacrifice every consideration of comfort to speed, or that have not been thoroughly tested and tried out in actual models.

For this reason it will be best for the amateur to rely to a considerable extent upon the judgment of the skilled marine designers and builders who have made modern boatbuilding almost an exact science. If he is not already in touch with such firms a communication addressed to any of the hull builders or marine engine manufacturers named in this work will put him directly in the way of all desired information.

We do not wish to be understood as discouraging amateur designing. On the contrary, some very successful models have resulted from the work of amateurs, but amateurs should have especial regard to the matters of safety and staunchness.

All boatmen have their preferences—and their dislikes —as to types and designs of boats for any particular purpose. The development of motor-boating has stimulated and, in fact, has awaked the inventive or designing abilities of many a man, so that today successful models of power boats are innumerable. The illustrations shown in this work are of a necessarily limited number of the most popular designs. With the large number of boat-building concerns now making stock models, the yacht designers, and last, but not least, the amateur designer, the most critical boatman can find a style of boat which, with slight changes, suits his particular fancy.

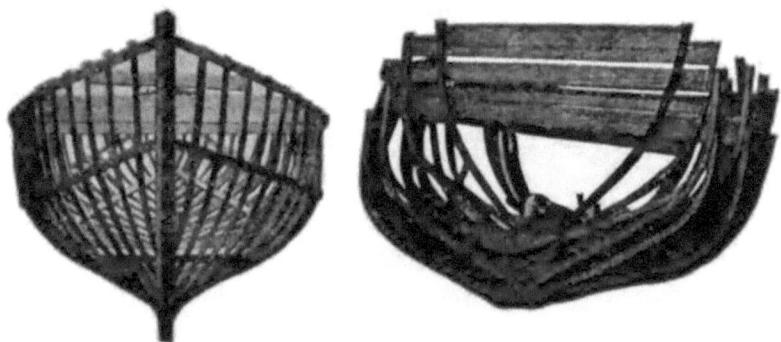

Pioneer "Perfect" Frames, Set Up and Knocked Down.
(Pioneer Boat & Pattern Co., Bay City, Mich.)

The amateur builder who wishes to pursue only a half way course in construction and to avoid the heavier work of frame building can avail himself of the knock-down frame method. There are reliable boat-building firms which supply motor-boat frames that can be assembled without boring a hole or cutting a shaving. In fact, the builders furnish boats in any stage of construction from patterns to completed craft, ready to put in the water and run. Thus, the amateur can put in any amount of individual construction work that he may desire. He can build his boat entirely by himself; he can assemble the frames, in whole or in part, and put on the finishing touches according to his own ideas or the plans of a naval architect; he can buy a bare hull or a completed hull, of wood or steel, and install his own engine; or he can purchase a boat already powered with a suitable engine and ready for the water.

Why Build Your Own Boat?

The question is often asked, is it cheaper to build one's own boat? Glance at any boat-builder's price list. Suppose you want a 25-foot launch. Patterns will cost you, say, $6.00; hardware of iron, $5.00; planking and decking, about $20.00; oak for frame, about $8.00. Say $45.00 to $50.00 to cover everything except your time, and this you take at odd hours, and the result is a boat that the builders sell at $325.00 and cannot afford to sell cheaper. In most cases you build your own boat at from one-quarter to one-fifth the money cost of a completed boat.

Can a man who is not a mechanic use boat patterns and build a boat? Any man or boy who can read the instruction sheets and is capable of sawing a board off or driving a nail, can build a boat by the pattern system, and an extra good one at that.

What advantages are there in building one's own boat? First, the advantage in cost stated above. Second, the satisfaction anyone feels in being able to construct something, particularly if it is that something which has always aroused the keenest instincts of man's nature to overcome the elements, namely, a boat. Then one's enjoyment in sailing a boat of his own construction is double what it would be were he to buy a boat of another's make. That is human nature.

The modern boat patterns are in every feature an improvement on those heretofore offered. The best builders offer nothing freakish, nothing untried, nothing that they wish to sell simply because it is new, but a pattern system that is the very best that experience and expert design and construction can produce. They believe in common sense and the steady and solid progress which comes from building on a solid foundation of known facts.

The amateur builder should scrupulously avoid freaks. This is a well known term in the boating world and is applied to the craft that is built around a single good feature to the exclusion of all others, to satisfy a passing popular fad.

The Boat Pattern System.

Bay City, Michigan, is conceded to have been the birthplace of the pattern system and there it has been developed from a mere experiment into a business of gigantic proportions—and this, it is claimed, by the inherent merits of the boat pattern idea. The system is now a demonstrated success and large boat-building concerns in the eastern states, as well as the pioneers of the Middle West, now furnish excellent boat patterns for the use of amateur builders.

During the period of development some of the defects in boat pattern systems have been due to the patterns themselves, but more often to the fact that boats from which they were taken were not designed with a view of securing patterns of the greatest simplicity and which would present the least difficulties to the amateur in the reproduction of the craft.

After years of careful study and experiment the leaders in the industry have incorporated into their methods, both as to patterns and knock-down frames and boats, those features which have commended themselves to the trade and have demonstrated their practicability and excellence after years of trial, and have added thereto such new ideas as they have gained by years of experience, observation and experiment. Their patterns are not taken from models built promiscuously for a number of years, but every set of patterns is taken from a boat constructed for the purpose of obtaining the simplest and most perfect patterns involving the least possible difficulties for

Built From DeFoe Patterns.

the amateur in their use, in the construction of a boat which, when completed, will embody the latest and most approved ideas of design and construction.

The DeFoe Boat and Motor Works of Bay City, Mich., well known among the boatbuilders of the Great Lakes, explaining the boat pattern system, say: "We have endeavored to make our pattern system a system in fact, not only as to the construction and use of the patterns, but in the design and method of construction of the boats from which they are taken. While there is no real reason under our system why he cannot build a large boat as easily as a small one, yet the amateur builder, as a rule, first undertakes the construction of a small boat and then almost invariably builds a larger one the next season. But if every size and style of boat is constructed on wholly different principles and by different methods, the experience gained in the construction of the first boat will be of little assistance in building the second. Under our modern system, however, every boat we build, either

DeFoe Speed Launch No. 630.

large or small, and regardless of the style, is built upon the same general plan or system. Thus the stern, keel, pipelog, and other portions of the frame are always made and put together in the same way, and the same general method is followed in planking, etc.

"This is a vast improvement, and one which puts the modern system a good long stride in advance. For when the amateur has built his first boat by this system he can build a second, regardless of size or design, with scarcely a reference to the instruction sheets and illustrations, making a great saving in time and expense, as he will know from his first experience the position and fastening of every part of the frame, the manner in which it is set up, and the method of planking and completing the hull.

"Many of our customers, we find, get their boats free in a novel manner. They first build a boat and sell it and with the proceeds purchase patterns and possibly a motor for the second outfit for their own use. Others go a step farther and turn a good business in this way, and come in for a fair discount from our prices by ordering patterns or frames in lots of a half dozen at a time."

Paper Patterns.

The amateur then may purchase, from a concern like that mentioned above, simply the paper patterns and do

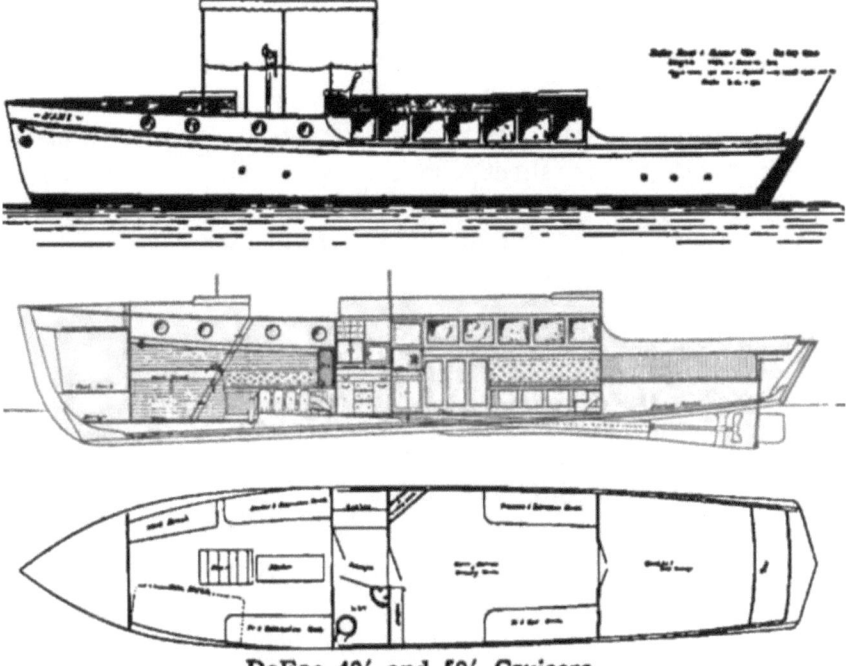

DeFoe 40' and 50' Cruisers.

all the work himself. Remember, these patterns are not blue prints to scale, but are full sized patterns for every piece in the boat.

For example, you are given a full sized pattern for the keel. This you lay upon your plank and mark out the keel. There can be no mistake. In the same way you cut every piece of the hull, planking and all, as there is a separate pattern for every piece and every plank.

The blue print idea has been tried and found wanting, as it naturally would, except in the hands of a skilled mechanic and boatbuilder, and even there, it is claimed, it falls short of equaling the pattern system.

With every set of DeFoe patterns are included full instructions and illustrations for doing the work. These are printed on a large sheet of paper that may be tacked against the wall of your shop. This sheet is complete in every detail and worded in such a manner, and with the illustrations so plain, that any man or boy can work by it without the slightest trouble. Remember, this is not a technical sheet, but is worded in the simplest, everyday language, with illustrations that could not be misunderstood. This sheet contains also full instructions for painting and varnishing and all finishing work, how to mix your stains and fillers, and how to put them on for the best possible results.

The Knocked-down Frame System.

In case the amateur does not wish to do all the work, he can purchase the knock-down frame with which patterns, instructions and illustrations, to complete the boat, are included, without extra cost.

Some boatbuilders furnish knock-down frames in two grades—the Standard frame and the Special frame.

The Standard Frame.—In this frame every part is worked to shape. Everything is dressed, stem and stern knee bolted together and entirely finished, rabbet and all; keel is finished completely, stem and stern is fitted on, and rabbet worked out; ribs are dressed and steam bent. In fact, all tool work is done on the frame and it is ready to set up. They do not set this frame up in the shops. When the purchaser gets it he sets up the keel, stem, stern, and molds, and fits in the ribs, and is then ready to put on the planking. This is by far the most popular frame, partly because of the attractive prices quoted, and also because freight is slightly less than on the set-up frame. If the amateur is not pressed for time he will be just as well satisfied with a Standard as with a Special frame.

The Special Frame.—This is a finished frame in every respect. The builders set it up in the shops, finish every item of tool work, fit in the ribs and bevel them properly, put on the top plank (or sheer-strake) and bolt in the clamps, making it a most complete frame. Molds or ribbands are not necessary in erecting this frame. When the purchaser gets it he uncrates it and it goes together like a buggy or a piece of machinery that comes to him

DeFoe Compromise Stern Launch With Hunting Cabin.

crated. He simply puts in the bolts and screws where the builders took them out. These frames, if under 20 ft. in length, can be shipped erected if so ordered, though freight rates will be somewhat higher than if the frame is knocked down and crated.

A frame consists of the following parts with all tool work done:

Launches.—Stem, keel, stern, and deadwoods, finished and put together; ribs steam bent, clamps, breast hooks, deck beams, floor timbers, fenders, keelson, skeg with pipelog bored, bolts for stems, keel, etc., together with bill of materials, patterns, etc., for completing the boat. In Runabouts the transom finished complete is included.

Canoes.—Keel, stems, gunwales, fenderwales, seat-risers, seat bars and decks.

Rowboats.—Stem and knee, keel plate, skeg, stern post, transom and knee, breast-hook, gunwales, fenderwales, risings, ribs and oarlock blocks.

Sailboats.—Keel, stem, stem knee, transom, transom knee, trunk logs or pocket-pieces, head ledges, stern post, skeg, clamps, deck beams, fenderwales and ribs.

A Special frame consists of all parts included in the Standard frame and the sheer-strake additional, set up and finished as stated above.

The Bare Hull.

You may also purchase a bare hull. The builders usually carry these hulls in stock, ready for completion. The nails are not set and they are not faired off, as this is work anyone can do, and the average purchaser would not care to pay for having it done. The boat yards will do it, however, at a slight extra cost. The clamps and deck beams are put in. This is an attractive offer to many, and especially to the amateur who wants something better than the rest, is particularly skilled in the use of tools and has expert knowledge in putting on stains and varnishes. You can purchase a perfect hull, and as time is the main element in a perfect job on the top and interior work, you may by the use of fine woods that you will be able to procure, and perhaps a few original ideas, turn out a boat that will be the pride of a sportsman's heart.

A 25-foot compromise stern boat, for instance, with a cockpit arranged with secret drawers and cupboards, an icebox, a gasolene stove of one burner or two, secreted when not in use behind a movable panel, and numerous other devices, products of your own ingenuity, will give you an outfit that will yield you an amount of satisfaction that money could not purchase in the way of a completed boat from any factory in the land. You may reach this same result by starting with patterns alone, or a knock-down frame; or, if you wish to avoid the more difficult parts of the work, get the bare hull. Freight on a bare hull would be at the same rate as on a completed boat, but, of course, the bare hull is much lighter and freight would be about cut in two.

If you order coaming from the boatbuilders indicate which wood you desire, either oak or birch. If a more costly wood, such as mahogany or cherry, is ordered, an additional charge will be made, depending on the size of coaming. Either oak or birch is the standard wood for this purpose.

Bill of Materials.

With every knock-down frame or set of patterns a list of all hardware, lumber, etc., necessary to complete the boat is usually included. The builders will quote you a price on this hardware that is perhaps better than you will be able to get in your home town, unless you have the advantage of extra low prices. Hardware of iron is sufficient for fresh water; for salt water you will need hardware of galvanized iron or of copper and bronze.

Ring Buoy, Steering Wheel, etc.

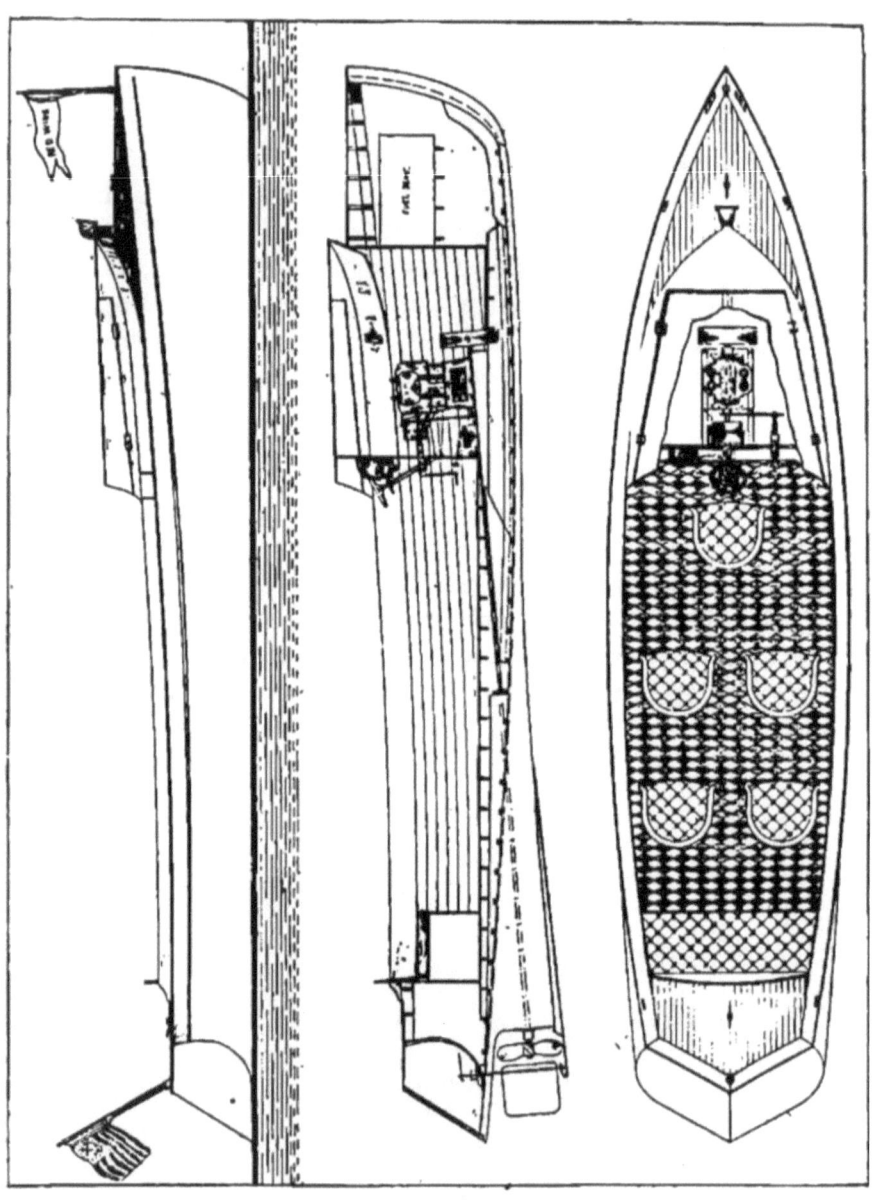

Red Wing Auto Boat—Red Wing Boat Mfg. Co.,
Red Wing, Minn.

CHAPTER XIII

PRACTICAL BOAT-BUILDING—Continued.

2. Form and Strength of Hull.

The general principles underlying the work of the boat-builder and the methods whereby these principles are carried into effect, are not difficult to comprehend.

The main objects of the builder are to realize the desired form and to provide the necessary staunchness and stability in his craft. In other words, form and strength are the main objects to be attained.

The form of the boat is a matter of design and involves geometrical principles and the study of such matters as utility, safety, appearance and air resistance. The amateur who builds his boat from patterns already prepared for him has little or nothing to do with the matter of design, since that was settled for him when he chose his model and bought his patterns. To realize the desired form, he has simply to follow the patterns.

The provision of the necessary strength in a boat is, however, a matter of mechanics and involves not only the selection of proper materials and the use of good workmanship, but the observance of sound mechanical principles to overcome the strains and stresses to which the boat structure will be subjected.

There are secondary matters, of course, to be considered before the boat is completed for use, but these relate mostly to the boat user's convenience or comfort and depend a good deal on personal taste. It is unnecessary to dwell on these secondary matters, which may be left to the individual boat-builder, and we can therefore confine ourselves here to the realization of the form desired for the boat and the provision of the strength required.

It should be clearly understood that while these main objects are separate and distinct, they must be regarded together in the attainment of the result desired, which is to realize both objects with the same set of structural members.

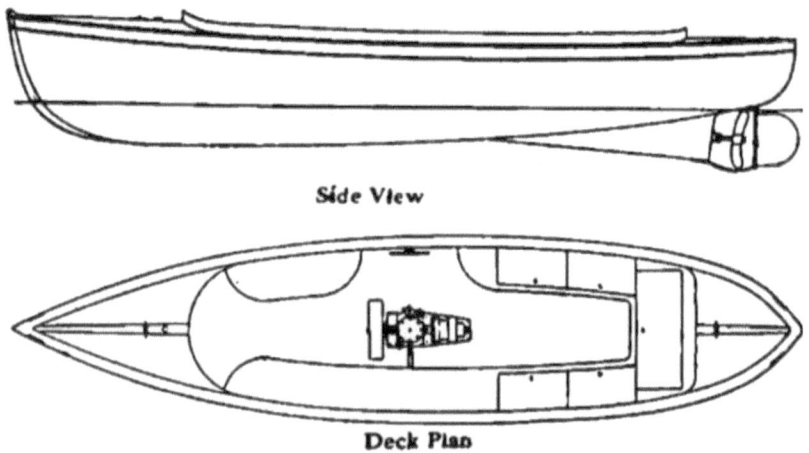

Side View

Deck Plan

**Compromise Stern Motor-Boat.
(Racine Boat Co.)**

The actual form of the surface of the hull depends entirely upon the outer planking or skin. To assemble this planking in the form desired an inner frame of some kind is necessary, over which the planking may be bent and secured in shape, also some form of internal stiffening to assist the planking in preserving the desired shape.

Thus, we must have these three factors in boat construction:

(1) An internal straightening framework.

(2) Frames or molds over which the planking is bent to the desired form.

(3) The outer skin or planking.

In practical boat-building two different methods of construction are employed. The first is a common method of building small craft, such as rowboats and the smaller motor-boats and launches. In this method the frames over which the planking is bent are temporary wooden molds and their object is fulfilled when the planking is put together in the proper form for the outer skin of the boat.

In the second method, used for the larger motor-boats, a framework composed of various members, including frames and cross ties or deck beams, is first constructed and set up to form a sort of skeleton of the boat model desired. The planking is then bent over and secured to this framework to form the outer skin and the framework thereupon becomes an integral part of the boat.

In building a boat from knock-down frames, as described elsewhere, these frames when set up constitute the permanent framework referred to above and it is no inconsiderable part of the entire construction of the boat. In other words, the use of knock-down frames saves the amateur builder most of the heavy carpenter work, besides assuring him of securing the form desired.

We may call the first method of boat-building the mold method and the second the frame method, it being clearly understood that molds are for temporary use only, to determine the form of the planking, while frames form a permanent part of the boat structure.

Provision of Required Strength.

In providing the necessary strength for the boat hull, it is well to remember that strength is required in three different respects, namely, longitudinally, transversely and locally.

Longitudinal strength may be defined as the capacity to resist bending along the fore and aft lines of the boat, such as hogging or sagging of the hull as a whole.

Transverse strength is the ability of the structure to resist bending or distortion to right or left with reference to the fore and aft axis,—in other words, to resist transverse strain or the strain produced in the planking or other member by a force operating at right angles to its length.

Local strength is the capacity of the various members of the hull to resist stress exerted at any particular point; that is, such a stress as might injure the hull at that point, but might not produce any distortion of its general lines.

In a boat without permanent frames or internal bracing, the planking is the principal factor which secures longitudinal strength. Various supplementary factors are required, however, to secure the necessary stiffness

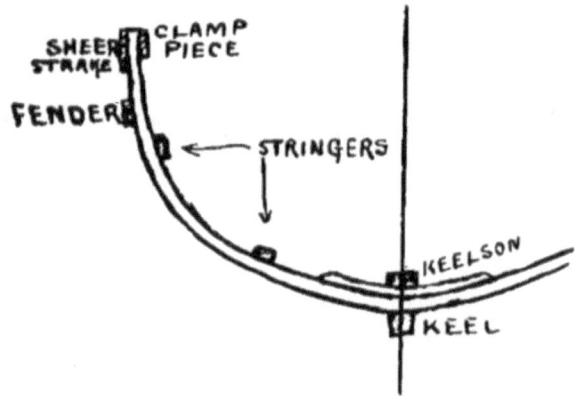

of the hull as a whole and these may include the combination of the keel and keelson, the sheer strake, stringers, clamps, and fender pieces or strips. The various positions in which these appear are illustrated. They are not usually all found in any one boat, though some are common to all designs.

In the provision of transverse strength the planking with its internal framing forms the principal factor, thus serving a double purpose, namely, determining the form or shape of the boat and providing a good deal of the strength required in the structure. The top sides of the boat, which are the weakest parts of the hull, may be strengthened by the use of deck beams or stringers, which prevent the sides from opening outward or collapsing inward, either of which by changing the form of the boat would destroy its general effectiveness. Where deck planking is used this adds to the transverse strength as opposed to inward strain. Though this planking is not often relied upon for the purpose, it likewise adds to the longitudinal strength of the boat and may be regarded, therefore, as one of the factors, though not an important one, contributing to the general stiffness of the decked hull. The flooring laid in the boat likewise contributes its share to the transverse strength, giving additional stiffness along the keel and bottom of the boat and forming a support for the lower members when these are subjected to transverse stress.

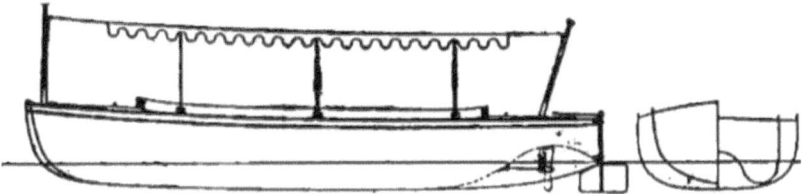

Turbine Boat—Shallow Draft.

As far as local strength of the various members of the hull is concerned, but little special attention is usually required apart from the use of good materials, especially sound timber. Near the bow, however, where the sides of the boat may come in contact with the dock or other craft, also beneath the engine and at the stern where the propeller shaft requires support, special construction is needed to secure local strength at these points.

At the bow of the boat and in other points local strength is usually secured by means of chock or angle pieces, as will be seen in our illustrations showing longitudinal sections of motor boats. The sides of the boat may be strengthened by means of special fender pieces or strips. The part of the boat beneath the engine is strengthened to perform its duty usually by a special foundation of longitudinal timbers or of steel, attached to the structure of the boat in such a way as to distribute through the hull the local stresses occurring through the running of the engine.

The methods in use for this purpose are clearly indicated in the chapter devoted to the installation of engines. Generally speaking, it may be said here that the engine foundation should be long and large enough not only to provide the local strength required, but also to distribute the stresses properly.

Red Wing 16' Runabout.

CHAPTER XIV

PRACTICAL BOAT-BUILDING—Continued.

3. Structural Members and Materials.

In the construction of small power boats and launches of wood, the following are the structural members required in ordinary practice and the materials commonly employed for each member.

Keel—Usually of oak, of square or nearly square section for the older standard form of stern; sometimes rectangular with the greater dimension vertical. A flat keel is used for the torpedo boat stern, which is a more modern form of construction.

Stem—Commonly of oak and fitted to the keel with knees of oak or hackmatack (the American larch or tamarack). When the sternpost is fitted to the keel, the same method and materials are used.

Frames—Also commonly of oak from $\frac{1}{2}$ inch to 1 inch square and set from 6 to 9 inches apart (between centers), the size and spacing depending upon the size of the boat and varying in accordance with the character of the construction.

Deck Beams—These are usually of oak, though spruce or sometimes pine is used, and must be spaced to suit the frames. Their size may vary in section with the size and character of the construction from $\frac{1}{2}$ to 1 inch wide by 1 to 2 inches deep.

Planking—The side planking for boats of small size may be of cypress, cedar or pine, and either a single or double set of planking may be used, varying in thickness from a mere shell $\frac{1}{4}$ inch thick to 1 inch or even more.

according to the size of the craft and character of construction. Mahogany is also sometimes used for the side planking. Ordinarily a single layer of planking from $7/8$ to $1\tfrac{1}{8}$ inches thick is good practice, where it is not necessary to regard the weight of the structure. This constitutes a serviceable and perhaps the least expensive form of construction. In this form of outer skin for the boat, the seams must be carefully attended to and calking and painting are also points that need looking after.

A better water-tight construction is secured by the use of 2 layers of planking, each from $3/8$ to $1/2$ inch thick, having white lead between, and care being taken that the joints of the two layers do not come together.

In building high speed boats special planking of cedar or mahogany in layers about $1/4$ inch thick is used, often with a layer of oiled or varnished silk or other fabric between the layers of wood.

Deck Planking—Is usually of cedar or pine $3/8$ to $3/4$ inch thick, often waterproofed with a canvas covering laid in white lead or varnish.

Fastenings—The fastenings used in boats of wood may be copper rivets and burrs, copper nails clinched or riveted over burrs, screw fastenings of various kinds, plain galvanized iron nails and ordinary screws. In the best practice for first class work, all fastenings are of copper, brass, or bronze and these are "through and through" fastenings instead of being merely driven into the wood.

Bulkheads—In modern construction of first class boats it is usual to divide the hull into water-tight compartments by means of bulkheads. It is evident that these, in order to be water-tight, must be designed and fitted with the utmost care and must possess considerable strength. Several such compartments are found in the best models, especially for seagoing craft, and the object is usually to provide that the boat will float when any single compartment is filled with water—and also support the occupants of the boat.

No matter what the size of the boat, the question of providing water-tight compartments is an important one. Boats so fitted give the owners and occupants a comfortable sense of security, adding greatly to their pleasure in the use of the boat. It is sometimes difficult to find room for such compartments at the bow and stern of the ordinary boat with open cockpit, particularly when plenty of seating capacity in the cockpit is required, but to secure safety under all circumstances, especially in case of emergency or accident, it is well to cut down or limit the size of the open cockpit, so as to enable compartments to be provided at the bow and stern by means of water-tight bulkheads, and these compartments should be large enough to enable a boat to float, even if the cockpit is filled with water.

The necessity for water-tight compartments is of course less in boats intended for use in shallow, smooth waters than in craft used on the seaboard, deep lakes or large rivers, but the matter should be always carefully considered. It is satisfactory to note that in the best modern practice the provision of water-tight compartments of sufficient size to float the boat under all possible contingencies is regarded as being of the first importance. Very often, of course, the highest possible degree of safety can be secured without sacrificing a single other feature of utility in the design of the boat.

Typical Material Specifications.

The following are typical specifications for the materials used in moderate speed motor boats of 18 to 30 feet in length:

Frame—Keel and keelson of solid white oak, one piece, white oak natural crook stem, securely fastened to keel. Solid oak stern. Frames of clear, straight-grained white

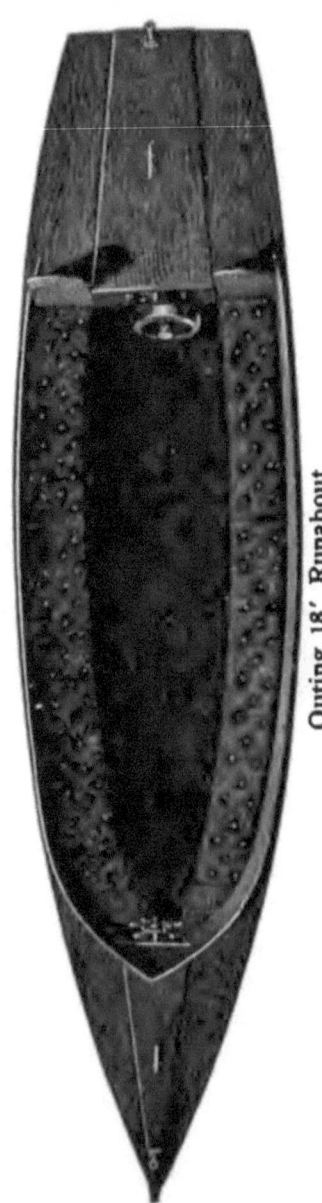

Outing 18' Runabout.

Outing 18' Runabout.
(Outing Boat Co., Ashland, Wis.)

oak, spaced closely together. Extra heavy frames at motor foundation to strengthen and reduce vibration.

Decking—Coaming, guard rail, covering boards of clear, finely figured, white oak. Decks of quarter-sawed white oak, finished natural or canvas covered.

Trimming—Combination bow chock and flagstaff socket. Cleats, chocks, deck sheaves, stern flagstaff socket, brass nickel plated. Steering wheel at bow, brass nickel plated and mahogany. Wire tiller line runs through brass nickel-plated sheaves and leaders.

Planking—Clear, red cypress, cedar or white pine. The garboard and sheerstrakes are of clear white oak, put on in long lengths, fastened to frames with brass screws or copper rivets. All holes in both planking and frames are bored to prevent cracking.

Cockpit—Entire cockpit sealed up with white oak or cedar, fastened with copper nails. Seats on sides and across at stern end of cockpit. Lockers under all seats. Fronts from seat to floor nicely paneled. Lids on all seats, fastened with brass hinges, to make all such space under seats useful for storage.

Finish—The entire boat is sanded to a smooth surface and given a coat of hot linseed oil. Over this are applied three coats of copper paint below water line. With three coats of pure white enamel marine paint above to sheerstrake, the entire interior with frames is treated to one coat of linseed oil, put on hot, and two coats of pure red lead paint. Sheerstrake, fenders, covering boards, decks, coaming and interior of entire cockpit finished natural in three coats of best spar varnish above filler.

Construction of High Speed Boats.

There is a wide difference in practice when we come to the construction of motor-boats designed exclusively for speed. The high speed racing machines are so constructed as to realize the main object of their design with the minimum of weight in the hull and engine.

In the high speed boat the frames are comparatively smaller in section than in the ordinary moderate speed runabout. The material must be carefully selected. The frames are also set somewhat closer together than in the ordinary boat, in order to offset the reduction in thickness of the side planking and the consequent lessening of local strength. This reduced spacing involves an increase in the number of the frames, but with proper design and the reduction in section of the frames there may be an important saving of weight in the hull as compared with the ordinary method of construction.

The side planking of high speed boats is usually fitted in two layers, each about ¼ inch thick. Occasionally only a single layer is used and the seams are covered on the inside of the boat with strips, which also serve the purpose of stringers. Where this method is employed, calking is not necessary and the weight of the hull is considerably reduced. Careful workmanship is required in such construction.

Special bracing is sometimes worked into the structure of high speed boats, this being placed diagonally inside the frames. It adds to the transverse strength of the hull, supporting it against torsional stress and consolidating the framework into a structure best suited to withstand the vibration caused by the working of a powerful high speed engine.

In other cases of special construction for racing craft light girders are worked along the interior sides of the hull to give additional longitudinal strength. These girders may include top and bottom chords, timber struts and steel wire braces. They add but little to the total weight and increase the resistance of the hull to longitudinal stresses.

In many notable cases, special forms of framing have been used for racing boats. These have usually been designed with the object of saving weight in the hull. A typical case of special framing is thus described by "Marine Engineering:" "The length of the boat over all is 60 feet and on the water line 48 feet, with an extreme beam of 7 feet 6 inches. The planking is of single thickness Honduras mahogany 3-16 inch thick, and with edges secured by flush screws to continuous longitudinals of Oregon pine. The framing is carried out on a special double system consisting of inner and outer frames and longitudinals. The longitudinals are notched over the outer frames, and all three parts of the structure are through riveted, giving great transverse strength on a minimum of weight. The inner frame is furthermore carried continuous up the side and across, forming the lower member of the deck beam, while the upper member of the same runs across from side to side and ends at the planksheer. The longitudinal strength of the boat is obtained chiefly from two truss girders running from end to end in the wings, and consisting of upper and lower continuous longitudinals, wooden compression struts and galvanized wire diagonals set up tight."

The local stiffening provided for high speed boats is also reduced as compared with that used in the ordinary moderate speed boat, but this is done at a sacrifice of a certain amount of safety in this respect and only after careful design, so as to secure the greatest possible strength of the least possible weight.

The forms of special construction briefly indicated above have resulted in producing boats in which the hull has about one-third the total displacement of water after the engine is installed as compared with the weight of the hull in ordinary boats of one-half to two-thirds the total ultimate displacement.

Typical Specifications.

The following are typical specifications for a high speed motor-boat:

Frame—Keel and keelson of solid white oak, one piece, white oak natural crook stem, securely fastened to keel. Solid oak stern. Frames of clear, straight grained white oak, spaced closely together. Extra heavy frames at motor foundation to strengthen and reduce vibration.

Planking—Clear red cypress, cedar or white oak The garboard and sheerstrakes are of clear white oak, put on in long lengths, fastened to frames with brass screws or copper rivets. All holes in both planking and frames are bored to prevent cracking.

Decking—Coaming, guard rail and covering boards of clear, finely figured white oak. Decks of quarter-sawed white oak.

Cockpit—Entire cockpit sealed up with white pine or cypress, fastened with copper nails. Seats on sides and across at stern end of cockpit.

Steel Boats.

Very many motor-boat hulls are now built of steel In this form of construction the general characteristics are similar to those found in wooden construction. The framing includes longitudinal keel plate and stringer angles, transverse angle iron frames, deck beams and steel plating, the latter being fitted similarly to the planking of wooden craft.

All these members of the framing of steel boats fulfill the same general functions as the similar members in wooden hulls.

CHAPTER XV

PRACTICAL BOAT-BUILDING—Continued.

4. Laying Down and Assembling—Finishing.

The process of assembling the structural members of a boat may now be considered. First, however (unless modern full-sized boat patterns are used), the water lines and sections at each frame must be laid down full size. This is done on the floor of the amateur builder's shed or loft and chalk marks are usually employed for the purpose, these being often done over with black lead to prevent rubbing out. The lines are taken from the designer's

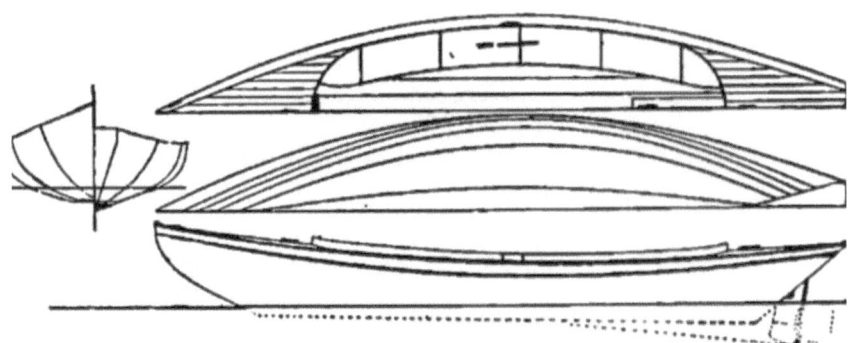

Lines of a Dory Launch.

plans, including the half-breadth body and sheer plans, but are made full size, all proportions being duly observed. The sections when transferred to the floor will indicate the sectional form at various stations to be regularly measured off along the line of the keel. These should be numbered for convenience.

It should be noted whether the lines of the design relate to the outside of the frame or to the actual water surface of the boat. If the latter, the thickness of the planking must be deducted all along the section lines in order to obtain proper form for the frame.

If the boat is to be built with fixed molds, after laying down the lines we must next determine the form of the molds. At least five such molds are required between the stem and stern post and it will often be found advantageous to use not less than eight molds for boats of small size. A series of twelve molds is frequently used for a small launch.

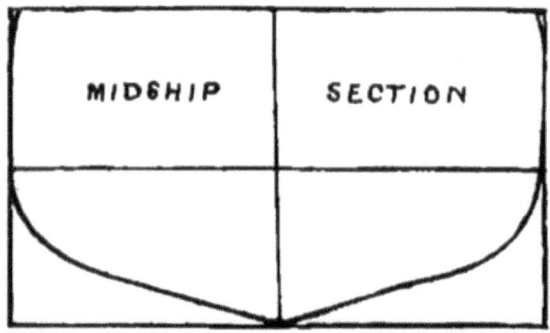

The form of each mold is obtained from the full-size sections. A single board of sufficient width is used to form one-half of the mold. A duplicate of this being made, the two are placed together to form the complete mold.

To obtain the form of the half section on the board used for the purpose, nails may be laid down with their heads on the section line and the bodies at right angles thereto, the board being then gently laid down upon the nails and tapped with a hammer or pressed upon them. An imprint of the nail heads will thus be made on the under side of the board and it will then be an easy matter to reproduce the form of the half section on the board by means of a batten sprung through the continuous imprints of the nail heads.

The half of the mold is then cut along the lines indicated. The vertical section lines having been noted, the duplicate half is cut and the two may be joined in the manner indicated in the illustration, with a cross-pawl or horizontal piece of timber at the top.

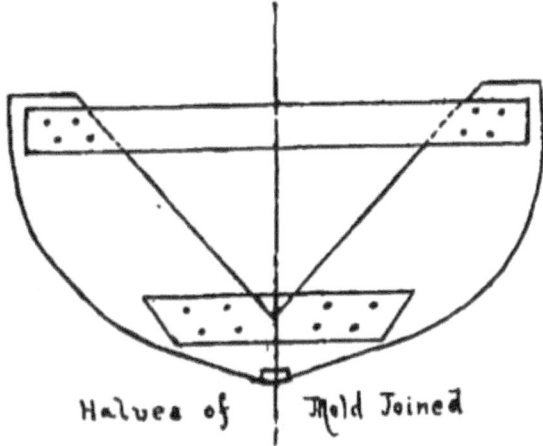

Halves of Mold Joined

The rest of the molds are made in a similar way, until the entire series is complete. They are then ready to be assembled on the keel, and we may proceed to prepare the keel.

To support the keel a two-inch plank should be set up on end and blocked securely. The upper edge must be cut or trimmed to correspond with the design for the sweep of the keel. This supporting plank forms no part of the boat structure, but is simply a convenient foundation for the work. If this support is adjusted in such a manner as to bring the intended water line of the boat horizontal with reference to the floor of the shed or loft, it will be found a great convenience to the builder.

A pattern for the stem is taken from the floor in the same way as the form of the molds is secured, and it may be noted here that while the molds are on the floor, the height of the deck line, if any, and the load water line should be marked on them.

The keel, stem and stern posts should now be prepared according to the dimensions required and must be rabbeted to admit the edge of the garboard strake, or first range or strake of planks laid on the bottom of the hull next to the keel, and its ends at the stern and stem. They are then erected in turn on the keel support and the stem and stern posts are secured to the keel by means of chocks and fastenings through and through.

For the stem a white oak plank may be used, cut to shape of the pattern. A center line should be scratched along its face and also another line on each side of this to show width of the face when finished. The thickness of the stem usually tapers to the point where it joins the keel. Position of the load water line taken from the body plan should be scratched across the face of the stern.

The stem and stern knees should be cut as shown on the plan and bolted to the stern with ¼ inch galvanized bolts, care being taken to set the bolts at cross angles across the scarf to draw the stem and knee together. If the boat is to be fitted with the old form of stern the deadwood and shaft-log may next be cut to dimensions and fitted to place. The deadwood is a body of timber built up on top of the keel to afford a firm fastening for the planks rising obliquely from the keel. The shaft-log must be of clear, straight-grained oak, having a longitudinal hole cut through its center of a size suitable to accommodate the shaft tube. It is usually formed by a couple of timbers bolted together with galvanized iron bolts.

In assembling all these members of the structure care should be taken to see that the joints between timbers are perfectly tight. They should be treated with white lead and closed with "through and through" fastenings.

Erecting the Molds.

The next step is to erect the section molds, made in the manner already described. After placing them at the proper stations, which should be marked at regular intervals on the keel, they must be centered and squared up with the keel and then fastened in place securely by means of braces and ties.

Each mold should be carefully plumbed fore and aft and sideways before being braced in place. A straight edged board several inches wide should then be nailed on the center line of the cross-pawls, one edge being just at the center line. By means of this straight edge, each mold can be squared athwartship and should be nailed at the top to a batten extending longitudinally around the molds from stem to stern. To insure the molds being plumb sideways, a spirit level may be set on top of each cross-pawl to see that it is level from side to side. Then the mold can be braced securely from above on each side.

The molds having been secured in place, we may now proceed to put in the ribbands.

These are strips of wood bent over the molds and fastened to them from stem to stern along the lines of the planking. They help to retain the molds in place, and when fitted will also serve to show any defects in the lines of the hull. The molds should be of sufficient height to allow the upper ribband to be fixed above the point designed for the sheer strake and thus serve to support the frame until the sheer strake and clamp piece are in place.

The ribbands may also be made large enough and numerous enough to enable the frames to be bent in against them to the proper form. This, however, is only done in the case of small boats.

Bending in the Frames.

Bending in the frames will be the next operation. The material for these should be carefully selected and extra pieces should be provided, as some are likely to break in bending. A good material is tough clear white oak. In order to make the frame timbers bend evenly, they should be made of uniform thickness by being run through a planer after being sawed out. As already stated, small frames may be bent directly to the required form against the ribbands, but usually the frame after being properly sized, must be first steamed. It is then taken immediately to its place, bent in to the required form, then secured to the keel, clamped to the ribbands and carefully adjusted in the proper position.

For the purpose of steaming frame timbers, a steam box is required. This may be about 14 inches square and 12 feet long. It can be made from common pine boards, well cleated on the outside and one end closed tight. The other end is left open to receive the frames, but when in use is closed by a temporary door or even by a bundle of rags stuffed in tight. In order that the frames may be set in the hottest steam, slats should be fixed across the inside of the box and the frames placed on them. An ordinary wash boiler with a tight wooden cover will give plenty of steam and it can be taken to the box through an iron pipe or rubber tube. Frames should be steamed about an hour and the steam should not be allowed to go down, but should be kept hot until the frames come out. See Steam Box in following chapter.

For larger boats, when the frames can not easily be bent in against the ribbands, they are usually formed on a bending floor or by means of frame molds. When they are formed on the floor the exact shape of the frame on the inner or concave side is laid down on the floor. Pegs or nails are driven into the floor along the line of the design and the steamed frame is then bent to the required shape against these pegs or nails. Sometimes special molds are cut for each frame and with this as a foundation the frame is bent to form.

Whenever the shape of the frame will permit, it should run in one continuous piece from rail to rail without any joint at the keel, but this can apply only to the frames in the midship section of the boat. Nearer the stem and stern, where the angles at the keel are sharp, the frame is necessarily bent in in two parts, these being secured together by a chock at the bottom. When bent to form, either as one continuous piece or in two parts, however,

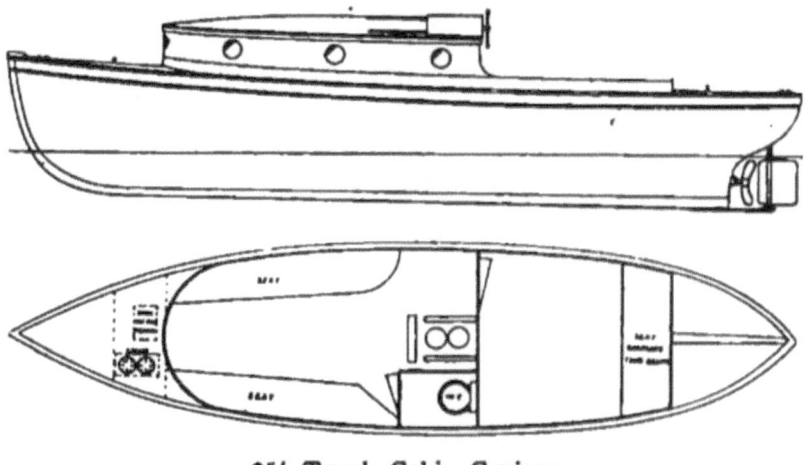

25' Trunk Cabin Cruiser.
(Racine Boat Co.)

the two sides of the frame are firmly secured by cross ties, so that when erected in the hull, it will retain its form.

When in place at the proper station on the keel, each frame should be permanently fastened thereto, with a temporary fastening to the ribbands by clamps. The heel of the frame may be fastened to the keel by two galvanized wire nails, which should be bored for and have their heads countersunk. The fastenings to the keel will include the fitting of chocks and bent floors with keelson, the latter being a continuous strip running fore and aft, securely fastening the flooring to the keel. The floors, which may be of one-inch timber, are usually fitted to the shape of the frames and notched closely over the keel. They must extend high enough to reach to the bottom of the cabin or cockpit floor, which is fastened to them, and they may be bolted to the keel with ⅜ inch galvanized bolts and riveted to the frames with two rivets on each side.

Limbers must be cut in them and these should be of sufficient size to prevent them clogging up, small ones being of little use. For the benefit of the novice, it may be stated that these "limbers" are holes cut through the floor timbers to permit the draining of water to the bilge or pump well.

When the frames are well set, the molds can be taken out, care being taken before doing this work on the frames which are the height of cross-pawls, to put stay laths across at each mold, well fastened to the upper battens, and transfer the overhead braces to the stay laths.

Planking and Seating.

The skeleton of the hull being now set up, it is ready for the planking or outer skin. This should be prepared in lengths as long as possible, each plank being tapered toward the bow and stern, so that there may be the same number of strakes from stem to stern. The edges of the planking will then come as nearly as possible at right angles to the frames.

If the method of construction involves a double layer of planking, the outer layer should be so arranged that the joints will not correspond with those of the inner layer. After the inner layer is put on, its outer surface may be painted thickly with white lead, special care being taken to cover the end joints and seams. If the joints and seams of the second or outer layer of planking are also similarly painted or covered, it will help to make the skin perfectly water-tight.

Before fitting the longitudinal planks, the ribbands formerly noted must be removed with the exception of the topmost ribband, which, as we have stated, should be sufficiently high to clear the sheer strake and clamp piece.

When the planking has progressed as far as the sheer strake, the latter is carefully fitted. This covers the topmost strake of planking and is securely fastened to the frames and the construction strengthened by means of the clamp piece or longitudinal member on the inner side of the frames, the whole being firmly bolted together.

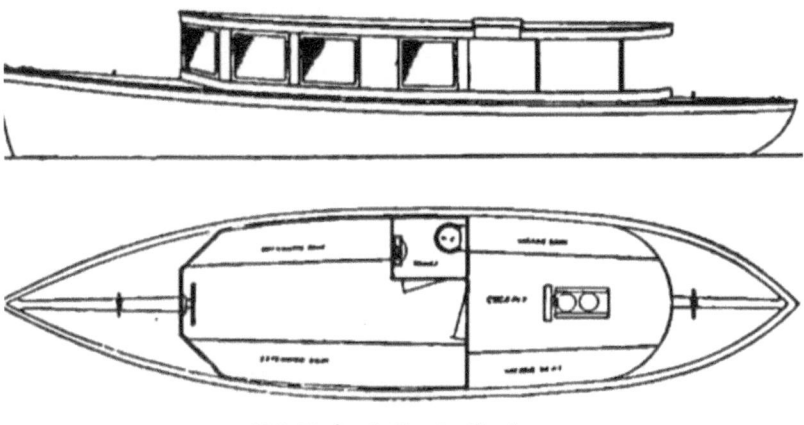

30′ Raised Deck Cruiser.
(Racine Boat Co.)

The upper ribband may now be removed, after a few ties have been run across from one side of the hull to the other. The tops of the frames are then cut off and the molds, if still standing, are removed.

The rail is then finished and may be made with a cap piece to cover the sheer strake, clamp and space between them formed by the frame ends; or the space between the frames may be filled in flush with the sheer strake and clamp pieces; or the combination of sheer strake, clamp and frame ends, may be left to form the rail.

In most cases, bilge and side stringers should be put on to add to the longitudinal strength of the hull.

With regard to the foundation for the engine, complete instructions will be found in the section devoted to installation of engines. Details of this work depend altogether upon the size, weight and design of the engine.

As already stated, however, care should be taken to put in a foundation of sufficient size and length to distribute the stresses caused by the operation of the engine as far as possible throughout the hull.

Seating—In order to support the seats called for by the boat design, whether these are fore or aft or across the boat, suitable stringer pieces are fitted on the inside of the frames and securely fastened to them. The seats being carefully fitted and fastened to these stringers, will add to the strength of the structure, acting as braces for the side, especially in the case of transverse seats, which, when properly fitted, add greatly to the lateral strength of the hull, preventing compression of the sides or bulging as the case may be.

Fore and aft seats, when properly fitted, add to the longitudinal strength of the sides, as well as increasing the transverse strength. When fore and aft seats are fitted, their inner edge is supported on posts standing on and fastened to a stringer piece secured to the frames.

Chocks or brackets may also be fitted under the seats to add to the strength of the construction.

If the boat is to be decked or partially decked, the next step is to put in the deck beams and then the deck planking over the space to be covered.

If gasolene tanks or air tanks are to be installed beneath decks, these must, of course, be set in place before the space is finally closed.

Finishing the Exterior.

When the work of construction has reached this stage, the exterior of the hull is ready for planing and finishing. The first step is to rough plane the planking and then to calk and fill the joints carefully with thick white lead or other suitable material; then the entire exterior can be finally planed, smoothed up and prepared for painting and puttying.

In the case of single planked boats with a thin skin, great care must be taken in the final planing not to weaken the structure by removing too much of the surface of wood, as the thickness of the timber will not stand it. Judgment must be used in such cases, in order to secure the best results in the form of the finished exterior without sacrificing the strength of the structure.

It will readily be seen at this point that special care must be taken in all the earlier stages of the work, so as to secure the precise form designed. Hence, at every stage, especially in preparing the molds and frames, dimensions must be carefully observed and workmanship must be exact, in order to secure the form required. After the frames are in and the planking fitted, it is too late to correct any error in the external lines of the boat and this fact should be borne in mind from the moment of laying down the keel.

If the boat has been built on approved lines with careful attention to details of workmanship and design, the exterior of the hull will emerge from the operations of planing, scraping and sand papering in a form to delight the eye of the builder.

When double planking is fitted, the operation of calking is not always necessary, but in the case of thick planking it is usually best to calk. The operation of calking is the driving of cotton or oakum into the seams with a calking iron, or broad form of chisel and a mallet, in order to prevent the penetration of water. The oakum or cotton is forced below the surface by means of the iron. In the construction of large boats and in shipbuilding, the seams are usually covered with melted pitch.

With thin planking, less than half an inch thick for instance, the seams would hardly retain the cotton, hence, when the thinner forms of planking are used, it is necessary to use it in two layers with shifted seams, this construction obviating the necessity of calking. White lead is freely used to protect the seams.

Painting—Care should be taken to use only the best kinds of marine paint. Three or four coats can be given, each coat being rubbed down before the next is applied, and plenty of time being allowed for drying between coats. If this is properly done, the result will be a smooth, hard surface of lasting quality.

A typical course pursued by boat-builders in finishing is as follows: The entire boat is sanded to a smooth surface and given a coat of hot linseed oil. Over this are applied three coats of copper paint below water line. With three coats of pure white enamel marine paint above to sheer strake, the entire interior, with frames, is treated to one coat of linseed oil, put on hot, and two coats of pure red lead paint. Sheer strake, fenders, covering boards, decks, coaming and interior of entire cockpit are finished natural in three coats of best spar varnish above filler.

In the above we have referred particularly to the construction of small boats and launches made over molds with the old form of stern and deadwood.

In the construction of larger boats of the same general design, the frames are heavier and stiffer in proportion and being molded or bent to form on the floor after steaming, the use of molds is unnecessary.

The keel, stem and stern posts are set up in the manner described above and the frames being then erected in place and ribbands fastened along the sides, the boat is "in frame" and the further steps of construction, including planking, decking, seating and finish, are conducted in the same general way as in building smaller boats.

When a more modern form of stern is adopted in the design, such as the well-known torpedo stern, the various steps of construction are practically the same as in the older model, but the keel is usually a flat timber, rather than square as in the old style boat. Provision also has to be made to support the shaft tube and shaft properly where these pass through the bottom of the boat. Supports must be provided, not only for the shaft bearing at the point of passage through the bottom, but also at the point where the shaft emerges into the water, just forward of the propeller. This may be in the form of a steel or bronze bracket securely fastened to the stern to support the shaft bearing.

Launch Equipped With 7 H. P. Clifton Engine.

It being impossible within the scope of a work of this size to describe in detail all the varied processes required in the building of the innumerable models now seen in American waters, we have endeavored to give a general practical idea of the methods of procedure commonly employed in building boats and launches of types generally regarded as normal, and designed for moderate speed and cruising purposes. At the same time we have shown the peculiar forms of construction used in building speed craft, such as the special methods of framing, the use of extra thin planking, sometimes with varnished silk or other fabric between layers, and other features tending to secure the rigidity of structure required where lightweight, high-speed engines are installed.

Our description of the methods commonly employed will suffice to start any amateur who possesses a slight knowledge of carpentry on the right road to success in building his own boat.

Equipped with the knowledge furnished in the preceding chapters, he will be stimulated to an intelligent study of the plans from which his boat is to be constructed and will know how to set about the routine of operations required in all boat construction.

Specific instructions for the building of a typical power boat from patterns will be found in detail in the next chapter, and these will furnish any points that may not be included in the general outline of operations already given.

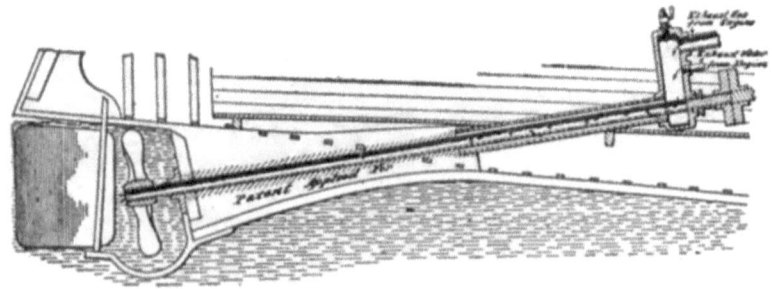

Under Water Exhaust.
(Outing Boat Co.)

CHAPTER XVI

PRACTICAL BOAT BUILDING—Continued.

5. How to Build a Boat from Patterns.

Complete instructions for building from paper patterns a motor boat or launch from 16 to 30 feet or more in length are given in the following pages. A typical boat for a novice to build would be, say, an 18-footer of standard stern, about 4 feet 2 inches beam, designed to carry six or eight persons and to run $8\frac{1}{2}$ or 9 miles an hour when equipped with a 3 H. P. motor.

The necessary patterns (or knock-down frames, if desired) for building such a boat or indeed a launch of any size or style can be obtained from the boat-builders who make a specialty of such business. The instructions and forms of design given in the various sections of this chapter apply particularly to the patterns furnished by the DeFoe Boat & Motor Works, of Bay City, Michigan, where the pattern system originated.

Section 1.—How to Handle Patterns.

If the sheets are large and unwieldy cut them up into convenient sizes, taking care not to cut the lines of any pattern. Lay the pattern you wish to use on your material, hold it carefully in place with weights or tacks, and trace the lines with a tracing wheel, bearing on sufficiently to leave the imprint on the wood. Remove the pattern and cut out the piece. Be careful to leave enough wood outside the pattern lines so that the piece will smooth up to the exact size of the pattern.

Another method is as follows: Prick holes through on the lines of the pattern with an awl. Make them about 18

166 MOTOR BOATS:

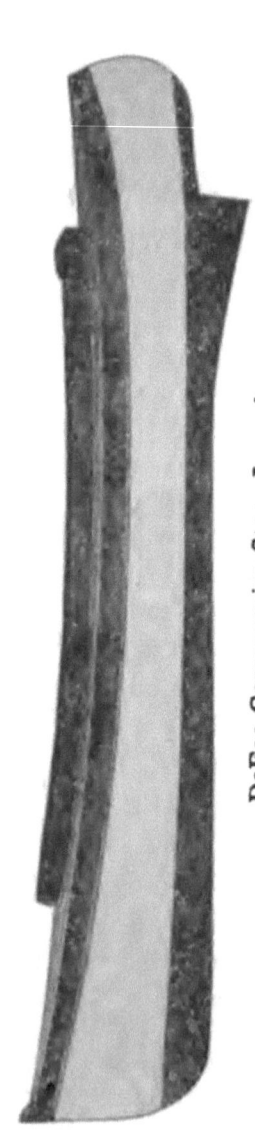

DeFoe Compromise Stern Launch.

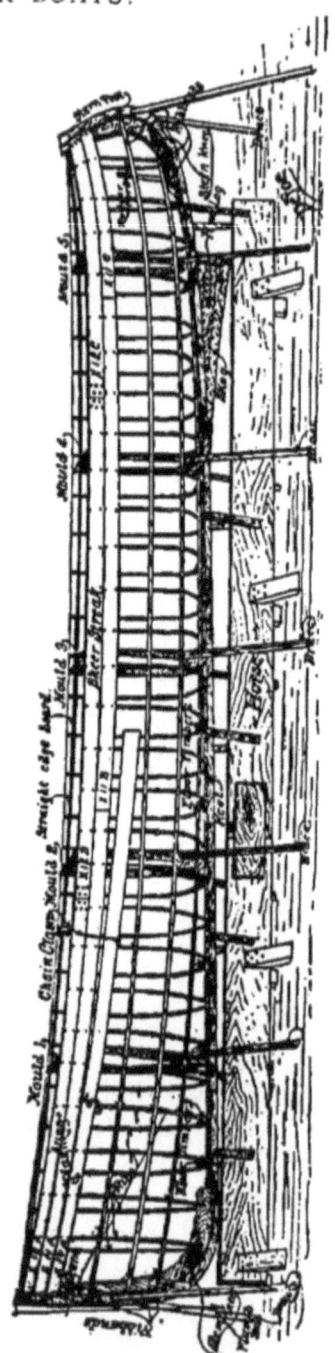

DeFoe Method of Construction.
FIG. 1.

inches apart on lines slightly curved and from that to very close together on lines greatly curved. Remove the pattern, stick nails into the awl holes, bend a thin batten along the nails and mark the line by it.

Be careful to use your material to the best advantage, and cut the parts out in a way to leave the least waste. You can make a big difference in the cost of your boat in this way.

In placing your pattern on the wood be careful that the grain runs in the proper direction to give the greatest strength. For example, the grain in the breast-hook (Fig. 6) should run crosswise, in the transom-knees (Fig. 3) diagonally, etc.

Do not cut your paper patterns out to exact size, as a long narrow pattern, such as a plank pattern for example, would be apt to lose its shape. It is a good plan, after each part is finished, to place it on the pattern again and see that no mistakes have been made. Do this every time without fail.

Section 2.—Materials to Use.

All lumber should be well seasoned and air-dried rather than kiln-dried, as kiln-drying makes it brittle.

White oak is by far the best material to use for the frame-work of the boat. Rock elm may be used. Fir may be used for stem, keel, etc., but it will not bend for ribs.

For planking use white pine, cypress, or cedar if it can be obtained and it generally can. Southern pine may be used, but it splits easily and is difficult to work and to hold in place. Avoid basswood, poplar, etc., unless your boat is to be canvas covered, as they will not stand the water. Fir or spruce may be used.

Buy good lumber. Wide boards cut with less waste than narrow ones. Cross-grained, knotty or shaky stuff will split and you will waste more in working it up than you will save on the lower price.

Section 3.—Keel, Stem, Stern-post and Skeg.

Keel—The first part to construct is the keel. Using patterns as directed, cut the keel to shape, and if made of two pieces (as in the larger boats), fasten together with a butt splice (Fig. 2 a). The keel is now finished.

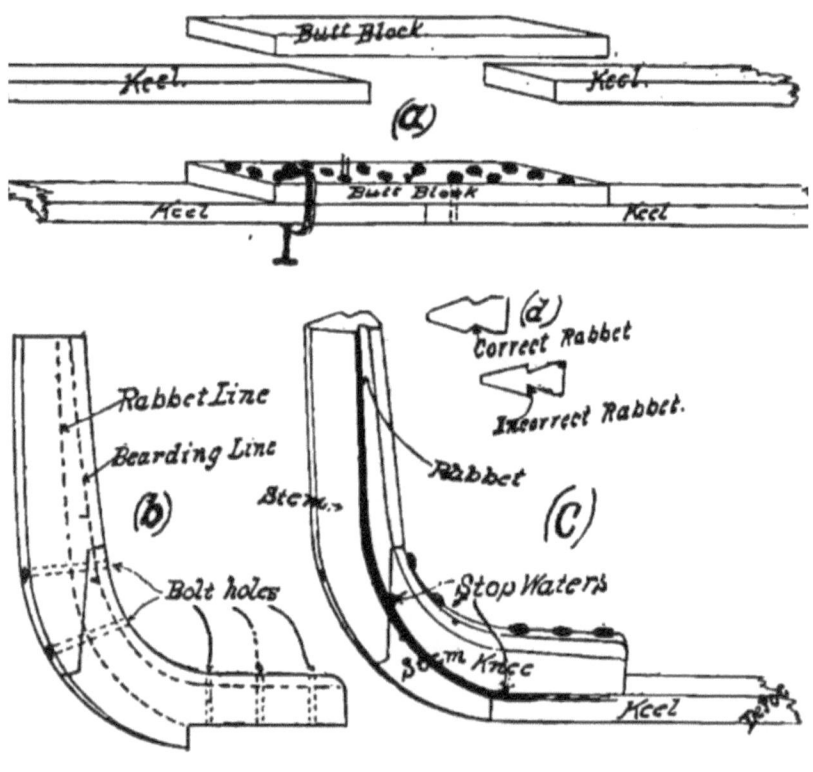

FIG. 2.

Stem—First saw out stem and stem-knee from the patterns, and bolt them together as shown in Fig. 2 (b). Mark the rabbet line on both sides, and with a chisel cut the groove, called the rabbet, as shown in Fig. 2 (c). The ends of the plank are to be fitted into the rabbet, and hence it should be as deep as the plank is thick.

Cut the rabbet with plenty of bevel as shown in Fig. 2 (d), so that the plank will slip in easy. The rabbet line and bearding line are shown on the stem pattern. In compromise stern boats the stern-post is put together and rabbeted exactly as the stem.

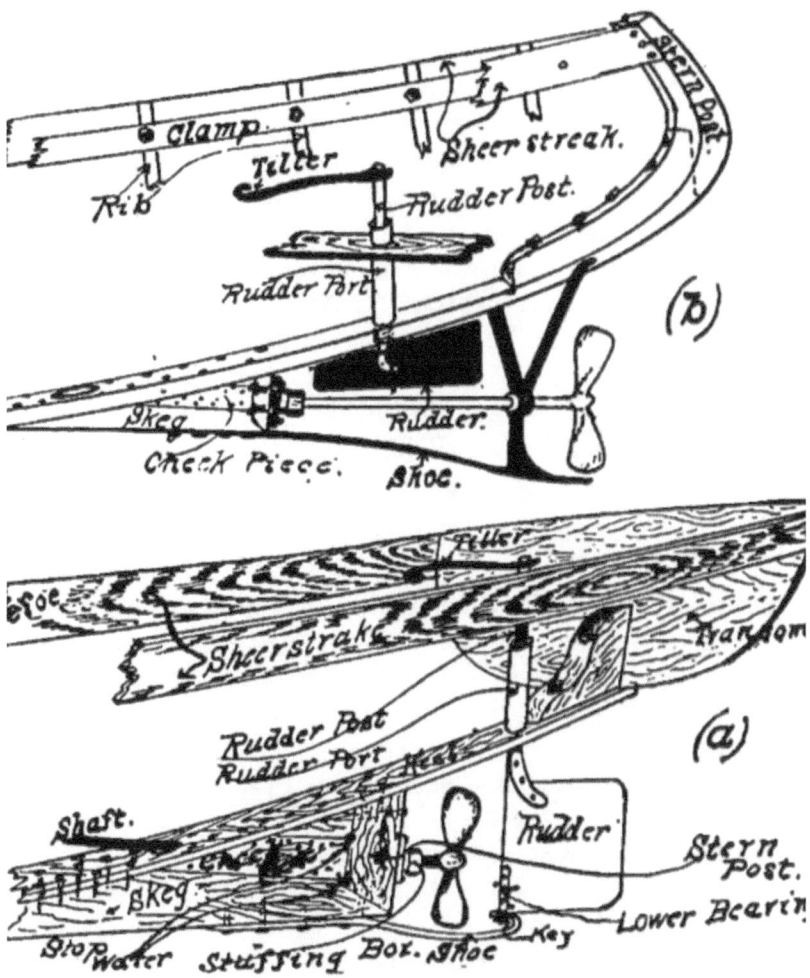

FIG. 3.

Fig. 3 (a) shows construction of the transom stern. (For torpedo and fantail stern construction special instruction sheet is sent.)

The skeg is made of stuff two to four inches thick, depending on size of boat. Have it thick enough that there is plenty of room for the shaft hole, though not so thick as to be cumbersome. If you haven't the means of boring the shaft hole rip the skeg in two on the line of the shaft and gouge out the shaft hole. Then fasten the two pieces together again by means of a flat cheek piece screwed firmly on each side. Fig. 3 (b). Fit this piece on carefully and bed it in white lead and you will never be troubled with leaks. The stern post is put in to make a better fastening for the shaft bearing, as the screws would not hold in the end of the timber of the skeg. The figure shows how to fasten stern post to skeg and put in stopwaters. Paint the skeg and keel where they are to be joined and lay a thin sheet of rubber or canvas between them to prevent leaks, and fasten skeg to keel by nailing down through keel. Nail thoroughly, boring a small hole for the nails to prevent splitting.

A stopwater is a small pine plug driven into a hole bored for it, to prevent a leak in a spot that cannot be reached to calk. Fit them carefully and they will swell enough to prevent the leak. A little study of the illustration will show you just why they are put in certain places.

Section 4.—Setting Up Frame.

Molds—The next step is to make the molds. They may be made out of any rough cheap stuff, as they are not a part of the boat, but simply forms to build it over. Wide boards will work up handier. Fig. 4 shows two molds. The pattern of but half the mold is given. Cut out one half of the mold and use it to mark the other half by. Get the distance across the top from the pattern, and also mark the center of each mold.

Next, from a two-inch plank 8 to 12 inches wide, construct a long horse for the purpose shown in Fig. 1. Make it straight on top, and nail the legs to the floor so as to brace it straight in line. Compromise and torpedo stern boats draw more water forward than aft and it is

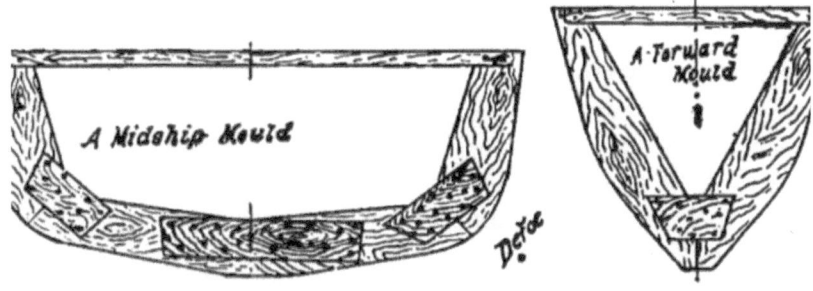

FIG 4.

better to raise the horse on longer legs at the stern end so that the boat will set while building about as it is supposed to set in the water. The builder can then better judge of his work while he is building.

Bolt the stem and stern-post and skeg to the keel, place the whole on the horse and fasten keel down to the horse so that it will be in line, that is with no kinks or bends in it.

Fasten the molds to the keel (keel pattern shows where they belong) by nailing a block on the keel and the molds to this block. Fasten them square across the keel and perpendicular to it. Nail a board with a straight edge (splice two together if need be) from stem to stern on top of the molds, bringing the center line of the mold to this straight edge, Fig. 1. This is to hold the mold square across the keel and perpendicular to it.

Plumb up the stem and stern with a plumb bob, and brace the whole thing either to the roof or floor as shown in Fig. 1.

The sheer strake is the top plank of the boat and the sheer line is the top line of this plank. The top of each mold will just come to the sheer line if you make them exact size of pattern and the point where the rabbet line ends on the stems is the sheer line.

Next put on the ribbands. These are narrow strips of straight grained stuff free from knots, about ⅝"x⅞" for small boats to ⅞"x⅞" for larger ones. Put at least five ribbands on each side, screw them to the stem and stern and nail them with light nails to the molds. Neither molds nor ribbands are a part of the boat, but are simply used for putting in the ribs.

Section 5.—Bending and Putting in the Ribs.

Everything is now ready for the ribs. These are to be steamed and bent over a form, or forms, and allowed to cool before using. It is generally best to use two or three different bending forms, as the ribs do not all have the same bend in them. Make these forms out of a piece of ⅞" board, and use the molds for patterns. It is not

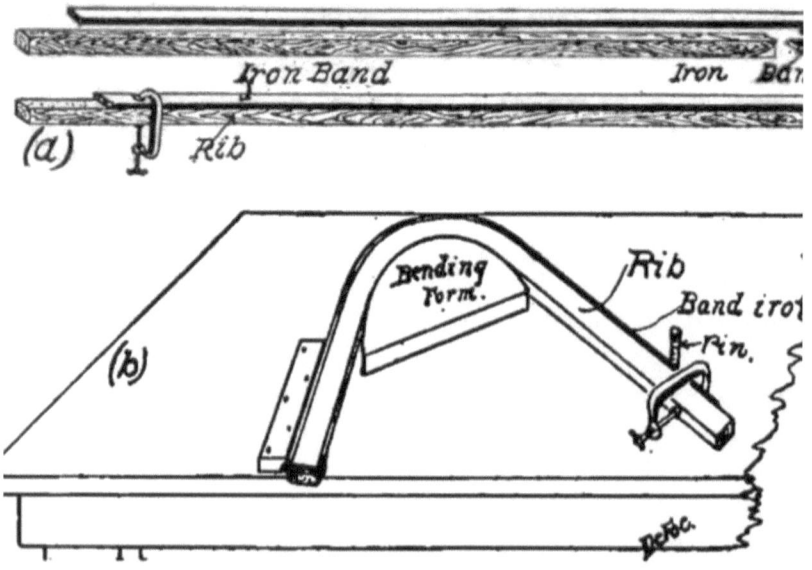

FIG. 5.

necessary to make a form from every mold, but select the mold with the greatest bend and one or two others. Make the form so that the rib will have a little more bend than the mold, as it will spring back a little after it is bent. And it is a simple matter to straighten it farther if it does not spring back enough. Nail these forms down to the bench.

Procure a piece of thin band iron about the width of the rib and bend a hook in one end that will just fit over the end of the rib, Fig. 5 (a), Steam the ribs thoroughly for an hour Clamp the iron strap quickly on a hot rib as shown in Fig. 5 (a), and immediately bent it around the bending form as in Fig. 5 (b). Tack a stay lath across to keep it from straightening out and the iron strap may then be removed, the rib taken off the form, and the operation repeated on the next rib. Leave the ribs about an hour until they are thoroughly cooled.

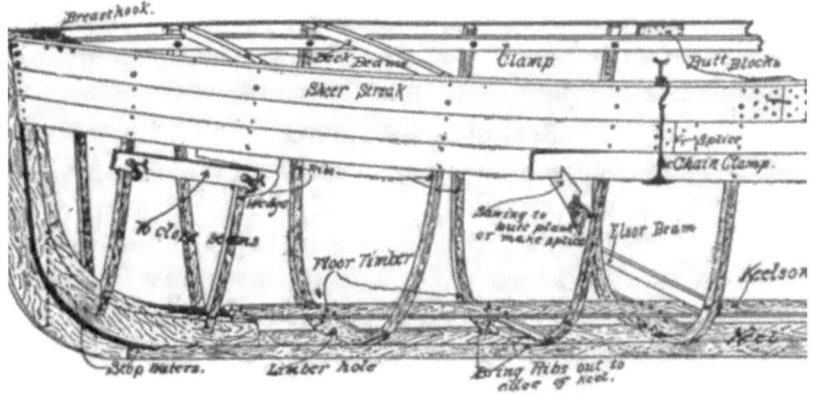

FIG. 6.

Then the stay-lath may be knocked off and the rib is ready for use. Be careful that each rib touches every ribband or the outside of your boat will not be smooth. Fit the lower end to the keel, nail it fast, boring for the nail through the rib to prevent splitting it, and tack them temporarily to the ribbands. Cut ribs 5 or 6 inches longer than required length to be sure of a fit. Be sure to get the bend in the proper place, so that one end of the rib will not be too short. The ribs near the stems must be notched into the sides of the stem knee, as shown in Fig. 6.

Floor Timbers—Figures 1 and 6 show floor timbers. They are used to fasten the ribs together and to fasten them more firmly to the keel. Use oak about the thickness of the ribs and about $1\frac{1}{2}$ to 3 inches deep. Lay the piece alongside the ribs and mark it. Then take it out and cut it to shape. In this way a good fit can be very easily obtained. Nail it firmly to ribs and to keel. Be sure to cut a limber hole in each one to let water run back to pump. Put a floor timber on every other rib. It is scarcely necessary to put them on every rib. The molds may be in the way of some of the ribs. If so, put these ribs in after the molds are taken out.

Be very careful to do all this work exactly to the patterns, for if your molds are not made correct in size and placed correctly, and if the ribs are not fitted exactly to the ribbands, of course the plank patterns will not fit.

Section 6.—Planking.

The plank patterns are marked and numbered as follows: They are numbered 1, 2, 3, 4, etc., up from the keel, No. 1 being the plank next to the keel. This plank is called the garboard. No. 2 is the next plank above and so on. In large boats each plank will probably be in two or three pieces. The end of the piece that goes toward the bow is marked with an X and the pieces of a plank are lettered from the bow. For example consider the 12th plank on a 30-foot boat (see Fig. 1). You will find that it is in three pieces. One piece is numbered X, 12, A, the X meaning that this end points toward the stem, the 12 that it is the 12th plank from the keel, and the A that it is the first piece of the plank toward the bow. The next piece is marked X, 12, B, the X and 12 indicating same as before, and the B that this is the 2nd piece of the plank from the bow. In shorter boats this plank would be in but two pieces. The proper edge of the plank is up when the number and letters on the patterns are right side up as the boat sets on her keel. Be sure to get the proper edge up. Mark the upper edge as you take the pattern off the board. The first strake of plank to be put on is the sheerstrake (See Figs. 1 and 6). Place the top edge even with the top of the molds and where the rabbet line ends on stem and sternpost (or top of transom in square stern boats). Most builders prefer to finish this in natural wood. In such a case all screws and bolts should be plugged. (See section on Painting, Varnishing and Finishing.) Screw the top edge to the ribs (as shown in Figs. 6 and 1). The bottom is not necessarily fastened until clamp is put in (see section 7). In putting on any strake fit up and nail to the stem and stern first, then splice. (Fig. 6).

As each piece of plank is got out and fitted, use it as a pattern to cut a like piece for the other side of the boat. Be very careful to finish up both pieces the same size, so that both sides of boat will be exactly alike.

Fig. 6 shows method of splicing plank. The plank patterns are all made about 6 inches longer than the finished plank is to be, to allow for sawing for the splice. Nail both pieces to the ribs except for the two or three ribs near the splice, and, holding the saw square across, saw both pieces off at once. This, of course, leaves the two pieces fitting perfectly, the saw cut leaving a space of about 1-16 inch between them to allow for calking. Make butt blocks (Fig. 6) of oak, as it will hold the nails well, and make them about the thickness of the ribs. Nail plank to both butt blocks and ribs from the outside with clout nails that will reach through and clinch. If sheerstrake is to be varnished, screw to butt blocks and plug screw. When the sheerstrake is on, put on the rest of the plank down to the bilge (i. e., where the bend comes in the ribs). Then the most convenient method is to turn the boat over, horse and all, (leaving the horse on will keep the keel in line) plumb up the stem and stern, and put on the plank next to the keel, called the garboard. This is the most difficult plank to put on and takes some careful fitting. Then plank from both ways, leaving about the 3rd plank from the keel to go on last. This plank is called the shutter. Unless your work has been very accurately done the pattern for this piece will not be apt to fit. It is safest anyway to cut it larger than the pattern and then dress it down to fit. The only object in turning the boat over is to make it handier to work at. If you prefer you may plank it entirely right side up.

Fig. 6 shows two methods of holding plank to place and closing the seams tight while nailing. The chain clamp may be purchased of the pattern makers. The other method, though serviceable, is not as convenient. It often requires quite a pressure to make these seams tight. They should come up tight on the inside, but the edges should be beveled before putting on, so that the seam will be open about 1-16th of an inch on the outside to allow the calking to be driven in. (See section on Calking.) After the plank is sawn out dress up the edges with a plane, and hold it up in place to see that it fits. At the same time bevel the edges a little to allow for the calking seam.

The planks that go on the bilge must be hollowed out a little on the inside to fit the curve of the ribs. This is easiest done with a round bottom plane. If you haven't a round bottom plane, gouge out with your chisel where the rib goes, till you get a fit.

With few exceptions all planks will go on without steaming.

Section 7.—Clamps and Breast-hooks.

When planks are all on remove the horse from the keel, right the boat up, and take out the forms. Place the boat at any convenient height for work, plumb up the stem and stern, and brace in position.

The clamps (Fig. 6) are located just the width of the deck beams below the top of the sheerstrake. They are straight pieces (preferably oak) and are sprung into place. They should be about ½ the width of the sheerstrake, and from ⅞ inch thick in 16-foot boats to about 1¼ inches in 30-foot and 35-foot boats. They are bolted through every rib, the same bolt fastening lower edge of sheerstrake, Fig. 6.

The breast-hooks (Fig. 6) are of oak, with the grain running crosswise, and rest on top of the clamps. Bolt and screw them in as shown in illustration. Make them thick enough that they will dress down even with the sheerstrake so that the deck will lie flat on top of them. Place breast-hook in stern also of compromise launches.

The keelson is shown in Fig. 6. Have your floor timbers level so that keelson will lie flat on top of them. A ⅞ piece about the width of keel should be used. Fasten securely at stem-knee and stern, and to every floor timber, as this is the main strength of the boat. A keel and keelson construction such as this is immeasurably stronger than a solid keel piece such as some builders use, and absolutely prevents vibration.

Decks—But one deck-beam pattern is given, as this is sufficient. Cut deck beams to required length and get the shape from this pattern, since the curve will of course be the same in each beam. Deck beams are nailed on top of clamps and along side of a rib (Fig. 6) where a secure fastening may be made. Before nailing them in be sure the boat is spread out to proper width, according to forward mold which you have removed. Nail deck knees (Fig. 7) in a little high and then shape down even with deck beams so that decks and covering board lie level. It is best for the amateur to cut a true circle for the coaming, as the coaming will then go in much easier. A few trials with a pencil and string, as shown in Fig. 7, will get the proper center. Strike the circle to come exactly tangent to the covering board, for if there is a short jog here the coaming cannot be brought up to fit.

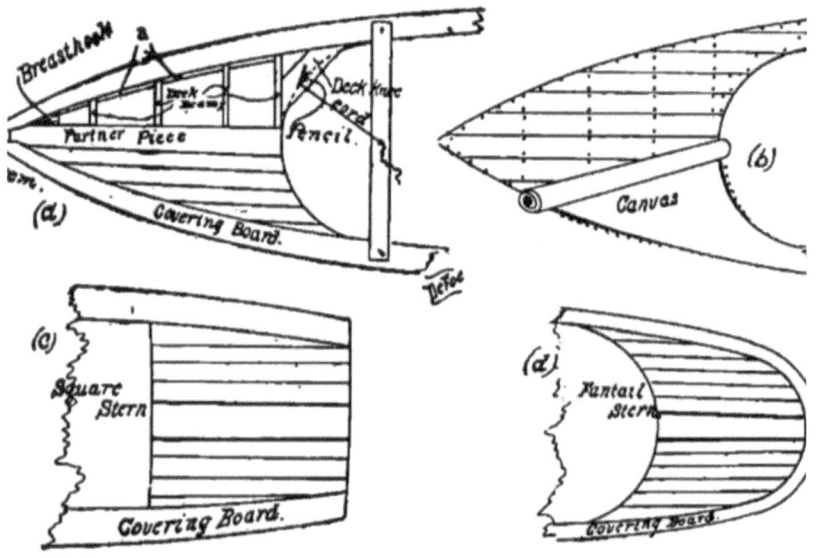

FIG. 7.

Place the deck beams from about 6 inches apart in smaller boats to about 10 inches in larger ones. The distance apart of deck beams may depend also on thickness of decking used. Decking should be from ½ to ¾ inch.

Fig. 7 shows a method for putting on deck for a varnish finish. Put on partner piece first, then covering boards. Put little blocks of proper height on the clamp along the sides to hold the covering board.

If you wish you may make the partner piece from 3-16 to ¼ of an inch thicker than the rest of the deck, letting it project above the rest of the deck this much. Cut the covering boards to shape. Nail the short pieces marked (a) Fig. 7, between the deck beams, and flush with them to hold the ends of the decking. Begin to put the decking on at the partner piece, and fill out to the covering board. This deck should be calked. Hence, leave seams open about 1-16 inch at the top and close them tight at the bottom. Calk with a cotton cord. Be careful to get these seams all true and even. Set the nails. Plane the deck smooth and scrape it before putting on coaming. Careful work is necessary for a good job on this deck, but it can be done by anyone who will take plenty of time and care to it. The seams are then puttied over the calking, either with putty to match the rest of the finish in color, or of another color that will give a pleasing contrast.

Fig. 7 (b) shows method of making a canvas-covered deck. This makes a very serviceable deck, and is easily put on. Matched pine flooring is good stuff for the decking, or waste material from the planking may be used. No partner piece or cut out covering boards are used. Nail stuff on and then cut out for coaming circle, and trim off edge flush with sheerstrake. Paste canvas down with a paste made of rye flour. (Stir up flour with cold water and cook till it thickens.) Draw it tight as possible and tack over the edges where fender strake and coaming will hide the tacks. Paint canvas with several coats of thin paint. Green is a good color.

Fig. 7 (c and d) shows stern decks of transom and fantail boats. The coaming may be put in either round or square to suit the taste of the builder.

Coaming—Fig. 8 shows method of bending coaming. Strike a semicircle on the floor somewhat smaller than the circle cut in the deck, to allow for the coaming springing out a little after taking it off the bending form. Cut out some wood brackets and nail them firmly to the floor on this semicircle. Bend the coaming around the

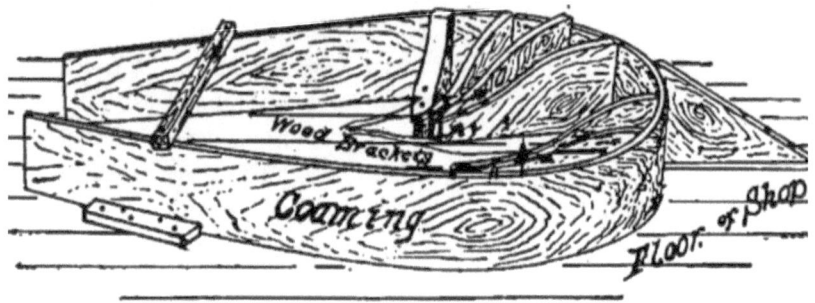

FIG 8.

brackets as shown. When cool remove it and screw it into place, and then dress it down to the proper height. Plug the screw heads for a good appearance. Use butt blocks 7 to 8 inches long to put pieces of coaming together, and put them on the outside (Fig. 10).

Interior Arrangement and Finish.

There is ample choice of a number of seating arrangements. The builder may suit himself in this matter, though the style with seats running all around cockpit is recommended as the best for boats under 22 feet in length, while any of the styles are suitable for larger boats.

Put in the floor beams (Fig. 6) so that the floor will come about at the bend of the ribs. To get them all level put in a beam at each end first and be sure that they are at right angles with the perpendicular of the boat, so that the floor will be level as the boat sets in the water. Also place them at such heights that the floor will be level fore and aft. Then stretch two lines connecting the ends of these beams and fit in the remaining beams so that they just come up to these lines at each end. Then lay the floor on these beams and it will be level.

A good interior finish is made by ceiling the cockpit with narrow strips of ceiling about 1½ to 2 inches in width. This is put in lengthwise, starting at the coaming, and is easily sprung into place. If you wish to make lockers under the seats ceil up with the same stuff, running the strips up and down. This when filled and varnished makes a very nice-looking interior.

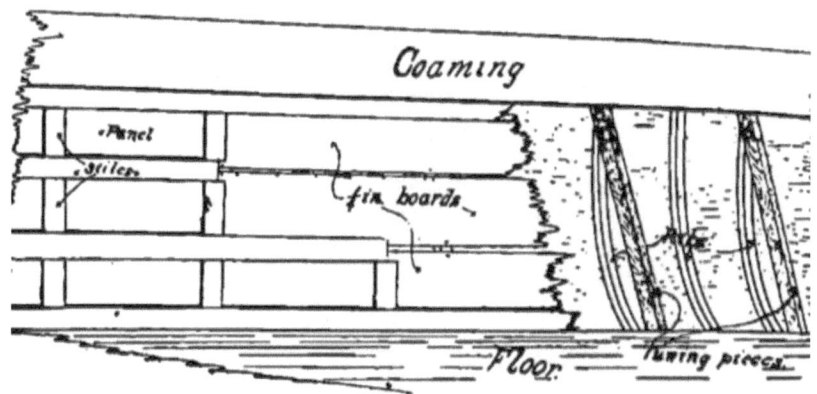

FIG. 9.

If you want an extra fine job, panel the interior in the manner shown in Figs. 9 and 10. Get your stuff out from ¼ inch to ⅛ inch thick. Put in the tuning pieces, reaching from the top of the rib to the floor, of oak or any timber that will hold a nail well. Use small brads and countersink them with a small nail set. Nail the panels on first and put the stiles on afterward. Put the lengthwise stiles on first and put in the up and down pieces afterward. This takes some careful fitting to make a good job, but anyone can do it if he is willing to take the time, and will throw aside a piece if it does not fit and make a new one. Paint the backs of the panels before putting them on. Panels of this make are just as durable as the tongue-and-groove panel, and are lighter and much more easily made. Make the width of the panel from 2½ to 3 times the width of the stile, and make the panel from 2 to 3 times as long as it is wide. In paneling the side of a cockpit, for example, where the panels must be wider at one end than at the other, make the stiles the same width on the whole job and vary the

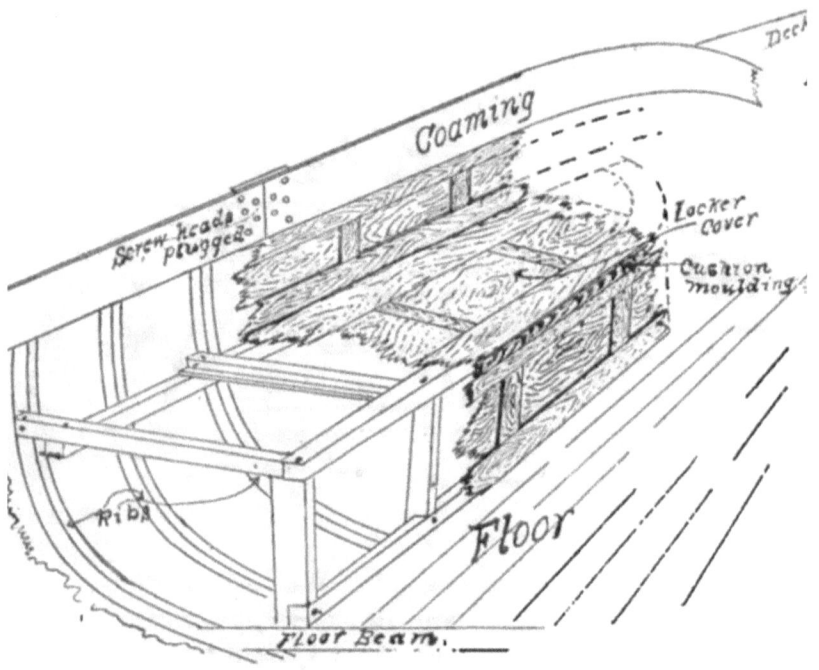

FIG. 10.

width of the panel only. In paneling a cockpit use from 2 to 3 panels up the sides and 1 or 2 deep around the lockers. The builder may have ideas of his own, for an artistic arrangement of the panels, as there is no set rule to follow.

Calking.

Use a small calking iron and a mallet. Calk the butts first and where plank joins stems. Use calking cotton if the seams are uneven, that is, wider in some places than in others. Do not put it in in long straight strands, but drive it in in little tucks or loops first. Go over about a foot or two of the seam in this way first, and then go back over it and drive it in solid. Be sure to get enough cotton in the first time, as it is a poor plan to put more in the seam after it has been once gone over. It is apt to work out if you do. Fill the seam about half full.

If the seams are fairly even you can do a much easier and perhaps better job of calking with a soft cotton cord instead of the calking cotton. Do not tuck this in, but run it in straight, and drive it down tight with a calking iron. Use only a single strand. If you have carelessly left a seam too tight to get the calking in, open it up first by driving the calking iron along it.

When the calking is done paint the seam with thick paint, being careful to touch all the cotton. This will keep it from coming out.

Calk before the boat is painted. After first coat of paint, putty the seams and nail heads.

Engine Bed for DeFoe Motors.

Fig. 11 shows how to make an engine bed. Make this of oak from 2 inches to 4 inches thick. Fasten the pieces together with lag screws.

The cross pieces must fit down to the planking and be nailed fast. Nail from the outside of the boat. Bolt the cross piece through the keel. Put the bolt head outside and sink it flush in the keel. Fit a block between the keel and keelson where the bolt goes through so that the bolt will not bend them together. Fasten the motor to the lengthwise pieces with bolts or lag screws. Dotted line shows position of motor. Of course this bed must be just the proper height and pitch to bring your engine in line with the shaft. Stretch a line through the shaft hole to the point where the forward end of engine shaft will come, and make the top of the bed come level with this line. As DeFoe motors have the flange pieces for fastening to the bed on a line with center line of the shaft, the engine will then be in line when it is placed on the bed. As the line must be taken down before the engine is placed, mark the points, by nailing pieces (marked X, Fig. 11) up to the line from the keelson where each end of the engine shaft should come in order

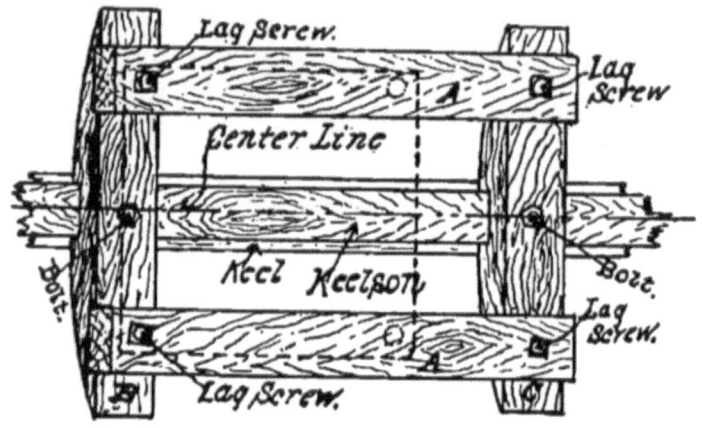

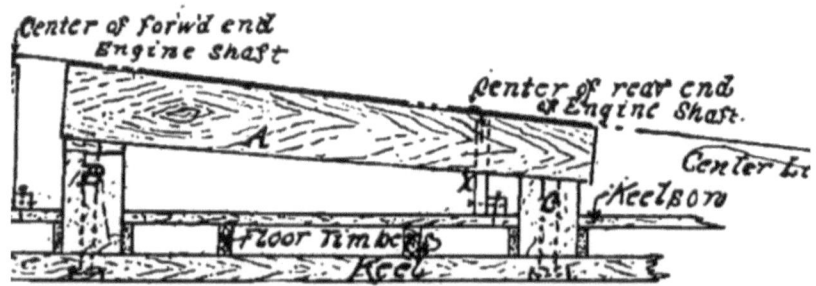

FIG. 11.

to be in exact line with the stern bearing. Of course the engine shaft should lie exactly where the line was. This will bring it if you are careful. Measure the engine shaft and get the two points just this distance apart. The lag screws that fasten the fore and aft pieces to the forward cross piece will in most cases fasten the engine down also. The dotted line shows the position of the engine on the bed.

Steering Gear.

Figs. 3 (a) and 3 (b) show two methods of putting on the rudder. Use a piece of gas pipe for the port, thread it on one end and screw it into the wood. Make the rudder of common sheet steel about $\frac{1}{8}$ inch thick, and make the rudder post and lower bearing of round iron about $\frac{3}{4}$ inch in diameter in smaller boats to $1\frac{1}{4}$ inches in larger ones. Square the upper end of rudder post to fit the tiller. Split the lower end to straddle the rudder, and rivet it on securely. Attach the lower bearing, Fig. 3 (a), in the same way, where a shoe is used, and make the shoe of iron. Turn the end of the shoe over as shown and put a key in the end of the bearing to keep rudder from jumping out.

The stuffing-box may be put either inside or outside—better outside on small boats at least, as it needs no Moreover, if it is properly packed it will not need further lubrication there, and if it should need repacking 'it would be no great task to raise the boat up to reach it. attention for a season at least.

Use cotton sash cord to connect tiller with steering wheel. The best arrangement is to keep the tiller below the deck, and run the cords around just below the coaming on each side to the steering wheel. Use blocks at the four corners where there is a quick turn, and small screw eyes under the coaming. Some prefer to have the tiller and ropes above the deck. In this case use four small cheek blocks and small brass eyelets to carry the cord. It will be necessary to bore holes in the coaming forward to get the ropes to the steering wheel if they are put above deck.

Steam Box.

Fig. 12 shows a very simple and yet very effective steam box. Use a common laundry room boiler, or a good sized kettle or pail will do for a small box. Make the box of ⅞ inch boards. Nail it solidly and make the joints very tight to hold the steam. Leave the ends open. A seven-foot box that will take a 12 inch board is large enough for most purposes. Cut a cover for the boiler from a ⅞ inch board and make it just large enough to slip into the boiler and fit snug. Nail the cover to the bottom of the box. Put two or three inches of water in the boiler and set the whole thing on the stove. If you have no stove handy set it over a fire built out of doors. Get it as hot as possible.

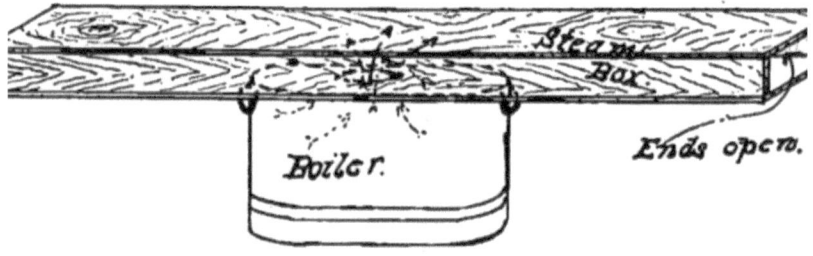

FIG. 12.

Put the material to be steamed in the box and plug up the ends tightly with rags. If you are steaming a long piece, such as a coaming, let the ends stick out of the box and pack around them with rags to keep the steam in. The amateur may work out a scheme of his own that will answer equally well; but this box, though crude in appearance, will answer all purposes.

By far the best way to treat the ribs for bending is to procure a metal trough that is long enough to hold them, and boil them in it for a half hour or so. Put a cover on the trough and boil them hard, and they can be made very pliable. The steam box will answer, however, unless ribs are of poor stuff.

Shop, Tools, Etc.

If you have a shop and a full set of tools, so much the better, though the ordinary tools to be found in most every household with very few additions will be sufficient. A hammer, handsaw, ripsaw, screwdriver, jackplane, smooth plane, a chisel or two, a brace and a few sizes of bits, about a half dozen clamps from 4 inches to 8 inches and a draw-knife. If you haven't all of them borrow them of your neighbor and give him a ride in the boat when it is finished. Keep your tools sharp.

A light, warm shop is of course the most desirable place in which to build your boat. But if you haven't such, fit up the basement, the woodshed, or the barn. Put a bench along one side about 14 feet long. Use planks for the top, and it should be about the height of the builder's hip joint. Have a vise at the left hand end. Of course the more convenient the shop, and the better the tools, the more pleasant will be the work, and naturally the better will be the results.

Painting, Varnishing and Finishing.

Use white lead and oil mixed very thin for a priming coat of paint. Next putty all nail heads and seams. A good boat putty is made by mixing whitening with white lead, (not the dry lead, but the ordinary kind which is ground in oil) until it is the proper consistency. Add about a teaspoon of Japan dryer to every pound of it before mixing. A quick drying and very durable putty is made by mixing equal parts by bulk of whitening and dry white lead with varnish. Any varnish will do; some old stuff, perhaps, that you may have around the house. This putty is sticky and hard to apply smooth, but will dry hard in three or four days. Sand the hull down perfectly after puttying, and apply at least two or more coats, sanding between coats. Be sure that each coat is thoroughly dry before you apply the succeeding one.

For a varnished finish proceed as follows: All screw heads, bolt heads, and the like, should be plugged with wood plugs. These plugs can be purchased at most hardware stores, or you can purchase a plug cutter, a cheap tool, and cut them yourself. They should be of the same wood as the remainder of your work and should be put in so that the grain runs in the same direction. Dip them in shellac and drive them into the hole and they will stay. When dry dress them off with a plane or a chisel. Then scrape and sandpaper the wood to a perfect surface, as any little blemish will show up badly after the finish is on.

Next apply the filler. If you are building only one boat, it will be better to use prepared stains and fillers; and if you tell your dealer what results you want, light oak finish, dark oak, mahogany, cherry, or whatever it may be, he will furnish you with the proper materials. The boat and frame builders also carry these things in stock and will make immediate shipment if you order from them. Directions will usually be found on the package for applying the filler. A rub filler is recommended as giving the best results, and a water stain. There are many good fillers, but be careful if you use a stain, for they are apt to raise the grain of your wood or fade out in time unless they are exactly what they ought to be.

Sand the filler with fine sand paper, putty all nail heads, seams, etc., and when dry apply a coat of spar varnish, (get the best putty and use no other varnish than spar) and sand carefully, rubbing lengthwise of the grain only. Follow with a second coat in the same way, and finish with the third coat. Three coats of any good spar varnish are sufficient. Let the filler and each coat of varnish dry thoroughly before the succeeding coat is put on. Otherwise it will check and may peel.

An excellent rub filler is made by mixing equal parts of whitening and cornstarch and adding turpentine until it becomes the consistency of paste. This will give a colorless filler and when applied will leave the wood its natural color and appearance. However, fillers are generally colored. In using a coloring matter, either dry or in oil, always dissolve it in turpentine before adding it to your filler or paint.

There are a variety of shades of finish for golden oak, mahogany, cherry, etc., and the best way to proceed is to purchase a few dry colors of brown, pink and red, and a little experimenting will produce a color that will suit your individual taste.

To apply the filler thin it with turpentine (use also about 4 teaspoonfuls of paint oil and a spoonful of Japan dryer to a quart of turpentine), and apply it with a brush, like paint, putting it on about as thick as paint. In from one to five minutes you will notice that dry spots will begin to show in the filler. Then take a handful of waste or an old cloth and rub off all the surplus filler, rubbing always across the grain of the wood in order to fill the pores. Finally use a clean cloth and rub off all the filler that will come off. The filler should then dry about 12 hours before the varnish is applied.

If you want a decided color, such as a very dark oak or a dark mahogany, use a stain first. You can make this yourself by simply mixing your dry powders with water and applying them to the wood with a cloth. Care must be taken not to leave the wood looking streaked. Apply the filler after the stain is on.

Useful Hints.

Nail planking on with clout nails. Bore through or nearly through the part to be fastened, and have the nail long enough to reach away through and clinch over about $\frac{1}{8}$ or $\frac{1}{4}$ of an inch. Hold an iron against the spot and nail through against it to clinch or double the point of the nail over.

Always bore for a nail where there is any likelihood of splitting. Bore the hole about two-thirds the size of the nail.

Always bore for a screw full depth, with a bit slightly smaller than the screw; and countersink for the head of the screw.

White oak bends with steaming better than any other timber. For this reason it is often used for garboards (the plank next to keel) that are difficult to put on. For this reason also, and by reason of its toughness and durability, it is used almost entirely for frames. Dry timber bends better with steaming than wet timber.

Clamp the whole sheerstrake on before you fasten any part except to the stem and stern. You can better line it up in this way.

In using a bolt always put a washer under the nut.

Special Building Instructions for an 18-foot Standard Stern Launch.

In setting up the frame, keel should run straight from stem to fore end of skeg. Then raise the aft end of keel 3½ in. above this straight line. Do not let the keel curve down between the stem and skeg. (See Fig. 1, General Instructions above.)

Lumber—See General Instructions for the kind of lumber to use for the different purposes, such as planking, ribs, decks, etc. Purchase as follows: For planking, 200' of ½" stuff (may use ⅝" if you desire). For keel, one piece, 1½"x5", 10' long, and 1 piece 1½"x5", 8' long, or, instead of the two pieces, 1 piece 18' long. For keelson, 1 piece 17' long, or 2 pieces same as keel. For ribs get 250 running feet of white oak, ⅞"x⅝", or get 25' of ⅞" stuff and rip out ribs by hand. Space them 8" apart. For clamps, 2 pieces, ⅞"x1⅜", 14' long, run at top of sheerstrake and only from deck to deck. For transom, 1 piece ⅞"x21½", 3' long; or 1 piece ⅞"x11", 6 long. For stem, stern post, skeg, etc., 1 piece ⅞"x10", 12' long. For fenders, 38' of ⅞" half round. For coaming, 2 pieces ½"x8", 12' long, and one piece 3' long. For covering boards, 2 pieces ⅜"x8", 10' long. For flooring, 60' of ½" stuff. If you wish to use a different wood for sheerstrake, get 2 pieces ⅝"x7", 9' long, and 2 pieces ⅝"x7", 12' long.

See General Instructions for interior finish.

Make forward deck about 4' long; aft deck about 2½' Space deck beams same as ribs, 8" apart.

Hardware—6 lbs. 1½" clouts, for planking. 1 lb. fourpenny wire nails to nail plank to stem. Use ¼" bolts in stem and keel; 40 bolts, ¼"x2¼" for clamps. Six ¼"x2" bolts for splice in clamp. One hundred 1¼" No. 12 screws for sheerstrake.

Some small items will be needed in addition and should be purchased as the work progresses.

"Going Some."

CHAPTER XVII

PROPELLERS.

The propeller is one of the most important parts of the boat and is generally the least understood even in its most elementary principles. An improperly designed or selected propeller for a given hull will cause a loss of power, fuel and speed, and many of the troubles that are commonly charged to the account of the engine can be traced directly to an incorrect wheel. The selection of a wheel depends on the engine speed, boat speed, duty for which boat is intended, water in which it is to be used, and the local conditions governed by the wheel location and the form of the hull. In buying a propeller it is by far the best method to consult a responsible propeller maker and acquaint him with all of the conditions under which the proposed wheel is to work.

In default of such information the owner will be confronted by two of the first terms used in specifying a propeller, that is, diameter and pitch. The diameter, which is the distance from tip to tip of opposite blades measured across the center of the shaft bore, is easily measured. The pitch, however, is a term not so easily understood and therefore is a matter that must be described more in detail.

In certain respects a propeller may be compared with a machine screw working in a nut. Every revolution that the screw is turned it advances a certain distance in the direction of its length. The distance traveled per revolution is called the "pitch" of the screw. In the same way a propeller screws its way through the water, the propeller blades acting in the same way as the threads on the screw. The difference between the two lies in the fact that the water is not a solid rigid substance like the nut on the screw and therefore the propeller slips or fails to advance by the amount of the theoretical pitch. The difference between the theoretical advance of the wheel and the actual advance is known as the "slip" and is usually given in terms of the theoretical pitch. The slip sometimes amounts to as much as 50 per cent of the theoretical pitch, or 50 per cent of the distance that the boat should move through the water for every revolution of the wheel were there no slippage. The speed that a boat would make were there no slippage is called the theoretical speed.

The slope of the blade with the line of the shaft is usually an index to the pitch, that is, the greater the blade angle, the greater the pitch. Measurement of the pitch by means of the blade angle is not so simple a manner as would be thought at first glance, since on close examination it will be noted that the angle rapidly increases from the tip to the hub. Take a 45 degree triangle and slide it along the working face of the blade until one edge of the triangle is parallel to the shaft line in hub. This is the 45 degree point on the blade and will be approximately half way between the tip of the blade and the hub, and generally at the widest part. At this point the pitch will be the same as the length of the circumference of the imaginary circle that passes through this point. **Rule.** Measure the distance from the 45 degree point on the blade to the center of the shaft hole and multiply this dimension by 6.28. This will give the theoretical pitch.

Example—The distance from the 45 degree point to the center of the shaft was found to be 14½ inches. Find the pitch. $14.5 \times 6.28 = 91$ inches $= 7.58$ feet, the theoretical pitch.

The theoretical speed of the boat in feet, with no slip,

can be found by multiplying the speed of the engine by the pitch as found above. Taking the pitch as found above and an engine speed of 600 revolutions per minute the theoretical speed will be, $600 \times 7.58 = 4548$ feet per minute. Since there are 5280 feet per mile, $4548 \div 5280 = 0.86$ miles per minute, or $60 \times 0.86 = 51.6$ miles per hour.

Stated in a simpler form, this will be

$$\frac{PN}{88} = \frac{7.58 \times 600}{88} = 51.6 \text{ miles per hour, where } P = \text{pitch}$$

in feet, $N =$ number revolutions per minute, and 88 is a factor derived from $\frac{5280}{60} = 88$. Assuming a slip of 50 per cent, the true or actual speed will be $51.6 \times 0.50 = 25.8$ miles per hour. Inserting the slip or efficiency, E, into the above formula we have the actual speed of

$$\frac{PN}{88\,E} = \frac{7.58 \times 600}{88 \times 0.50} = 25.8 \text{ miles per hour.}$$

It must be understood that the efficiency of 50 per cent does not apply to all cases and was only chosen for the sake of having a concrete example.

The ratio of the pitch to the diameter of a propeller is called its "Pitch Ratio," and this ratio varies in propellers designed for different classes of service. A high speed boat requires a higher pitch ratio than a slow speed boat for heavy duty such as a tug or work boat.

The diameter of a wheel is of the greatest importance since the thrust of the wheel is concentrated on the face of the blades or rather the disc area (diameter squared $\times 0.7854$) and as this must not exceed a certain amount in pounds per square foot to prevent breaking through the water we must have ample area. In general, it is desirable to have as large a wheel as can be swung for another reason, that is, a large wheel is more efficient in the utilization of power.

The pressure per square foot on the surface of the blades should not exceed 400 pounds. If this pressure is exceeded the slip stream of the propeller will be broken and "cavitation" or holes produced which will reduce the thrust or push and increase the power. Dividing the total thrust by 400 will give the area of the blades (area of all blades) in square feet. The value of the thrust at the given boat speed may be had from the builder of the boat, or may be found experimentally by towing the loaded hull behind another boat at the given speed, the thrust being measured by a spring balance or ice scale attached to the tow rope. Care should be taken in making this test to place a weight in the hull equal to that of the combined weight of the engine, fuel and crew. Always tow at the highest speed that you intend to make, against the wind, current and with everything adjusted in its normal position. When the boat is to be used in shallow or rough water, the factor 400 should be reduced to 250 to 300. When thrust is determined divide by above factor thus obtaining total blade area.

Knowing the thrust, area of propeller, and boat speed we can obtain the approximate slip from the formula

$$S = \frac{TV}{Av}$$

where S is the slip in feet per second; T is the thrust in pounds, V is the boat speed in feet per second; A is the area of propeller disc (.7854 × diameter squared) in feet, and v is the velocity of slip stream relative to boat speed. The total slip S is added to the boat speed to obtain the theoretical velocity of the propeller. When reduced to feet per minute and divided by the engine revolutions, the result will be the theoretical pitch given the propeller.

While the propeller should be as large as possible it

should not break through the surface of the water nor be below the skeg so as to run chances of striking rocks or lying in the mud. A good propeller has only a slip of from 20 to 30 per cent.

In regard to the number of blades in the wheel there is a certain diversity of opinion. In work boats and large cruisers in which the wheels should be as large as possible the engine can turn a larger two blade than three blade, thus placing the results in favor of the two blade wheel. For the same reason small boats generally have two bladed wheels since it is possible to have them larger and therefore act on larger bodies of water. This reduces the churning. Where the thrust per square foot of blade area must be high owing to limitations placed on the diameter by the construction of the boat three blades will generally be found necessary. On large boats with very heavy thrusts, slow speeds, and small head room, four blades will often be found necessary.

In boats where the dead wood is very thick and acts as a shield to the wheel, three blades will act better than two as there will always be two blades active while the third is in the shadow of the dead wood. The propeller should be placed a sufficient distance from the stern post, rudder and other parts of the boat to insure easy access of water to the wheel. The stern post should be tapered and as narrow as possible to prevent the effects of shielding. Boats with wide bluff sterns should have wheels with small throats and large balloon ends because the stream does not turn into the center of the wheel.

It should be remembered in this regard that the friction of the hull in the water causes the water to follow the hull at a certain speed (following wake) so that the propeller acts on water that is moving at about half the boat speed and in the same direction. For this reason the propeller at the back is more effective in producing speed than one at the bow; pitches being equal in both cases. With the wheel at the rear the actual boat speed is equal to the actual propeller speed in open water plus the velocity of the frictional wake.

The blades for normal service should be elliptical in shape, the width of the blade being about 0.4 of the length, the width being the minor axis of the ellipse.

High speed boats require clover leaf wheels with almost circular blades, usually three in number and so wide that the edges almost overlap. The widest point of a blade for normal service should be at the 45 degree point while with high speed blades this greatest width comes nearly to the root of the blades. For average high speed the blades should flare out from the root to the center and should never taper from root to tip.

Thrust Bearings.

When at work, the thrust of the propeller tends to force the propeller shaft toward the hull or in a direction opposite to the thrust of the blades when the boat is moving forward. When the boat is moving astern the direction of the pressure is also reversed. It is customary for the engine builder to build a special thrust bearing into the engine for taking up this axial force, which is by no means of small degree.

In the smaller motors the thrust bearing is of the ball or roller type, one race being imbedded in the engine frame while the other race is fastened to the shaft in such a way that steel balls or rollers fill the space between the two races. Two independent sets of thrust bearings are provided by some builders, one set taking the thrust from the forward drive while the second set takes the thrust from the reverse.

Right and Left Hand Propellers.

As a propeller blade has only one efficient driving face and for the reason that this limits the direction in which the wheel may rotate when driving full ahead, it is necessary to give the direction of engine rotation in ordering the propeller. This often leads to misunderstanding and mistakes in delivery for the reason that the customer seldom knows in which direction to face the engine when taking the rotation, nor in fact, how to read the direction at all. For the benefit of those who have not had this experience we will illustrate and describe what is practically a standard method among engine and propeller makers.

Standing in front of the engine, and facing the fly-wheel, look aft while the engine is running. If the top of the fly-wheel turns from the right to the left a right hand wheel is needed. If it turns from the left to right, a left hand wheel is needed. A left hand engine needs a right hand propeller, if rotation is viewed while looking aft.

Construction of Propellers.

In the practical propeller there are a number of differences from the true screw propeller just mentioned, the

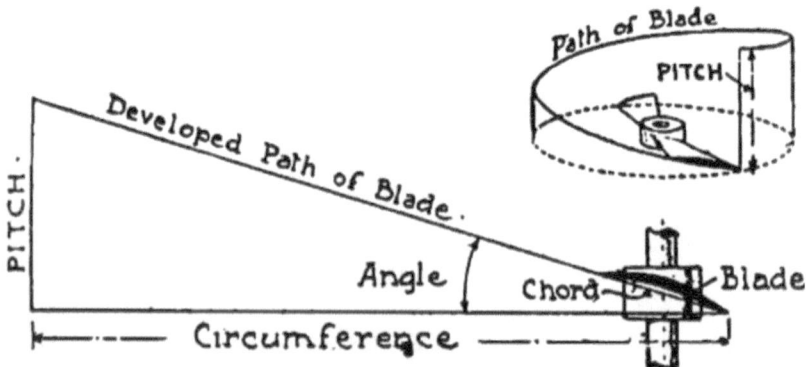

FIG. 1.—Graphical Representation of Pitch and Blade Angle.

differences depending principally on the service to which the blade is to be put, the speed at which it rotates, etc. In some, the angle of the blade is constant from tip to root (constant angle propeller), in others the blade angle increases from tip to root (uniform pitch), and in some cases the blade angle varies according to the addition of some constant angle to the angle of the uniform pitch system. Constant angle propellers are as a rule not efficient for the reason that the inner portions of the blade drag in the water and therefore do not exert a propulsive force throughout the greater part of their length. That this is true will be proved by the following description of the true screw or uniform pitch propeller.

A simple propeller is shown by Fig. 1 in which the path, blade angle and pitch are shown in their relative positions. In the upper right hand corner is shown the cylinder diameter swept by the blades, the height of the cylinder being equal to the pitch, or to the distance traveled by the boat in one revolution. In traveling this distance, it is evident that a point on the tip of the blade will not only revolve about the center but will also advance forward by a distance equal to the pitch. This results in the tip of the blade actually traveling along the inclined curve, the latter being known as a "helix." In other words, the blade climbs up an inclined plane.

Say, for example, that the cylinder of revolution is cut along the pitch dimension and straightened out as shown in the figure in the lower left hand corner giving an inclined plane or wedge in which the height is the pitch and the base length is equal to the length of the circle formerly described by the tips of the blade. The hypotenuse, or inclined line of the triangle is the exact path followed by the tip of the blade, while the angle between the base and the hypotenuse is the blade angle. Actually the angle of the blade is slightly greater than the pitch angle to allow for slip. Thus by knowing the pitch required and the circumference of the circle swept by tips it is possible to construct the theoretical blade angle by the means shown.

As shown, this blade would have a constant angle from tip to root which would not fulfil the conditions since the inner portions would drag on the outer. That this is true can be proved by drawing a series of triangles taken at different points in the blade length, the base of the triangle being taken as equal to the circumference of the circle passing through the blade at that point while the height or pitch is kept constant in all triangles. The latter condition is necessary for the reason that all parts of the blade must travel forward a distance equal to the pitch in one revolution. When these triangles are drawn it will be seen that the blade angle is different in each one, the angles increasing as the root of the blade is approached. With a constant angle the root portions of the blade would not pass the water fast enough to correspond with the water displaced with the tips. At the center of the hub, the blade would be at exactly right angles to the center of the shaft.

Fig. 2 (Diag. A) shows this construction more in detail, ABCD being known as the "pitch" or "displacement" cylinder. The diameter D^1 of the cylinder is made equal to the propeller diameter while the pitch is shown by P, and the propeller blade by Z. In progressing from X to X along the cylinder center line, a point on the tip of the blade Z traces a "flight" curve, or helix, XFYEX in which the direction of progress is indicated by the small arrow heads on the curve. The progress of the propeller is indicated by the arrow W, that is, the whole propeller moves from right to left. In passing from F to E, a distance equal to the pitch, the propeller has made one complete revolution along the curve FYE. A front elevation of the propeller is shown by Diag. B in which M and N are the blade tips, O is the shaft, Q is the hub, and S-T is the circle described by the tips, equal to the cylinder diameter D^1.

Suppose that we wish to find the blade angle condi-

CONSTRUCTION AND OPERATION 201

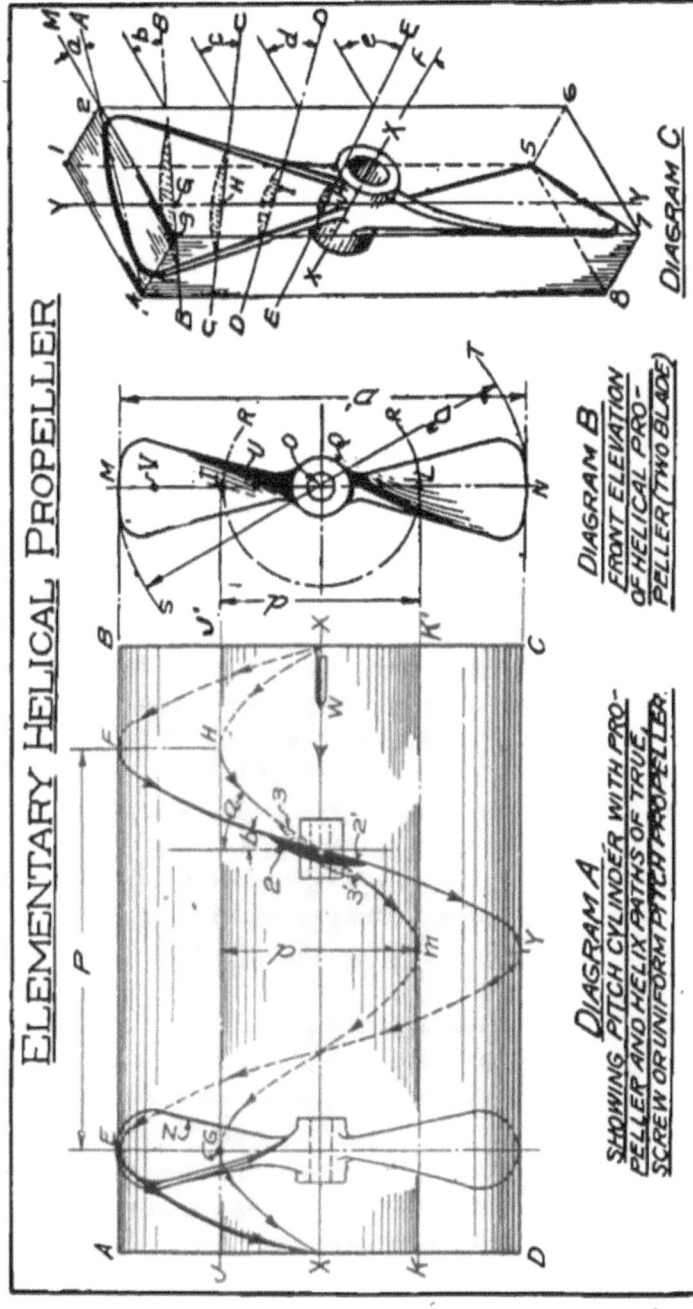

Fig. 2. Development of the "True Screw" Propeller Blade. Diagram A Shows That the Angle Must Be Increased Toward the Root of the Blade. Diagram C Shows the Blade in Relation to the Block from which the Pattern is Cut.

tions existing at the points I and L on the blade MN, the points being assumed to lie on the circle R-R, in Diag. B, and on the blade at G in Diag. A. The diameter of this auxiliary circle will be indicated by d, and its path cylinder is shown in Diag. A by the outline JJ[1]KK,[1] the cylinder being shaded to distinguish it from the surrounding lines.

As in the case of the blade tip cylinder, a second helix HMG is drawn for the inner circle path. This curve starts and ends on the same vertical lines as the first curve since the pitch distances GH and EF must be equal to one another and also to the pitch P. With the second HMG curve drawn on the smaller diameter d it will be noted, for equal pitches, that the angle with the vertical is considerably greater than the angle of the helix FYE. These angles are indicated by b and a, the first being the angle of curve FYE. An outline of the blade section at the tip is shown by the solid black section 2-2,[1] while the blade section at the points I and L on the propeller is shown by the dotted outline 3-3.[1] In this view we are supposed to be looking at the ends of the blade, and proves conclusively that, for uniform, or equal pitches we must increase the angle as we approach the root or hub Q. Performing the same operation with a circle drawn through the point V we will find that the blade angle is greater than at the tip, but less than at the point I. The variation is indicated by the shade lines in Diag. B.

Unfortunately the actual design is not as simple as this for very efficient results, owing to conditions about the hub, but a propeller built along these lines will give fairly accurate results for any amateur who wishes to build his own propeller. All angles must be increased over these theoretical angles by an amount equal to the slip, that is, by 20 to 40 per cent at the tip.

Propulsion is exerted by the pressure of the water

against the driving face of the blade and to obtain the best results with a given diameter equal work should be performed by every square inch of blade surface. That this is not possible will be seen from examining the ineffective area occupied by the hub and the exceedingly heavy blade angles near the root. Practically all of the work is done by the outer half or two-thirds of the blade.

Since the angle is theoretically 90 degrees with the shaft at the hub center, it is evident that no drive would be experienced at this point, even though it were possible to dispense with the hub. This heavy angle continues for quite a distance toward the tips, and is heavy enough to prevent much forward driving effort for fully one-third of the length. This, coupled with the disturbing effects of the wash from the hub, resolves itself into designing this part of the blade for low resistance to forward motion rather than for driving, although in some propellers the angle here is made less than the theoretical (expanding pitch).

A propeller of the uniform pitch type is shown encased in a rectangular block by Diag. C in order to illustrate such a propeller more clearly. The block 1-2-3-4-5-6-7-8 is assumed to be the block out of which the propeller pattern is carved, the widths 1-2 and 3-4 determining the tip angle 3-2-4, or "a." The line X-X is the center line of the hub and is at right angles to the block face 2-3. A series of sections through the upper blade are shown by G, H, I and J taken along the lines B-B, C-C, D-D, and E-E respectively.

At the tip, the blade angle is "a," this being the angle made by the blade with the face 2-3 of the block. Further down and on the line B-B is the section G which makes the angle "b" with the block face. The angles c, d, and e are taken in the same way, increasing as the root is approached, while the angle F made by the section J with the shaft center line X-X, is very nearly at a right angle with the block face 2-3.

In making a propeller pattern a block is chosen whose length is equal to the propeller diameter, as shown and whose width is equal to the widest part of the face. The length of the blade from the center line X-X to the tip is then divided into a number of equal parts as at G, H, I, and J, along the blade center line Y-Y. These spaces should not much exceed two inches for accurate work on small propellers, and preferably should be less. After the proper angles are computed for these points, saw cuts are made along the section lines such as B-B, C-C, etc., at the given angle. It is now a simple matter to chip out the wood between the saw cuts and work the blades down to the proper form.

In getting the angles, first determine the number of section points required for the length of blade, and then lay out a series of triangle diagrams as shown in Fig. 1. The base will be equal to the circumference of propeller, or equal to 3.1416 times the diameter. The vertical height of triangle will of course be equal to the actual pitch, the method by which this is determined being described elsewhere in this chapter.

Propeller Data.

The pitch ratio, which is equal to the pitch divided by the wheel diameter, depends upon the type of boat on which the wheel is to be used. A heavy boat with blunt lines fore and aft requires a small pitch ratio, from 1.1 to 1.3, with broad blades and a low speed motor. A medium weight boat with moderately fine lines requires a medium pitch propeller with a pitch ratio of from 1.4 to 1.6. A speed boat with a high speed engine, shallow draft, narrow fine lines, and of the racing type requires a pitch ratio of 1.8 to 2.0.

It should be remembered in this connection that the

pitch is equal to the diameter multiplied by the pitch ratio. Thus the pitch of a 16 inch propeller with a pitch ratio of 2 is equal to 16x2 or 32 inches. The pitch ratios offered by firms handling stock wheels runs from 1.10 to 2, the former being for towing while the latter is specially adapted for racing hydroplanes. These sizes cover the commercial range.

The ratio of blade width to the diameter of the wheel varies but slightly in any type, say from 0.25 to 0.40.

With the exception of the towing wheel which has triangular blades, the wheels listed above are of the true screw type with elliptical tips.

Pitch and Power.

The power consumed varies with the pitch, wheel diameter, and number of blades, an increase in any of the three items resulting in greater power consumption. Roughly speaking a three blade propeller will absorb approximately 1.5 times as much power as the same size

Type of Wheel	Pitch Ratio	Boat Type	Blade Width % Diam.	Type Engine
Towing	1.10	Heavy-Slow	33	Slow Speed
General Use	1.40	Yachts-Launch Fast Work Boat	25	
Moderate Speed	1.50	Runabouts	25	High Speed
Speed	1.60	Runabouts and Small Racers	30	High Speed
Speed	1.80	Large Racers	33	Great Power
Speed	2.00	Hydroplanes Light Draft	33	Great Power High Speed

of two blade wheel. The pitch increases the power at a rapid rate. A small diameter wheel will not transmit as much power at low speed as at high, since the pressure per unit of blade area is greater at the lower speed. Within certain limits, the power transmitted by a given wheel is in direct proportion to the revolutions per minute, that is, doubling the speed gives twice the propelling power.

With a broad skeg or thick deadwood, a two bladed propeller transmits less power than a wheel with three blades since the supply of water is momentarily cut off from the two blades when they stand in a vertical position. With a three blade wheel there will always be two blades effective in driving, no matter what the position of the wheel. A two blade wheel acts on a greater volume of water at high speed for with three the water does not pass freely between the blades.

With a boat having full lines aft care should be taken not to have the pitch too great as a high pitch tends to scoop out the water from under the stern and causes the boat to "Squat."

In fitting propellers, especially to racing boats, it will often be found that the diameter is too great to allow the motor to run at its rated speed. The reduction in the motor speed will of course prevent the engine from developing its full power, and from giving the necessary pitch velocity. To reduce the drag and to allow the motor to speed up, the diameter can be cut down if the same shape and proportion of the blade is maintained. That is, if the width is reduced in the same proportion. This does not change the efficiency to any great extent in a true screw propeller.

In regard to cutting down a wheel it must be remembered that the blades must not be twisted so as to change the pitch and on the completion of the job that the wheel must be perfectly balanced. All blades must be of equal thickness at the same point and there must be no difference in pitch between the blades. Unbalanced wheels, blades of unequal length or thickness, unequal pitch, or very thin blades will produce annoying and destructive vibration, especially at high speeds.

CONSTRUCTION AND OPERATION

Horse-Power Tables.

The accompanying tables will give the approximate horsepowers corresponding to various pitch ratios, diameters, and numbers of blades and for different classes of service. In the first four columns will be found the "Type of boat," "pitch ratio," and the "pitch corresponding to a given pitch ratio and diameter." Thus a wheel for a towing boat with a pitch ratio of 1.10 and a diameter of 20 inches will have a corresponding pitch of 22 inches. The next four columns are the horsepowers for two and three blade wheels at both the maximum rated speed and at 100 revolutions per minute. Taking a 20 inch wheel with a pitch ratio of 1.10 it will be seen that a two blade wheel will absorb 2.25 H. P. at 100 revolutions and that the same pitch and diameter in a three bladed wheel will absorb 3 H. P. at the same speed.

At 400 revolutions per minute (the rated speed), the the power required will be four times as much, or 9 and 12 H. P. respectively. For any other speed not greatly in excess of 400 revolutions, multiply the power at 100 revolutions by the number of hundreds of revolutions. Thus if the two bladed 20 inch wheel is to be driven at 350 revolutions, the power will be 2.25x3.5 = 7.9 H. P., approximately. In this case the figure 3.5 stands for three and one-half hundreds. Since the maximum revolutions in this case are 400 per minute, the column "HP At Max. Revs." gives values four times as great as those in the first column.

Example: We desire to drive a boat 25 miles per hour, and from towing tests on this boat we find that 50 H. P. will be required to drive this particular hull through the water. We will assume a slip of 20 per cent and an engine speed of 800 revolutions per minute. Find the approximate size of propeller required.

With a 20 per cent slip, the actual pitch speed will be

POWER REQUIRED FOR PROPELLERS

Purpose	Pitch Ratio	Corresponding Pitch Pitch	Diam.	Two Blades		Three Blades	
				H.P. at 100 Revs.	H.P. at Max. Revs.	H.P. at 100 Revs.	H.P. at Max. Revs.
Towing	1.10 Max. Revs. 400	17.6	16.0	1.00	4.00	1.50	6.00
		19.8	18.0	1.50	6.00	2.25	9.00
		22.0	20.0	2.25	9.00	3.00	12.00
		24.2	22.0	3.00	12.00	4.00	16.00
		26.4	24.0	4.00	16.00	6.00	24.00
		30.8	28.0	7.50	30.00	9.00	36.00
		32.3	30.0	9.00	36.00	10.00	40.00
		39.3	36.0	...	....	15.00	60.00
Speed (Medium Wt.)	1.30 Max. Revs. 400	18.2	14.00	0.66	2.50	0.75	3.00
		20.8	16.00	1.00	4.00	1.25	5.00
		23.4	18.00	1.50	6.00	2.25	9.00
		26.0	20.00	2.25	9.00	3.00	12.00
		28.6	22.00	3.00	12.00	4.00	16.00
		31.2	24.00	4.00	16.00	6.00	24.00
		33.8	26.00	6.00	24.00	7.50	30.00
		36.4	28.00			9.00	36.00
		39.0	30.00	...	....	10.00	40.00
All Around Wheel (Yachts-Launches)	1.40 Max. Revs. 400	16.8	12.00	0.40	1.60	1.25	
		19.6	14.00	0.60	2.40	3.00	
		22.4	16.00	1.00	4.00	4.00	
		25.2	18.00	1.50	6.00	6.00	
		28.0	20.00	2.25	9.00	7.50	
		30.8	22.00	3.00	12.00	9.00	
		33.6	24.00	4.00	16.00	10.00	
		39.2	28.00	7.50	30.00	15.00	
		42.00	30.00	9.00	36.00	20.00	
		50.40	36.00	12.00	48.00	30.00	....
Racing Boats Only	1.8 Max. Revs. 800	21.6	12	0.38	3.0	0.57	4.5
		25.2	14	0.75	6.0	1.00	8.0
		28.8	16	1.25	10.0	1.75	14.0
		32.5	18	2.13	17.0	3.00	24.0
		36.0	20	3.63	29.0	5.00	40.0
		43.2	24	9.13	73.0	12.50	100.00
		46.8	26	13.75	110.0	19.38	155.00
Hydroplanes	2 Max. Revs. 1000	24.0	12.0	0.60	6.00	.80	8.00
		28.0	14.0	1.00	10.00	1.20	12.00
		32.0	16.0	1.50	15.00	2.00	20.00
		36.0	18.0	2.50	25.00	3.50	35.00
		40.0	20.0	4.00	40.00	5.00	50.00
		44.0	22.0	6.00	60.00	7.50	75.00
		48.0	24.	7.50	75.	12.00	120.00

1 1/5 times 25, or 30 Miles per hour. At 800 revolutions the pitch will be,

$$P = \frac{\text{Miles per Hour}}{.000947 \times N} = \frac{30}{.000947 \times 800} = 40 \text{ inch}$$

pitch, where P is the pitch, and N is the number of revolutions per minute. (See speed table.) As this is a speed boat the pitch ratio will be from 1.8 to 2.0.

Consulting the power table and with a pitch ratio of 1.8, we find that the nearest pitch is 43.2 inches, and that the diameter is 24 inches. Following to the right we find that a two bladed propeller of this size will transmit 73 H. P. This is ample for our needs but it is possible that it will slow down the engine so that the full speed will not be available. The next size smaller will give 36 inch pitch, 29 H. P. with two blades and 40° H. P. with three blades, both wheels being too small although the three blade wheel would allow the engine to speed up and gain power. Since the power is in proportion to the speed, the speed of the wheel would be increased 25 per cent since the power increase will be 25 per cent. We could use this wheel if it would be permissible to run our engine at 1,000 revolutions.

Assuming a pitch ratio of 2.0 a 20 inch wheel will have 40 inch pitch, and absorb 50 H. P. at 1,000 revolutions, or the same pitch ratio with a 22 inch wheel will give 44 inch pitch and will absorb 60 H. P. (Two blades.) Since 60 H. P. is 1.2 × 50 H. P, the latter wheel will transmit 50 H. P. at 20 per cent less speed, or 800 revolutions, the required speed. The pitch will also be reduced 20 per cent or to 35.2 inches, a little low.

As every engine can develop considerably over its rated power we can run a 24 inch diameter, 48 inch pitch propeller at 800 revolutions which will make the effective output 60 H. P. instead of 75 as shown and the effective pitch will be 38.4 inches.

TABLE OF BOAT SPEEDS IN MILES PER HOUR.

The following table gives the boat speed in miles per hour for different propeller pitches, revolutions and slip efficiencies.

To find speed for and pitch and R. P. M. look under R. P. M. column at left then follow to right through the known percent of slip, until the vertical column is reached which gives the pitch. The figures in the body of the table at this point will give the speed in miles per hour. For example, a 24-inch pitch wheel at 600 R. P. M. with 20 percent slip will give a boat speed of 10.91 miles per hour.

R.P.M.	% of Slip	14"	16"	18"	20"	22"	24"	26"	28"	30"	33"	36"	40"	45"	50"	55"	60"
400	None	5.30	6.06	6.82	7.58	8.33	9.08	9.85	10.61	11.36	12.50	13.63	15.15	17.05	18.94	20.83	22.72
	10%	4.77	5.45	6.14	6.82	7.50	8.18	8.87	9.55	10.22	11.25	12.27	13.63	15.34	17.05	18.75	20.44
	20%	4.24	4.85	5.45	6.06	6.66	7.27	7.88	8.49	9.09	10.00	10.90	12.12	13.64	15.15	16.67	18.18
	30%	3.71	4.24	4.77	5.30	5.83	6.36	6.89	7.43	7.95	8.75	9.54	10.61	11.93	13.26	14.59	16.01
600	None	7.96	9.09	10.23	11.36	12.50	13.64	14.77	15.91	17.05	18.75	20.46	22.73	25.57	28.41	31.20	34.08
	10%	7.16	8.18	9.20	10.22	11.25	12.27	13.29	14.32	15.34	16.87	18.41	20.46	23.01	25.57	28.08	30.68
	20%	6.37	7.27	8.18	9.09	10.00	10.91	11.82	12.73	13.64	15.01	16.37	18.18	20.46	22.73	24.96	27.28
	30%	5.57	6.36	7.16	7.95	8.75	9.54	10.34	11.14	11.93	13.13	14.32	15.91	17.90	19.89	21.84	23.87
800	None	10.61	12.12	13.64	15.15	16.67	18.18	19.70	21.21	22.73	25.00	27.27	30.30	34.09	37.88	41.66	45.24
	10%	9.55	10.91	12.27	13.63	15.00	16.36	17.73	19.09	20.46	22.19	24.54	27.27	30.68	34.00	37.50	40.72
	20%	8.49	9.70	10.91	12.12	13.34	14.54	15.76	16.97	18.18	20.01	21.82	24.24	27.27	30.30	33.33	36.20
	30%	7.43	8.48	9.54	10.61	11.67	12.73	13.79	14.85	15.91	17.50	19.09	21.21	23.86	26.52	29.17	31.67
1000	None	13.26	15.15	17.05	18.94	20.83	22.73	24.62	26.52	28.41	31.25	34.09	37.88	42.02	47.35	52.08	56.82
	10%	11.93	13.63	15.34	17.05	18.75	20.46	22.16	23.87	25.57	28.12	30.08	34.09	38.36	42.01	47.88	51.14
	20%	10.61	12.12	13.64	15.15	16.66	18.18	19.70	21.22	22.73	25.01	27.27	30.30	34.10	37.88	40.67	45.46
	30%	9.28	10.61	11.93	13.26	14.58	15.91	17.23	18.57	19.89	21.88	23.86	26.52	29.83	33.15	36.46	39.78
1500	None	19.89	22.72	25.58	28.42	31.26	34.10	36.94	39.79	42.63	46.89	51.16	56.82	63.95	71.05	78.16	85.23
	10%	17.89	20.45	23.00	25.56	28.12	30.67	33.23	35.78	38.34	42.17	46.01	51.12	57.51	63.90	70.29	76.71
	20%	15.92	18.19	20.47	22.74	25.01	27.29	29.56	31.84	34.11	37.52	40.93	45.48	51.17	56.85	62.54	68.19
	30%	13.93	15.92	17.91	19.90	21.89	23.88	25.87	27.86	29.85	32.84	35.82	39.80	44.78	49.75	54.73	59.67

PITCH OF PROPELLER IN INCHES

CHAPTER XVIII

REVERSING GEAR AND PROPELLER WHEELS.

A motor-boat which is not equipped with some means of backing up lacks an important factor of safety and convenience. Most owners nowadays require a reversing device, and there are various methods employed for the purpose. Where a reverse gear is installed the boatman enjoys the advantages of positive control of a forward and backward movement to the boat and also of a neutral point. Racing rules usually require power craft to be provided with means of changing positively and quickly from full speed ahead to full speed astern, this point being strongly insisted upon.

Reversing the direction of a boat may be accomplished by reversing the engine itself, by the use of the switch, but to do this successfully requires practice and considerable aptitude on the part of the operator. The two more direct methods generally used are a reverse gear or a reversible propeller.

A reversing gear is a system of clutches and toothed wheels by means of which the propeller shaft may be made to turn either opposite to or in the same direction as the motor crankshaft. The reversing gear uses a solid propeller, which may be made stronger than a reversing propeller wheel, and can take more hard blows and knocks without breaking, but its great advantage is that it places the reversing mechanism inside the boat, where it is less liable to meet with mishap and is accessible for repair in case anything does happen.

There are countless instances where it is necessary to bring a boat to a quick stop, reverse or slow down, then go ahead, and to perform these operations repeatedly. When operating a boat in crowded waters or making a dock, the feeling that one has a reliable reverse gear coupled to the propeller shaft gives the wheelsman confidence in his craft, which is wholly lacking when his boat is not equipped properly for reversing.

Another feature in favor of a reverse gear equipment, just as important as the forward and backward control, if not more so, is the neutral point.

Ferro Reverse Gear.

When the reverse gear is thrown into a neutral position the motor may be running, but this motion is not transmitted to the propeller, or in other words the motor may be going without the boat moving at all.

"This is a very desirable point," says a well known authority, "for the following reasons: First. If you wish for any reason to try out your motor to see how it is working, with a reverse gear equipment you may run your motor just as long and at any speed you wish without ever putting out from the boathouse or landing, and without having lines out from bow and stern to hold the boat stationary.

"Second. Often for various causes the boat is stopped for such a very short time, too short a time really to shut the motor down; with a reverse gear the motor may continue to run while the forward movement of the boat is stopped.

Parts of Ferro Reverse Gear.

"Third. Probably the very best reason of all for installing a reverse gear is **ease of starting**. By throwing the reversing gear into the neutral position, the effort required to turn over the flywheel of the motor when starting is very greatly lessened. Without a reversing gear it is necessary when starting a motor to turn over not only the flywheel and crankshaft of the motor, but the propeller shaft and propeller in the water.

"When an automobile is started the engine alone is started first before taking up the load of operating the car. This same idea is carried out in most machinery plants, that is, the load is not placed on the engine or motor until it is fairly started. Why should it be otherwise in a boat, especially when the motor used is of fairly large size?

"The advisability of installing a reverse gear being hardly disputed, the question to take up is the kind of gear to use. Like all mechanical devices, a poor reverse gear is worse than none at all.

"Some of the points desirable in a reverse gear are the following:

"The good reversing gear should couple the motor directly to the motor shaft on the forward drive; there should be no gears running, and the whole device should act simply as an extra flywheel or a straight unbroken shaft. To carry the power through gearing on the forward drive is often wasteful and noisy. When the gear is in the neutral, the motor runs free, without turning the propeller shaft; it makes no difference whether the gears run or not, as there is no load on them and therefore no wear. On the reverse position, the gears come into play and the power of the motor is transmitted and reversed by them. The gears should be 'in mesh' with the motor running. The changes from the neutral into the forward speed or from neutral into the reverse should be so arranged that the load is picked up gradually without a jerk. All brakes, clutches, and other parts should be easily adjusted and all gears should have bushings running on steel pins; the wear will then come on the bushings, which cost about one-tenth the price of spur gears.

"Gears should be of ample diameter, and stub tooth pattern. They should be inclosed in an oil-tight case, which can be filled with oil or packed with grease as may be required. The entire gear ought to have a rigid fore and aft bearing."

Reversible Propellers.

With a reverse gear, when it is reversed, the propeller shaft turns opposite to the motor shaft. With a reversible propeller, when it is reversed, the angle of the propeller blades is changed so as to pull the boat backward.

If the propeller blades are to change their angle they must turn in the hub; but as the diameter of the hub of a motor-boat wheel is small, it must be hollow to contain the device for shifting the blades and, if possible, it should present a smooth exterior. To fasten three blades, or even two, to the small hub, to get them so that they will turn easily when there is a pressure on them, to have no play and plenty of bearing surface to prevent wear, is not an easy matter, because there is so little room on the hub or inside of it.

The fastening of the blades to the hub is the vital point; the rest is easy. The usual method of construction is to make the propeller shaft in two parts: an inside, solid shaft, driven by the motor and keyed to the hub, and a hollow tube outside this shaft, which is shifted

Reversible Propeller.

forward and aft by the lever inside the boat. The shaft terminates in the hub, in which the propeller blades are pivoted. The tube terminates in a yoke which engages a lug or pin on each blade, and serves to shift the angle or pitch of the blades, when the propeller is either idle or in operation, hence giving the propeller a forward or reverse pitch.

The great advantage of a reversible propeller is the splendid control you have over the speed of the boat, from practically nothing at all up to full speed in either direction. The fisherman who trolls with his launch finds the reverse propeller advantageous for maintaining the slow forward motion which trolling requires. For other similar purposes the reverse propeller has its merits.

With the advent of auxiliary power in small and large sailboats, there has arisen a demand for a propeller which, when the boat is under sail, will not have any resisting tendencies in retarding the forward motion of the boat. Several reversible propellers on the market are therefore designed so that the blades can be turned edgewise. This is termed a "feathering" blade. Where this type of reversible wheel is constructed to give the strength and serviceability that is required, and to withstand severe usage, it can be used to good advantage by the yachtsman and the fisherman.

The reversible propellers furnished when desired with the well known Buffalo engines are illustrated herewith. They are made with round closed hub and smooth surface, creating the least possible disturbance of water and not entangling with weeds as easily as the open type. All parts are accurately machined and interchangeable. They are made of a very superior bronze which is extremely tough.

Buffalo Reversible Propeller, Showing Hub, etc.

CHAPTER XIX

HYDROAEROPLANES

Early in the history of aviation it was found desirable to conduct flying experiments over water in order to minimize the danger of such work and also to obtain a smooth surface for making the preliminary run. This demand led to the development of the hydro-aeroplane or flying boat, which is simply an aeroplane provided with floats or pontoons of the planing type just described. Owing to the efficiency of these hulls in regard to power consumption and weight they deserve more than passing notice even to those not particularly interested in flying.

In general these hulls may be divided into three principal classes: (1) The single pontoon; (2) the double pontoon; (3) a pontoon in which is located the passengers and sometimes the power plant. The latter type generally is referred to as a "Flying Boat." In the first two classes the passengers and power plant are carried in the body of the aeroplane proper, the pontoons merely taking the place of the usual chassis wheels and act as a support for the aeroplane. In all cases the drive is by an aerial propeller whether the plane is moving on the water or in flight.

A hull of the first type is shown by Fig. 1, and is commonly used in the Curtiss and Farman machines, the wings and aeroplane structure being shown above the hull. To prevent excessive strains due to hard landings it is now common practice to provide rubber cable shock absorbers located on the supporting members. As the hull is very narrow the side balance is accomplished by the wing surfaces when at speed, small floats at the wing tips serving to hold the machine upright when at rest.

218 MOTOR BOATS:

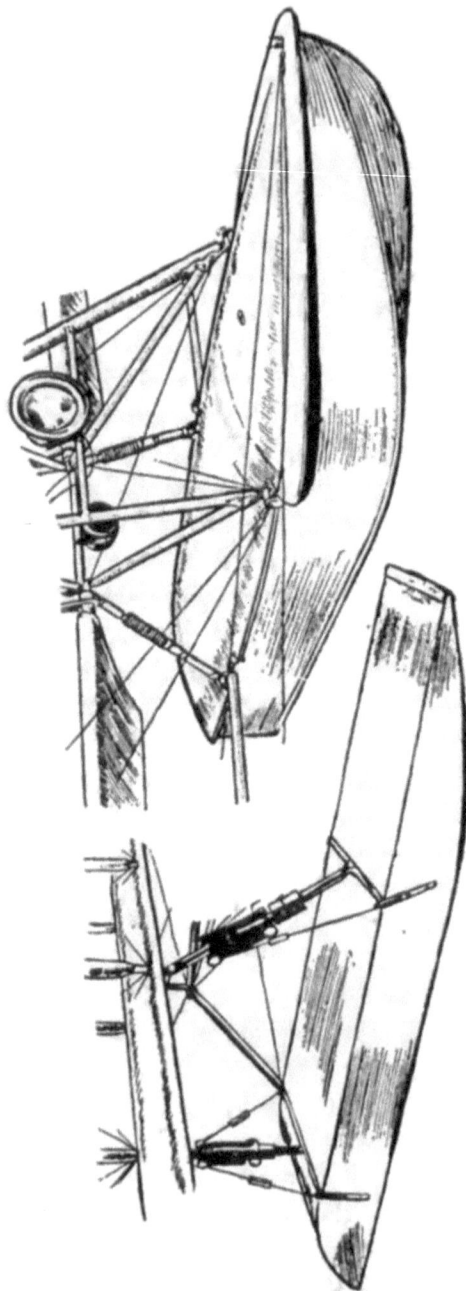

FIGS. 1-2. Types of Hydroaeroplane Hulls. The Single Pontoon of the Curtiss Type Is Shown at the Left. A French Single Pontoon Type Is Shown at the Right in which the Prow is of the "V" Form. This Parts the Water Easier and Is Better Adapted for Use in Heavy Seas.

To lift the hull out of water at the critical flying speed, the tail surfaces are depressed so that the planes tip up in front and therefore raise the nose of the hull. A constructional detail of the Curtiss pontoon construction is shown by Fig. 3 which gives the arrangement of the ribs and form of the surfaces. The hull is of a very thin veneer and is extremely light. A pair of battens are placed on the planing bottom to prevent injury in beaching the machine. Fig. 2 is a larger and more elaborate form used on the French Breguet Biplane. It will be noted that the bow is more nearly of the conventional boat type than in the preceding example.

Fig. 5 shows a Burgess-Wright double pontoon type of the biplane order, the double aerial screws being shown behind and between the two wing surfaces. The passengers and the power plant are carried in the "Nacelle" attached to the lower plane. As the two pontoons are placed at a considerable distance from one another no floats are required on the wing tips and no special balancing is required when planing over the water. Double pontoons have the disadvantage, however, of offering considerable air resistance when in flight and of being unstable in rough water. In rough water strain is occasioned in the frame by the floats striking waves of different height at the same instant, especially when running in the trough of the sea. This trouble is much reduced with single pontoons.

Fig. 4 shows the well known Curtiss Flying Boat, a type in which the aviator and passenger are located in the hull with the power plant well up between the wings. This hull is of the "stepped type." The step in this case is about two inches, while the side drift due to the wing surfaces is partially offset by the thin keel shown in the center of the planing surface. With a side wind, or in rough water, the machine is prevented from tipping sideways when at rest by the small cylindrical metal floats

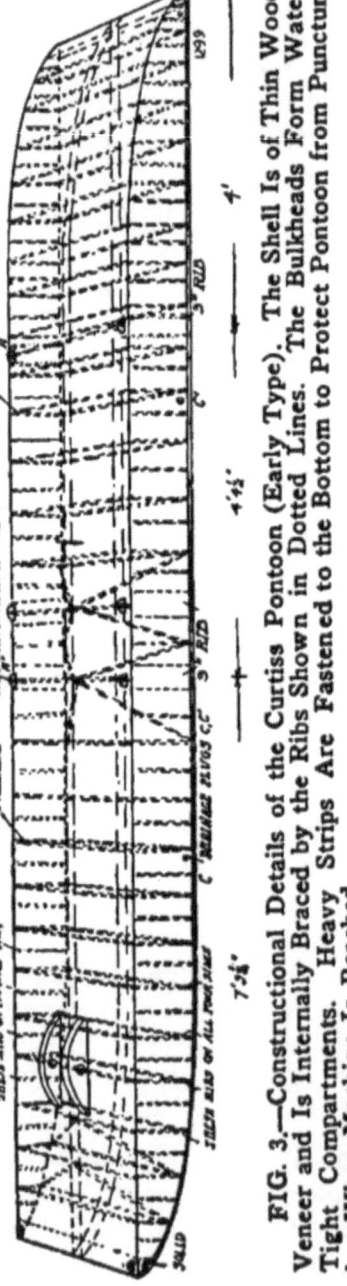

FIG. 3.—Constructional Details of the Curtiss Pontoon (Early Type). The Shell Is of Thin Wood Veneer and Is Internally Braced by the Ribs Shown in Dotted Lines. The Bulkheads Form Water Tight Compartments. Heavy Strips Are Fastened to the Bottom to Protect Pontoon from Puncturing When Machine Is Beached.

shown at the tips of the lower wing. When in flight or when running rapidly over the water balance is affected by the "Aileron" or small movable surface shown midway between the main planes and at the tip. The horizontal line shown under the wings is the center line of air

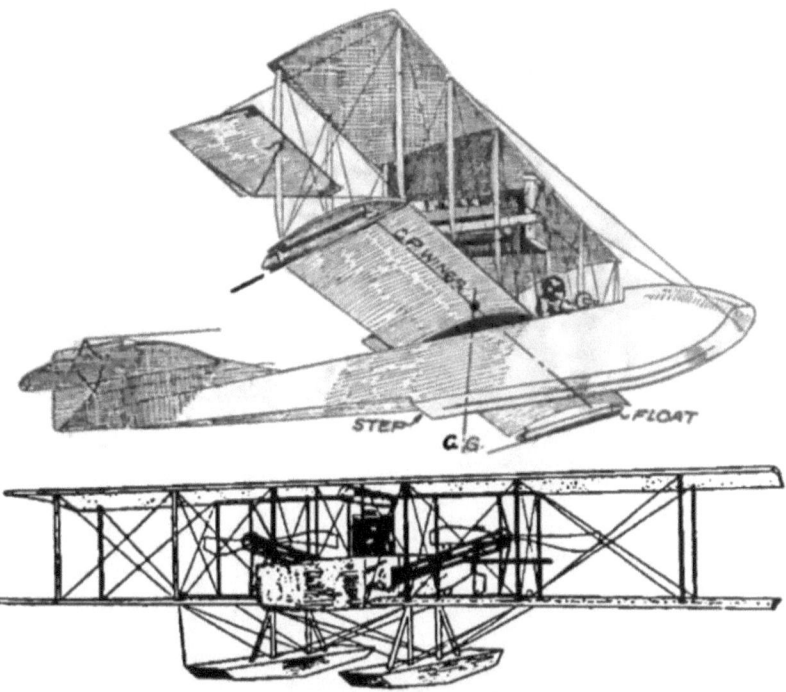

FIG. 4 (Above).—Shows the Curtiss Flying Boat.
FIG. 5 (Below).—Burgess Wright Double Pontoon Type.

pressure on the wings which is normally located near the center of gravity. The step is generally located slightly behind this point as shown. At the extreme rear end is the tail surface used in maintaining fore and aft balance and for elevating the machine into the air after the flying speed has been reached.

In the majority of cases both the flying boat hulls and the pontoons are provided with several water tight compartments to protect the plane when the hull is sprung

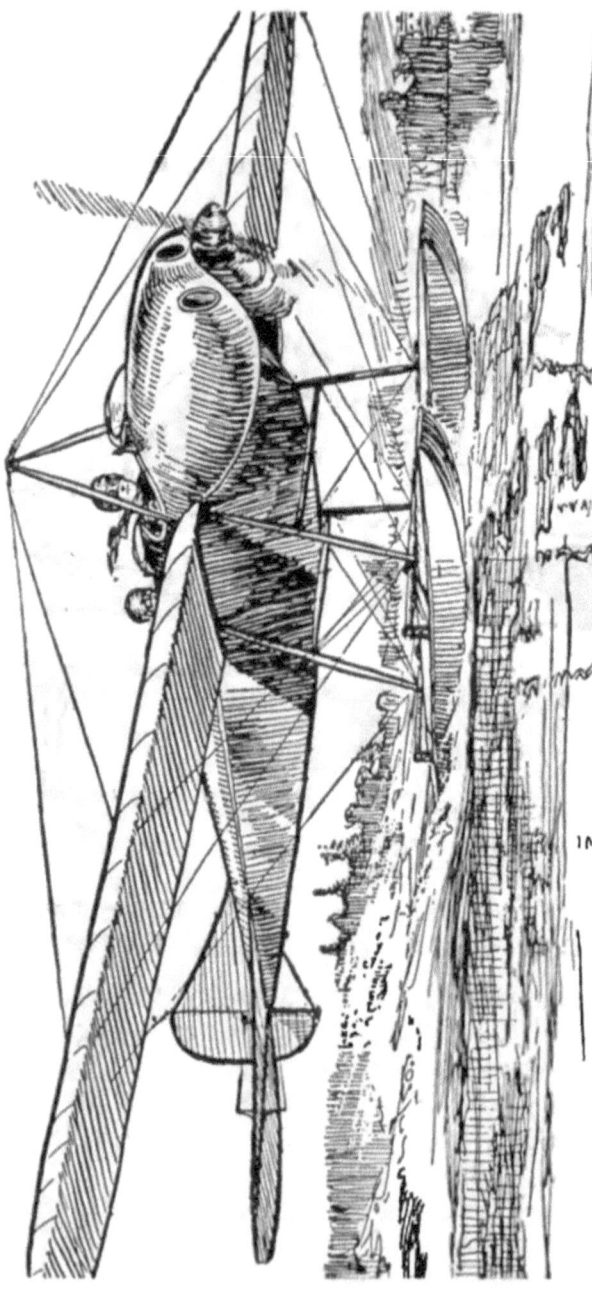

An English Hydroaeroplane of the "Monoplane" Type Which Has Two Pontoons. The Cut Clearly Shows the Planing Action of the Pontoon at the Time When the Machine Is About to Lift from the Water.

by a hard landing or by striking a snag. As the body of the hull is necessarily of very frail construction great care must be exercised in landing and maneuvering on the water to prevent leakage and misalignment of the flying surfaces. The power for flying this type is supplied by a motor rarely less than 125 H. P., and in several recent war machines in excess of 400 H. P. United States Government specifications generally call for sufficient fuel to make a continuous six hour flight and sufficient capacity for the carrying of an observer. This brings the total weight well over 3000 pounds for a war hydro-aeroplane. The speed is approximately 80 miles per hour. A recent Siborowski plane built for the Russian government carries two 300 H. P. motors and carries a useful load of over 6000 pounds.

The large battle planes and long range reconnaissance type seaplanes used by the United States Government are provided with "Twin" motors, each motor carrying a separate propeller. The motors are carried on either side of the central body about half-way out on the wings. Two engines and two propellers are made necessary by the fact that it is very difficult to build a satisfactory propeller that will transmit more than 160 horsepower. By subdividing the power plant into two units it is possible to transmit 300 horsepower total, with ease.

In case of accident, the twin can fly on one motor, although this throws an eccentric load on the machine that must be constantly corrected with the rudder. On account of the heavy motors placed at a considerable distance from the center of gravity, the twin has considerable inertia and is sluggish and "logy" in answering the controls. This, however, is not so much of a disadvantage with a sea plane as with a land machine.

On page 222 is shown a hydroaeroplane of the "monoplane" type in which there is only a single set, or "layer" of wings. As this type of machine has not much wing area it cannot support much of a load except at extremely high speeds. For high speed work, the monoplane is an excellent machine and is used extensively in scouting work and in combat service where enemy aeroplanes must be driven off. For bomb carrying or other heavy work they are useless.

The cut of the monoplane gives an excellent idea of the position of the pontoons when the machine is just about to leave the water. The bearing on the water is well to the rear of the pontoons, and a little further increase in the angle of the wings will "break her loose."

CHAPTER XX

ENGINE TROUBLES AND THEIR REMEDIES.

A thorough understanding of the engine will often enable the owner to prevent trouble. Most engines have their own peculiar idiosyncrasies and the conscientious owner will carefully study his motor and ascertain the conditions necessary for its operation. When he is thoroughly familiar with it, if he cannot always prevent trouble he will be better able to detect and rectify it.

Engine faults, causing deficiency of power or inability to start, may be divided into three classes: Mechanical troubles, ignition troubles and carbureter troubles, or those due to faulty mixture.

Mechanical troubles include those that may be included under the heads of Poor Compression, Weak or Broken Valve Springs, Valve Timing and Pipe Obstructions and Leaks.

The great majority of engine troubles may be charged up to ignition. Ignition troubles are easily distinguished from those due to imperfect mixture. If the spark fails or is very weak, the charge is not ignited at all. If the sparks are regular, too much or too little gasolene in the mixture will make the engine run weak, but there will be no misfiring unless the mixture is very bad indeed. If the explosions which occur are reasonably strong, the cause of misfiring is to be looked for in the ignition.

If the engine owner or operator has familiarized himself with the principles and adjustment of his carbureter, or mixing valve, he will soon learn what to do in case of trouble with the engine when the symptoms indicate defective mixture.

The most common engine troubles and their symptoms, may be very briefly summed up as follows:

Failure to Start.—Too much or no gasolene, or no spark at the plug.

Base Explosions.—Not enough gasolene; or too late a spark.

Pounding.—Generally a loose flywheel, or too early a spark.

Failure to Reverse.—Probably too much gasolene turned on, speed not caught right, or weak batteries.

Missing Explosions.—Defective spark plug, water in cylinder, poor contact at cam, weak batteries, too much gasolene, or vibrator of coil sticking.

How to Remedy Troubles.

In the following pages the symptoms of and remedies for all the troubles likely to be experienced in operating a marine gasolene engine are clearly indicated.

Leaks.

See that gasket is sound and no leakage from crank-case.

See that spark plug is screwed in tight, so there is no leakage around threads.

See that valves in carbureter seat properly.

Stops.

Regulate flow of fuel so there is no flooding or starving.
See that commutator is in tune with fuel supply.
See that spark is healthy, causing regular explosions.
See that cylinder is perfectly lubricated.

Failure in Starting.

If the engine refuses to start the following causes are possible:

1. Switch not closed.
2. Gasolene shut off; too much or not enough gasolene.

CONSTRUCTION AND OPERATION 227

3. Broken wire.
4. Water on spark plugs.
5. Dead battery.
6. Grounded low tension igniter.
7. Carbureter primed too little or too much.
8. Water in carbureter.
9. Stale gasolene.
10. Weak spark or no spark at the plug.

If high tension ignition is used, turn the crank slowly and note if the coil tremblers buzz. If not, look for broken primary wire or dead battery. If ignition is by make-and-break, short circuit one of the igniters by

"Standard" Engine, 25-32 H. P., 4-cycle.
Standard Motor Construction Co., Jersey City, N. J.

snapping a wire or screwdriver from the outside connection to the engine, and see if a spark results. If the engine has only one or two cylinders, short circuit the (high tension) spark plugs to test the spark. To do this, touch a screwdriver to the cylinder, then approach it to the spark plug binding post. By doing this you will avoid a shock. The foregoing tests will indicate whether or not the ignition is at fault. If it is not, look for mixture troubles.

If the engine fails to start after several trials, too much gasolene may be feeding, which can be determined by opening the air-cocks and turning the flywheel around slowly with the switch on until an explosion takes place through the air-cocks, then close them and start as before.

It very frequently happens that an engine becomes flooded with gasolene by allowing it to stand with the gasolene valves open, so the gasolene can work in and lie in the base of the engine. It will then be difficult to start on account of the excess of gas which is formed. To determine this, open the cock at the bottom of the engine and turn the flywheel around until an explosion occurs.

Missing Explosions.

Defective or dirty spark plug, water in cylinder, poor contact at cam, loose connections or weak batteries, sticky vibrator on the spark coil. Sometimes caused by feeding too much gasolene. Occasionally the timer may give a poor contact and cause missing, which can be easily remedied by putting in new contact pieces or stiffer springs.

Base Explosions.

Not enough gasolene. Turn on more gasolene and set the spark a little earlier.

Sudden Loss of Power.

If the carbureter has been giving good service and the mixture suddenly goes wrong, do not attempt to correct matters by changing the carbureter adjustment. Look instead for stale gasolene, for a sticking auxiliary air valve in the carbureter, or for dirt or water in the gasolene. If the carbureter has a wire gauze intake screen it may be choked with dust. If the carbureter floods, the float, if of metal, may be punctured, or if cork, it may have absorbed gasolene; or the float valve may leak and cause dripping. If the weather has suddenly turned cold and the engine will not start, probably a little hot water poured over the carbureter will evaporate the gasolene and start the engine off as well as ever.

Loss of Compression.

Failure to hold compression may be due to leaky exhaust valves, leaky gaskets or leaky piston rings. An extra dose of oil on the piston head will make the rings temporarily tight in case they leak, and oil squirted on the gaskets or around the spark plugs will betray leaks at those points. The seat of a leaky exhaust valve will be pitted and burnt, and will show by its appearance that it seats on one side only.

The compression may become weak for lack of sufficient lubrication. When this trouble occurs it is a good idea to pour a little cylinder oil through the spark plug hole, then see that the oil cups are feeding properly. In old engines the compression may become weak from the wear of the piston rings. New rings should then be fitted, which, after a little running, should wear to a good fit and give better compression. The flywheel should spring back after being pulled up against the compression.

Pounding.

When a pounding noise is heard the cause is most generally a loose flywheel key. Sometimes pounding is caused by early ignition, due to hot spark plug or sticking of the piston. If a hot spark plug is the cause the engine will run after the switch is thrown off. If caused by a sticking piston the latter will stick tight after a little running under full load and stop the engine. Plenty of oil fed to the cylinder will overcome the sticking of the piston. If any pounding is heard stop the engine at once and locate the cause of the trouble immediately, as above.

Deficient Power.

Occasionally, deficient power in one cylinder may be traced to the valve spring being too weak or too stiff, or a broken spring will cause a particular cylinder to act badly. If the springs are too weak the engine will be noisy and weak except at low speeds.

A possible cause of deficient power is small or crooked piping, inlet or exhaust. Pipe elbows should never be used; all bends should be of easy radius, and the intake piping should be smooth internally.

Gasolene Feed.

It is very important to feed the proper amount of gasolene at all times. If too little is fed base explosions will occur, and if too much is supplied the engine will slow

Carbureter.—The Watertown Motor Company, Watertown, N. Y.

down. The best way to regulate the gasolene is to open up the throttle wide, put in the clutch (where a clutch is used) to give the engine a full load, then adjust the gasolene by gradually closing it off until the highest speed is reached; then close it still further until the engine commences to slow down or miss fire. Then opening the needle valve a little should give the proper mixture. A little practice will enable one to determine the proper point at which to set the needle valve, which, when once set, should seldom require further adjusting, but it is well to try it occasionally to see if the engine will not operate on less gasolene.

Troubles are sometimes experienced by not getting enough gasolene through the pipes, caused by the pipes being partially stopped up or the tank too low, which can be easily remedied.

Spark Coil.

The only delicate part of the spark coil is the contact points on the vibrator. These points are liable to become burned and stick, causing misfires. These can be examined occasionally, and if they show rough surfaces they can be smoothed up with fine emery cloth or a fine file. The vibrator can be adjusted by the thumb-screw so it will give a good spark. It is best to screw it down as far as possible, but with weak batteries it will have to be screwed back to give less tension to the spring.

Make-and-Break System.

The procedure in tracing an ignition fault, says Mr. Herbert L. Towle, C. E., will depend somewhat on whether the low tension or the jump spark system is used. If the former, the first step is to test the adequacy of the spark. Disconnect all the igniters (by opening the cut-outs, if there are any) and touch one end of the wire from the coil to the cylinder. If there are cut-outs, touch a screwdriver to the cylinder and to the bus bar connecting all the igniters. If no spark results, the trouble is in the batteries or in the wiring. Test the batteries with an ammeter or voltmeter. Dry cells should test 5 amperes or more on short circuit. Storage cells should test 1.8 volts each or more, on open circuit. **Never test storage cells with an ammeter.** If the batteries show proper strength, hunt for broken wires or loose connections. Possibly the wire from the coil may be grounded on the engine.

Sooted Igniters.

If a good spark is obtained on test, it is still possible that the igniters may be partly grounded by soot. If the igniter plates have two lava bushings, one of them may be cracked, or soot may have accumulated in the air space between them. With mica insulation, soot gradually collects between the mica leaves. A ground in any individual igniter will have the effect of grounding all the others, and the engine will not run at all. A partial ground due to soot in one igniter will cause missing in all the cylinders. To locate a partial ground, cut out all the igniters except one and run the engine on one cylinder at a time with reduced throttle. If several igniters are slightly sooted, missing will be produced as though one igniter was considerably sooted, but each cylinder when running separately will run all right. The only remedy is to take the igniters out and clean them thoroughly. To locate a completely grounded igniter, connect one igniter at a time, taking care that it is not making contact at the spark point, and short circuit it with a screwdriver. If no spark is produced it is grounded. Another symptom will be a spark between the wire to the coil and the igniter binding post when the igniter points are not making contact.

Jump Spark System.

· If high tension ignition is used, first note by the sound of the engine whether missing appears to be confined to certain cylinders. If so, the cylinders at fault are quickly located by holding down with the fingers the tremblers of one or more of the spark coils. If all but one are held down the engine will stop, if the last cylinder is not working. When the faulty cylinder has been traced, first note whether the trembler gives a clear buzz. This can be done by opening the pet cocks, retarding the spark, and turning the engine slowly by hand until the desired trembler buzzes. If the sound is not clear and steady, adjust the contact screw by turning slightly. If the spark is much feebler than that given by the other coils, but there is no arcing at the contacts and the trembler is adjusted as well as possible, the coil is probably short circuited and must be sent to the factory.

Sooted Plugs.

If the trembler and coil are all right, the spark plug is probably sooted. With some engines and some spark plugs, this is a very common occurrence, and the plug is the first thing to be examined. If the plug is clean, it is still possible that the porcelain is cracked internally. Try a new plug or exchange with the plug from some other cylinder. If the same cylinder still misses, investigate the cable for leaks due to water or to defective insulation.

Synchronized Ignition.

If "synchronized" jump spark ignition is used—i. e., a single coil and a high tension distributer—the symptoms of different possible troubles will be substantially as above, with the exception that local misfiring can only be due to leakage in the spark plugs or spark plug cables, or to defective insulation in the distributer itself. The latter may be due to water or dirt or to metal particles, and should not appear if the distributer is kept clean. The trembler for such a system does duty for all the cylinders instead of only one, and its contact points therefore require frequent attention.

Sudden Stoppage.

If the engine stops suddenly without warning, the cause is probably a broken battery wire. If it gives a few weak explosions before stopping, the cause may be a suddenly slipped timer, or the gasolene may have given out. Water in the gasolene will stop the engine very abruptly, but there are usually a few spasmodic explosions before it ceases entirely. If the explosions grow weaker for some moments before the engine stops, and if on priming the carbureter and cranking, the engine starts again but presently stops, the flow of gasolene to the carbureter is probably obstructed by dirt or fluff, which may be in the gasolene pipe, in the carbureter intake, or in the gasolene filter (if the carbureter has one). See if the gasolene runs down freely when the float is depressed. If it does not, disconnect the gasolene pipe at the carbureter. Most carbureters have a draining connection or petcock, where the gasolene enters, and by opening this, the accumulated dirt or water may be flushed out.

Preignition.

Occasionally, the explosions in one or more cylinders will produce a sharp metallic knocking quite unlike the muffled thump due to loose bearings. This noise is due to spontaneous ignition of the charge before the spark occurs, and is caused usually by incandescent particles of carbon on the piston head. This carbon accumulates gradually as a residue of the cylinder oil and requires to be scraped out once or twice in a season.

Dirt in the Carbureter.

When you have tried all other things and failed to remedy the trouble, look for obstructions or dirt in the carbureter or gasolene pipe. Do not say, "Oh, I know they are all right," for you do not know until you examine them. A piece of waste, cork, chip, dirt, accumulations of paraffin or glue from gasolene barrels may work through the pipe connected to the carbureter, and while not stopping the entire supply will often cut down the supply, causing slowing down and back-firing, often stopping the engine, gradually filtering through and allowing the engine to start, but later giving the same trouble.

Test for Preignition.

On throwing off the switch, if engine continues to run the cause is preignition.

Removing Carbon.

Avoid trouble by using a good grade of gas engine cylinder oil. A good plan is to put about two or three tablespoonfuls of turpentine in each cylinder, and run the engine the same as you would when using kerosene to clean out the carbonization on piston cylinder and rings; do it after running, say, 200 miles or more, or at any time cylinders have heated or become carbonized. Kerosene is mostly used to clean out cylinder; either kerosene or turpentine will do.

Flooding Carbureter.

Flooding at the carbureter may be caused by dirt under the needle valve and sometimes can be removed by jarring the carbureter or pressing the float spindle against its seat and revolving, otherwise it will be necessary to remove the cover on the float chamber and lift the float out; the needle valve can then be inserted and moved around on its seat, thus removing the dirt. Be sure that the carbureter stands plumb.

A carbureter which drips continually when the engine is not running is hard to start, owing to over-richness of the mixture, especially if the engine has been shut down for a few minutes without closing the gasolene valve. If the gasolene level is more than 1/16 or 1/8 inch below the spray orifice it will not be as easy as it should be to run the engine slowly.

Carbureter Adjustment.

Irregular explosions may be caused from either improper mixture, or defective spark. The mixture can be adjusted by the needle valve at the bottom of carbureter. If the gasolene is turned off too much it may cause back firing, or base explosions, and therefore must be opened up again slightly. This rule should be borne well in mind. After the carbureter is properly adjusted it seldom requires any changing. Any defect in spark will be located in the coil, plug, battery, or timing mechanism.

TROUBLE HINTS AND TIPS.

Over-Stiff Vibrator.—An over-stiff vibration spring requires considerable current to make it work, and will cause misfiring before the batteries are spent.

Weak Battery.—A weak or worn out battery will cause irregular explosions and should be renewed. When testing a battery of dry cells use an ammeter, as it will show the condition of the cells much better than a voltmeter.

Misfiring.—An engine misfiring or exploding irregularly will sometimes cause a novice to think that some of the internal mechanism has become loose and is striking against some part of the cylinder, whereas the knocking or hammering noise is simply the result of the unsteady motion of the moving parts.

If the missing affects all the cylinders alike, it may be due to a weak battery, or to a loose connection or broken wire anywhere between the battery and the coil or between the battery and the ground connection on the engine. A loose connection may touch and break contact from vibration as the engine runs. If the missing is most pronounced at high speed, it is likely to be due to rough contacts in the timer if the latter is of the roller type. Irregular firing, with or without actual missing, may be due to the use of grease instead of oil in a roller contact timer, or to the body of the timer wabbling on its bearing from wear, or to lost motion in the connections operating the spark advance.

Irregular Missing.—Irregular missing may be caused by a dirty spark plug, a sticking coil vibrator, or wrong adjustment of vibrator, platinum points on vibrator or spark coil pitted or burned off, dirty or loose in the spring, bad commutator or ground; if irregular knocking also occurs, it may be a loose primary wire. Sometimes the jump spark wire has the insulation worn off or is poorly insulated, and the current jumps outside the cylinder. Primary wire (the small wire) may be broken inside the insulation, or may have dirty connection, or may be worn through and only a few strands holding.

Cracked insulation on either porcelain or mica spark plugs will give trouble.

When a good spark is had at the coil and none or a weak spark from the end of the secondary wire, there is a leak in the secondary wire.

If a good spark is obtained at the end of the secondary wire and none or a poor spark at the spark plug, the point or points need adjusting or the plug is short-circuited.

Back Firing.—The principal cause is delayed combustion of previous charge. When the mixture enters the cylinder and does not contain sufficient gasolene, it makes a low mixture, so slow in combustion that it continues to burn on both the working and exhaust strokes of the piston, the flame remaining in the cylinder long enough to fire the incoming fresh charge, which escapes back through the receiving pipe.

Remember, in case of weak mixture, feed a little more gasolene. If this does not control it, look for carbon deposits and remove them.

Weak Mixture.—Weak mixture or late explosions cause slow burning; delayed flame in cylinder, when inlet port from the by-pass is uncovered by the piston, causes crank case explosions or back-fire. When engine back-fires into the carbureter it is usually a sign that you are not getting enough gasolene. Throttling the carbureter too much often causes back-firing, which may be overcome when engine is running at full speed by feeding more gasolene and advancing the spark.

Back-firing may be caused by running with the throttle of carbureter wide open and spark level retarded too much. If that is not the trouble, open the needle valve a little at a time, until it explodes regularly.

Preignition.—Caused by sparking too soon, over-heated cylinders, over-advanced timer, over-heated projections or deposits of burnt carbon in cylinder or igniting chamber, producing a deep, heavy pound. If this is the cause, the pounding will cease as soon as the deposits are removed, or the spark made later. Always try changing time of spark before tinkering with the inside of the cylinder.

Tight Bearings.—A tight bearing occurs frequently in an engine which turned easily before installing. The cause for hard turning over is from springing the base of engine in screwing down on an uneven engine bed, throwing the crankshaft bearings out of line. To prove this, loosen the leg screw and turn flywheel over.

Temperature of Gasolene.—If a dish of gasolene is set out where temperature is at zero it will not evaporate. This should explain why it is often hard to start in cold weather.

Short Circuit.—If the wires connecting the batteries are carelessly attached so as to come in contact with zinc and carbon, short circuit will be the result if insulation is worn, or the zincs come together.

Testing Spark Plug.—To test the jump spark plug for fouling, injury or short circuit in plug, remove the plug from cylinders, lay it on a clean metallic part of the engine, usually on top of cylinder, with wires attached to the plug, being careful that only the outside metal of the plug containing the tread comes in contact with the engine, the same as if placed in the cylinder. Turn over the flywheel until contact is made at the commutator or timer. If the vibrator of the spark coil does not buzz, adjust by thumbscrew until it works. If it does not work, clean the points between the thumbscrew adjuster and vibrator. When vibrator works, notice the size of spark at the points of plug.

If the spark jumps the space between points the plug is all right. If not a good spark, try opening or closing the space a little.

Do not put your hands on plug when contact is on. You will be apt to get an unpleasant though not dangerous shock.

Valve Timing.—The exhaust valve of a four-cycle engine should open when the crank lacks about 40 degrees of its bottom position, and should close just after the crank has reached its top position. The inlet valve should open approximately when the exhaust valve closes, and should stay open until the crank is about 20 degrees beyond its bottom position. If the valves are wrongly timed the cause may be found in slipping of the valve cams on their shaft, or in wear of the cams or the valve lifters. There should be at least 1/32 inch clearance under the valve stems when the valves are shut. After an engine has been overhauled, the gears may be incorrectly assembled, so that all the valves open and close later or earlier than they should. Usually the gear teeth are marked with a prick punch to show the correct setting.

A FEW HINTS FOR ALL.

Do not attempt to fill a gasolene tank at night, unless an electric hand-light is used for illumination; the use of a light or lantern is only tempting danger.

Make a landing heading into the wind or against the current.

It is a good idea to always carry recharges for your battery or else a set of dry cells; better still is a magneto.

Before you start your motor in the spring, clean it thoroughly, removing all the old grease, and see that everything is in perfect order, free from rust. Pour a small cupful of kerosene in the cylinder through the priming cup. Turn the engine over a dozen times and then let it stand overnight. This will loosen the piston rings, if they have stuck, and greatly increase the compression.

In screwing down compression grease cups, do so while the motor is running, otherwise the lubricant will not enter the grease duct.

When you hear an unusual noise about your motor, do not keep on running. Something is wrong and requires attention. The old adage that "a stitch in time saves nine," well applies here. Stop and find out the cause and then remedy the fault, if possible.

There may be a number of reasons for the pounding in a motor—lack of lubrication, lack of water supply, spark advanced too far, too much gasolene, or the flywheel key loose. Drive in the flywheel key first; if this does not remedy the trouble, see that the pump is working; if the pounding continues, look to your lubrication, and finally see that the spark is not advanced too much. Sometimes, however, through the use of poor cylinder oil, the rings on the piston will become gummed and stick, thus causing a pound. In this case a little kerosene poured into the cylinder through the priming cup and the motor turned over several times will loosen the rings.

When your motor doesn't start on one or two turns of the crank, it is time to look around and see what you have forgotten—something, nine times out of ten. Thus, the Camden Anchor-Rockland Machine Co., of Camden, Maine, tell of a case where they sent a man 400 miles to put a customer right, and found that he had forgotten it was necessary to put in his switch—and he had been operating the boat a month at that.

It sometimes happens that a cylinder gasket becomes destroyed in removing the head of a motor, and that new packing is almost impossible to obtain. In such cases heavy manila paper saturated with shellac, will act very well. Thin copper, if obtainable, is still better. Asbestos is commonly used and is usually found where there is an engine. It is well to soak asbestos in linseed oil before using, and after the motor is run awhile the head nuts should be tightened.

Poor lubricating oil has been the cause of a good deal of trouble with gasolene motors. We have heard of a number of cases where oil men laid claim to having the best thing on earth, and the result has been that if this was purchased trouble occurred. There are good brands of oil in the market and it will pay to use the best.

Knox 4-cycle, 4-cylinder Engine, 40 H. P.

When you have trouble with your motor, don't do like the embryo hunter who was lost in the woods and ran around in a circle, hoping to find his way out. Follow one line to the end, and if you do not locate the trouble there, go to the next. This generally proves the shortest way out of the woods.

Every owner of a motor-boat should be equipped with an ammeter (ampere meter) for the purpose of testing batteries. There are voltmeters also, but these are useless; it is the amperage that runs down, not the voltage. The voltage is the pressure of current and the amperage is the quantity. The voltage may be sufficient when there is no amperage, and the result is that the charge of gas will not ignite. It is well to remember also that a spark apparently good in the open air is not so strong in the cylinder when under compression. This often misleads the unaccustomed in such matters. A spark sufficient to ignite gas must be of a blue or purple hue, which indicates its quality. A purely red spark is apt to be weak.

To store a motor away for the season, clean it thoroughly. See that all water is drained out of water jacket and pipes. See that the check valves are clear. Take out igniter, oil it with heavy oil and place it away where it will not rust. Pour about a cupful of cylinder oil into the cylinder through igniter hole, turn the engine over until the oil is well distributed over the inside of engine, oil all bearings with heavy oil, and grease thoroughly. Cover all parts exposed to the air, that will rust, with heavy oil mixed with tallow. Unpack pump and place motor, well covered up, in a dry place, free from dirt and rust.

A Ferro Motor Boxed for Shipment.

CHAPTER XXI

DON'TS FOR MOTOR BOATMEN.

Don't fill gasolene tank by artificial light.
Don't put gasolene in tank without straining.
Don't try to run engine without gasolene in tank.
Don't try to start the engine with gasolene valve closed.
Don't try to start engine with worn out batteries.
Don't try to run engine with soot fouled spark plugs.
Don't go without tools in the boat.
Don't cast off until engine is started.
Don't start without lubricating oil.
Don't neglect opening lubricators.
Don't allow base of motor to get out of oil.
Don't put too much oil in base.
Don't fail to observe if water pump works.
Don't neglect to oil clutch.
Don't adjust clutch unless it needs it.
Don't let batteries get wet.
Don't let wires run through bilge water.
Don't let wire connections get loose.
Don't stop motor until boat reaches mooring.
Don't stop motor and leave charging switch in contact.
Don't forget to close lubricator and gasolene valves when motor is stopped.
Don't hesitate to write or ask for needed information.
Don't use lighted match to examine contents of gasolene tank.
Don't pack stern stuffing box with asbestos.
Don't let bare wires come in contact with the motor.
Don't let wire connections and terminals get loose.

Don't blame the manufacturer or the motor for every little thing that happens.

Don't forget that you are a factor in the successful running of the motor.

Don't get nervous or excited—sit down and think a minute.

Don't forget that the builders are as much interested in the performance of the motor as you are.

Don't forget that eighty-five per cent of motor failure can be traced to electric trouble; either in the battery or the coil or the wiring or the plugs.

Don't try to start the motor with any "lead" on.

Don't run at too high speed just to show off, as you might burn out bearings.

Don't fool with adjustment of spark coil. The vibrator is properly adjusted at factory and seldom needs readjustment.

Don't take engine apart unless absolutely necessary and if you have to do so to get at inside of crank-case, simply tip cylinder over, not removing piston.

Don't expect to get best results from an engine working on a shaky foundation.

Don't forget to turn down grease cups every hour or so, forcing grease upon your bearings. Be sure there is plenty of grease in the cups.

Don't forget that extra can of oil if you are going on a long trip.

Don't try to start engine with the draining plug out of the bottom of crank-case or with drain cock open.

Don't try to use batteries after they are played out; it is a good plan to purchase an extra set of batteries after the ones you are using have been in service about two months. We have seen batteries that will run for six months and still be in good condition; but we have also seen them played out in a few weeks.

Don't forget to open sea-cock to pump, if you have one.

Don't try to start without first making sure that the spark lever, timer or commutator is retarded.

Don't try to start without the switch turned on.

Don't try to start an engine which has a reverse gear or clutch, without making sure the lever is set neutral.

Don't screw the spark plug in too tightly but only just enough to prevent leakage and hold firmly. You may want to take it out again.

Don't put your wrench on upper nut on spark plug when plug is in cylinder. You may destroy it.

Don't use other than the best gas engine oil. The best steam engine oil will not do.

Don't think that because too much oil is bad that too little is better.

Don't forget to throw out the switch or pull the button, and put in your pocket when not running.

Don't run engine unless the pump is working.

Don't expect engine to run if wire connections get loose, batteries weak, spark plug dirty or wire poorly insulated.

Don't put your face close to an opening in gas engine when switch is on, or to see the spark take place.

Don't run an engine if a hammering or knocking noise is heard; find the trouble.

Don't forget to turn on gasolene cocks both at tank and engine before starting.

Don't think it waste of time to clean off ignition points occasionally.

Don't wear yourself out cranking an engine; if it does not start after three or four turns after priming something is wrong.

Don't think that a thump, pound or thud about your engine is always due to some trouble in the cylinder or connecting rod.

Don't put a check valve between carbureter or vaporizer on a three-port engine.

Don't use 90-degree els, when possible to use two 45-degree, especially on exhaust pipe.

Don't forget that a union on each pipe as near to end as possible is good practice.

Don't try to start with carbureter throttle entirely closed or entirely open.

Don't adjust the carbureter as soon as the engine works badly; it may be poor ignition, poorly seated valves, poor water circulation, etc.

Don't expect gasolene to run up-hill.

Don't expect an engine installed below the water line with underwater exhaust to run, unless the exhaust pipe is carried above the water line, before entering the water line, and an air valve or relief cock placed at highest point.

Don't think a dirty, rusty engine will run as well or last as long as a well-kept one.

Don't forget that success or failure depends upon yourself.

Don't forget to turn off the gasolene cock when not running.

Don't forget to fill gasolene tank.

Don't forget to draw water out of cylinder in cold weather.

Don't wipe engine while running.

Don't use too much gasolene; more power is developed with smokeless mixture.

Don't pile anything on batteries.

Don't be afraid to fix your engine.

Don't get excited, but go carefully.

Don't trust wire screen strainer, but use chamois skin, and save trouble. If chamois skin is not handy, use handkerchief.

Don't look for the opening in your gasolene tank or a leak with a match.

Don't reduce the size of pipe after leaving the engine.

Don't have any more turns in exhaust pipe than possible.

Don't see how close you can run to another boat.

Don't cut in ahead of a ferry boat or any other boat just because you have the right of way. They may not respect any rule except the rule of might.

Don't forget that all sail craft, big or small, have right of way over power craft.

Don't forget to offer assistance to a boat in distress, and always ask it or accept it when offered when in distress yourself.

A Pacific Coast Type of Launch.

CHAPTER XXII

RULES OF NAVIGATION.

The following rules and regulations for steam vessels apply also to the navigation of the Naphtha or Gasolene Launch, and should be followed to prevent collisions:

Lights.

The lights mentioned, and no others, should be carried in all weathers between sunset and sunrise:

(A) At the bow, a bright white light, of such a character as to be visible on a dark night, with a clear atmosphere, and so constructed as to show a uniform and unbroken light over an arc of the horizon of twenty points of the compass, and so fixed as to throw the light ten points on each side of the vessel, namely, from right ahead to two points abaft the beam on either side.

(B) On the starboard side, a green light of such a character as to be visible on a dark night, with a clear atmosphere, and so constructed as to show a uniform and unbroken light over an arc of the horizon of ten points of the compass, and so fixed as to throw the light from right ahead to two points abaft the beam on the starboard side.

(C) On the port side, a red light of such a character as to be visible on a dark night, with a clear atmosphere, and so constructed as to show a uniform and unbroken light over an arc of the horizon of ten points of the compass, and so fixed as to throw the light from right ahead to two points abaft the beam on the port side.

The green and red lights should be fitted with inboard screens.

Diagrams.

The following diagrams are intended to illustrate the working of the foregoing system of colored lights:

First Situation.

Here the two colored lights visible to each, will indicate their direct approach ("head and head") toward each

other. In this situation it is a standing rule that both shall put their helms to port and pass to the right, each having previously given one blast of the whistle.

Second Situation.

Here the green light only will be visible to each, the screens preventing the red light from being seen. They

are therefore passing to starboard, which is rulable in this situation, each pilot having previously signified his intention by two blasts of the whistle.

Third Situation.

A and B will see each other's red light only, the screens preventing the green lights from being seen. Both ves-

sels are evidently passing to port, which is rulable in this situation, each pilot having previously signified his intention by one blast of the whistle.

Fourth Situation.

This is a situation requiring great caution; the red light of B in view to A, and the green light of A in view.

to B, will inform both that they are approaching each other in an oblique direction. A should put his helm to port, and pass astern of B, while B should continue on

his course or port his helm, if necessary to avoid collision, each having previously given one blast of the whistle, as required when passing to the right.

Fifth Situation.

This is a situation requiring great caution; the red light of A in view to B, and the green light of B in view to A, will inform both that they are approaching each other in an oblique direction. B should put his helm

to port, and pass astern of A, while A should continue on his course or port his helm, if necessary to avoid collision, each having previously given one blast of the whistle, as required when passing to the right.

Sixth Situation.

In this situation A will only see the red light of B in whichever of the three positions the latter may happen to be, because the green light will be hid from view; A will be assured that the port side of B is toward him, and that the latter is therefore crossing the bows of A in some direction to port; A will therefore (if so near as to fear collision) port his helm with confidence, and pass clear. On the other hand, B, in either of the three positions, will see both the red and green lights of A,

by which the former will know that A is approaching directly toward him; B will act accordingly and keep away if necessary.

Seventh Situation.

In this situation A will only see the green light of B in whichever of the three positions the latter may happen to be, because the red light will be hid from view; A will be assured that the starboard side of B is toward him, and that the latter is therefore crossing the bows of A in some direction to starboard; A will therefore (if so near as to fear collision) starboard his helm with

confidence and pass clear. On the other hand, B, in either of the three positions, will see both the red and green lights of A, by which B will know that A is approaching directly toward him; B will act accordingly, and keep away if necessary.

The manner of fixing the colored lights should be particularly attended to. They will require to be fitted each with a screen, of wood or canvas, on the inboard side, and close to the light, in order to prevent both being seen at the same moment from any direction but that right ahead to two points abaft the beam.

This is important, for without the screens any plan of bow lights would be ineffectual as a means of indicating the direction of steering. This will be readily understood by a reference to the preceding illustrations, where it will appear evident that in any situation in which two vessels may approach each other in the dark the colored lights will instantly indicate to both the relative course of each; that is, each will know whether the other is approaching directly or crossing the bows either to starboard or port.

This intimation, with the signals by whistle, as provided, is all that is required to enable vessels to pass each other in the darkest night with almost equal safety as in broad day. If at anchor, all vessels, without distinction, must exhibit a bright white light as far as possible above the surface of the water.

The lights carried by sailing vessels are the same as those given, except the white light.

Vessels under power are always required to give way to those under sail.

Alter course to starboard and pass on port side of other vessel when meeting end on or nearly so. Follow this rule at night whenever both side lights of approaching vessel are visible across the beam.

When crossing, the vessel having the other on her starboard side, must not obstruct the other's passage.

A power vessel shall not obstruct the passage of a sailing vessel.

Do not overtake and pass another vessel in a narrow passage.

The whistle signals indicating the course required are specified.

When a signal is received, answer with the same signal.

One blast signifies, "I am directing my course to starboard" (right).

Two blasts signify, "I am directing my course to port" (left).

Three blasts signify, "My engines are full speed astern."

When nearing a bend in the channel sound one long blast.

Give whistle signals by day or night only when other vessel signaled is in sight.

Fog signals only are given in thick foggy weather.

Upon being overtaken by another vessel, a white light must be shown astern, visible over twelve points of the compass aft.

Rules regarding sidelights are to be complied with when vessel is under way and not otherwise.

A white light is to be shown while at anchor, visible all around the horizon.

A whistle, siren, fog-horn or something of similar nature is to be used as a fog signal. A "prolonged blast" is from four to six seconds' duration.

One prolonged blast at one-minute intervals or less must be given when the boat has way upon her.

In sailing vessels, one blast at one-minute intervals or less must be given when on starboard tack; two blasts at one-minute intervals when on port tack; with wind abaft the beam, three blasts at similar intervals.

www.ingramcontent.com/pod-product-compliance
Lightning Source LLC
Chambersburg PA
CBHW050902300426
44111CB00010B/1341